Bloom's Modern Critical Views

Bloom's Modern Critical Views

Bloom's Modern Critical Views

TONI MORRISON

Edited and with an introduction by
Harold Bloom
Sterling Professor of the Humanities
Yale University

CHELSEA HOUSE
PUBLISHERS
A Haights Cross Communications Company
Philadelphia

©2005 by Chelsea House Publishers, a subsidiary of
Haights Cross Communications.

A Haights Cross Communications ✦ Company

http://www.chelseahouse.com

Introduction © 2005 by Harold Bloom.

Printed and bound in the United States of America.

10 9 8 7 6 5 4 3 2 1

Library of Congress Cataloging-in-Publication Data applied for.

Toni Morrison / Harold Bloom, ed.
     p. cm. — (Bloom's modern critical views)
  Includes bibliographical references and index.
  ISBN 0-7910-8136-2 (alk. paper)
  1. Morrison, Toni—Criticism and interpretation. 2. African Americans in literature. I. Bloom,
Harold. II. Series.
  PS3563.O8749Z89 2004
  813'.54—dc22
                                        2004012646

Contributing Editor: Grace Kim

Cover designed by Keith Trego

Cover photo: Associated Press/Charles Rex Arbogast

Layout by EJB Publishing Services

Contents

Editor's Note

My Introduction, composed as an affectionate homage to a superb writer, nevertheless expresses a reservation in regard to her insistence that her authentic context is African-American literature. Her actual precursors remain Virginia Woolf and William Faulkner.

Many of the essayists represented here would disagree with me. Madonne M. Miner finds in Pecola, protagonist of *The Bluest Eye*, someone "absenced" in relation to white, male norms, while Melvin Dixon traces in Morrison a redress for "black homelessness" supposedly not available in Ralph Ellison's magnificent *Invisible Man*.

Sula is read by Deborah E. McConnell as a "Black Female text", after which Marilyn Sanders Mobley emphasizes that *Beloved* calls African-American readers to return to their repressed past so as again to ponder slavery.

Trudier Harris invokes African-American folk traditions as the as the basis for *Sula*, while Philip Page finds in *Song of Solomon* (to me Morrison's best narrative) the return of American ghosts, and J. Brooks Bouson acclaims the modes in which Morrison bears witness to African-American traumas.

A more aesthetic kind of critical response is provided by Maria DiBattista's acute analysis of *Tar Baby*, and by Michael Wood's poignant reverie on *Paradise*. I am pleased also to commend this volume's final essay, where Rachel C. Lee contemplates the "aesthetic of ambiguity" in the admirable *Sula*, and in *Beloved*, a work I myself sometimes judge to be uneven and problematic.

HAROLD BLOOM

Introduction

Toni Morrison, in a speculative essay on literary canon-making, proposes the difficult critical quest of uncovering the hidden obsession with African-Americans that has haunted the American novel throughout its history. Her principal example is to sketch a reading of *Moby-Dick* in which Ahab's manic obsessiveness with the whiteness of the whale becomes a synecdoche for white America's compulsive relation to the African-American aspects of its culture, past and present. Morrison's reading is in the mode of D.H. Lawrence's *Studies in Classic American Literature*, where what Lawrence saw as the doom of the white race is prefigured in Ahab's compulsiveness. I am of many minds about Morrison's critical project, if only because it would give yet another dimension to the unhappy procedure of uncovering just how much of white America cannot be exorcised from African-American fiction. Morrison's five early novels, culminating in *Beloved*, are possible candidates for entering an American canon founded upon what I insist would be aesthetic criteria alone, if we still retain any such criteria after our current age of politicized response to narrative, dramas, and poems has passed.

Morrison, like any potentially strong novelist, battles against being subsumed by the traditions of narrative fiction. As a leader of African-American literary culture, Morrison is particularly intense in resisting critical characterizations that she believes misrepresent her own loyalties, her social and political fealties to the complex cause of her people. If one is a student of literary influence as such, and I am, then one's own allegiances as a critic are aesthetic, as I insist mine are. One is aware that the aesthetic has been a mask for those who would deny vital differences in gender, race, social class, and yet it need not be an instrument for the prolongation of exploiting forces. The aesthetic stance, as taught by Ruskin, Pater, and

Wilde, enhances a reader's apprehension of perception and sensation. Such a mode of knowing literature seems to me inescapable, despite times like our own, in which societal and historical resentments, all with their own validity, tend to crowd out aesthetic considerations. Yet, as an artist, Morrison has few affinities with Zora Neale Hurston or Ralph Ellison, or with other masters of African-American fiction. Her curious resemblance to certain aspects of D.H. Lawrence does not ensue from the actual influence of Lawrence, but comes out of the two dominant precursors who have shaped her narrative sensibility, William Faulkner and Virginia Woolf. Faulkner and Woolf have little in common, but if you mixed them potently enough you might get Lawrence, or Toni Morrison.

Lest this seem a remote matter to a passionate reader of Morrison, I would observe mildly that one function of literary study is to help us make choices, because choice is inescapable, this late in Western cultural history. I do not believe that Morrison writes fiction of a kind I am not yet competent to read and judge, because I attend to her work with pleasure and enlightenment, amply rewarded by the perception and sensation that her art generates. Reading Alice Walker or Ishmael Reed, I cannot trust my own aesthetic reactions, and decide that their mode of writing must be left to critics more responsive than myself. But then I reflect that every reader must choose for herself or himself. Does one read and reread the novels of Alice Walker, or of Toni Morrison? I reread Morrison because her imagination, whatever her social purposes, transcends ideology and polemics, and enters again into the literary space occupied only by fantasy and romance of authentic aesthetic dignity. Extraliterary purposes, however valid or momentous they may be for a time, ebb away, and we are left with story, characters, and style, that is to say, with literature or the lack of literature. Morrison's early novels leave us with literature, and not with a manifesto for social change, however necessary and admirable such change would be in our America.

Morrison herself has made very clear that she prefers to be contextualized in African-American literature, or in an American literature that ceases to repress the African-American presence. I am neither a feminist nor an African-American critic, nor am I a Marxist, a deconstructor, a Lacanian, a New Historicist, a semiotician. And yet I scarcely would agree with several of the contributors to this volume, who would maintain that my theories of literary influence simply reduce to yet another logocentric, capitalistic, white male symbolic system that has no validity or relevance for reading and understanding the work of an African-American feminist and Marxist novelist. Literary texts emerge from other literary texts, and they do not choose their forerunners. They are as overdetermined aesthetically as their human makers are overdetermined erotically. It is a great sorrow that we cannot choose whom we are free to love, and it is almost an equal sorrow that the gifted cannot choose their gift, or even the bestowers of their gift. We are free to choose our ideologies, but eros and art, however intertwined they are with cultural politics, cannot be reduced to cultural politics alone. As an African-American woman, Toni Morrison has developed a powerful stance that intervenes forcefully in the cultural politics of her time and place, the United States as it stumbles beyond the year 2000 of the Common Era. As a novelist, a rhetorical tale-teller, Toni Morrison was found by Virginia Woolf and William Faulkner, two quite incompatible artists, except perhaps for the effect that James Joyce had upon both of them. Morrison's marvelous sense of female character and its fate in male contexts is an extraordinary modification of Woolfian sensibility, and yet the aura of Woolf always lingers on in Morrison's prose, even as Joyce's presence can be felt so strongly in Woolf's *Mrs. Dalloway* and in Faulkner's *The Sound and the Fury*. Faulkner's mode of narration is exquisitely modulated by Morrison, but the accent of Faulkner always can be heard in Morrison's narrators, even as Joseph Conrad's authorial stance never quite left Faulkner. Consider the plangent closing passages of *The Bluest Eye*, *Sula*, and *Song of Solomon*:

> And now when I see her searching the garbage—for what? The thing we assassinated? I talk about how I did *not* plant the seeds too deeply, how it was the fault of the earth, the land, of our town. I even think now that the land of the entire country was hostile to marigolds that year. This soil is bad for certain kinds of flowers. Certain seeds it will not nurture, certain fruit it will not bear, and when the land kills of its own volition, we acquiesce and say the victim had no right to live. We are wrong, of course, but it doesn't matter. It's too late. At least on the edge of my town, it's much, much, much too late.
>
> —*The Bluest Eye*

> Shadrack and Nel moved in opposite directions, each thinking separate thoughts about the past. The distance between them increased as they both remembered gone things.
>
> Suddenly Nel stopped. Her eye twitched and burned a little.
>
> "Sula?" she whispered, gazing at the tops of trees. "Sula?"
>
> Leaves stirred; mud shifted; there was the smell of overripe green things. A soft ball of fur broke and scattered like dandelion spores in the breeze.

"All that time, all that time, I thought I was missing Jude." And the loss pressed down on her chest and came up into her throat. "We was girls together," she said as though explaining something. "O Lord, Sula," she cried, "girl, girl, girlgirlgirl."

It was a fine cry—loud and long—but it had no bottom and it had no top, just circles and circles of sorrow.

— *Sula*

Milkman stopped waving and narrowed his eyes. He could just make out Guitar's head and shoulders in the dark. "You want my life?" Milkman was not shouting now. "You need it? Here." Without wiping away the tears, taking a deep breath, or even bending his knees—he leaped. As fleet and bright as a lodestar he wheeled toward Guitar and it did not matter which one of them would give up his ghost in the killing arms of his brother. For now he knew what Shalimar knew: If you surrendered to the air, you could *ride* it.

— *Song of Solomon*

Even decontextualized, without the narratives that they culminate, these conclusions retain considerable lyrical and dramatic vitality. If I stumbled upon them anywhere, I would know them for Morrison's fictional prose, and I do not hear any voices in them except for Morrison's passionate and caring cry of the human, her own particular eloquence. And yet part of appreciating Morrison's command here of sensation and perception involves attending to the genealogy of her art. It is not a question of allusion or of echoing but of style, stance, tone, prose rhythm, and mimetic mode, and these do stem from an amalgam of Faulkner and Woolf, the father and mother of Morrison's art, as it were. Woolf and Faulkner are poets of loss, who search past and present for the negative epiphanies of vanished moments, possibilities, radiances, hopes. The narrative voice in Morrison turns always upon the negative magic of the romancer. Her perfect sentence is: "If you surrendered to the air, you could *ride* it." That is her epitome, but it would serve also for the most Morrisonian beings in Faulkner: Darl Bundren in *As I Lay Dying* and Lena Grove in *Light in August*. And it would illuminate also the perfect heroine of Woolf, Clarissa Dalloway, whose sensibility hovers at making that surrender in the air that Septimus Smith made, only to discover that he could not ride it. The pure madness of integrities of being that cannot sustain or bear dreadful social structures is as much Morrison's center (and not just in *The Bluest Eye*) as it is Woolf's and, with a difference, Faulkner's. The most authentic power in Morrison's work is the romance writer's sense that "it's much, much, much too late," that one's cry of grief and loss "had no bottom and it had no top, just circles and circles of sorrow." In some sense, all of Morrison's protagonists leap wheeling towards the death struggle, with the fine abandon of Faulkner's doom-eager men and women. Toni Morrison, in her time and place, answering to the travail of her people, speaks to the needs of an era, but her art comes out of a literary tradition not altogether at one with her cultural politics.

MADONNE M. MINER

Lady No Longer Sings the Blues: Rape, Madness, and Silence in The Bluest Eye

Robert Stepto begins a recent interview with Toni Morrison by commenting on the "extraordinary sense of place" in her novels. He notes that she creates specific geographical landscapes with street addresses, dates, and other such details.[1] His observations certainly hold true for Morrison's first novel, *The Bluest Eye*, set in a black neighborhood in Lorain, Ohio, in 1941. Reading *The Bluest Eye*, I feel as if I have been in the abandoned store on the southeast corner of Broadway and Thirty-fifth Street in Lorain where Pecola Breedlove lives, as if I have been over the territory traversed by the eleven-year-old black girl as she skips among tin cans, tires, and weeds.

Morrison's skill in creating this very specific place accounts, in part, for my sense of the strangely familiar, the uncanny, when I read her novel—but only in part. While reading, I am familiar not only with Pecola's neighborhood but also, in a more generalized way, with Pecola's story. The sequence of events in this story—a sequence of rape, madness, and silence— repeats a sequence I have read before. Originally manifest in mythic accounts of Philomela and Persephone, this sequence provides Morrison with an ancient archetype from which to structure her very contemporary account of a young black woman. In the pages which follow I want to explore intersections between these age-old myths and Morrison's ageless novel.

For an account of Philomela, we must turn to Ovid, who includes her

From *Conjuring: Black Women, Fiction, and Literary Tradition*, edited by Marjorie Pryse and Hortense J. Spillers. © 1985 by Indiana University Press.

story in his *Metamorphoses* (8 A.D.). According to the chronicler, this story begins with an act of separation: Procne leaves her much-loved sister, Philomela, to join her husband, Tereus, in Thrace. After several years, Procne convinces Tereus to make a trip to Athens and escort Philomela to Thrace for a visit. In Athens, Tereus barely manages to curb the lust he feels for Philomela. He caresses her with his eyes, watches possessively as she kisses her father good-bye, and uses each embrace, each kiss,

> ... to spur his rage, and feed his fire;
> He wished himself her father—and yet no less
> Would lust look hideous in a father's dress?

Arriving in Thrace, Tereus drags Philomela into a dark wood and rapes her. The virgin calls out the names of father, sister, gods, but to no avail. Having indulged his lust, Tereus prepares to leave this "ringdove ... with bloodstained plumes still fluttering" when she dares cry out against his sin:

> "I'll speak your deed, and cast all shame away.
>
> My voice shall reach the highest tract of air,
> And gods shall hear, if gods indeed are there."[3]

Tereus cannot tolerate such sacrilege against his name, so he perpetrates yet another rape: with pincers he

> ... gripped the tongue that cried his shame,
> That stammered to the end her father's name,
> That struggled still, and strangled utterance made,
> And cut it from the root with barbarous blade.[4]

Deprived of speech and lodged in "walls of stone," Philomela weaves the tale of her plight into a piece of fabric, which she then sends to Procne. When Procne learns of her sister's grief and her husband's treachery, she determines upon a most hideous revenge; she slays the son she has had with Tereus and feeds his remains to the unsuspecting father. While Ovid's story ends with this feast, popular mythology adds yet another chapter, transforming Philomela into a nightingale, damned forever to chirp the name of her rapist: tereu, tereu.

Obviously, male violating female functions as the core action within Philomela's story. Under different guises, this violation occurs several times:

first, when Tereus ruptures the hymen of Philomela; second, when Tereus ruptures the connecting tissue of Philomela's tongue, and, finally, when he enters her body yet again ("Thereafter, if the frightening tale be true,/ On her maimed form he wreaked his lust anew"[5]). With each act Tereus asserts his presence, his sensual realm, and denies the very existence of such a realm (encompassing not only sensuality, but the senses themselves) to Philomela. As if to reinforce the initial violation, Tereus, following his act of rape, encloses Philomela in silence, in stone walls. He thereby forces her to assume externally imposed configurations instead of maintaining those natural to her.

If man-raping-woman functions as the most basic "mythemic act"[6] in Philomela's story, the most basic mythemic *inter*-act involves not only this pair, but another: father and sister of the rape victim. When, for example, Ovid notes that Tereus, lusting for Philomela, "wished himself her father," and when the chronicler describes Philomela, in the midst of the rape, calling out her father's name (for help, of course, but for what else?) he sets the act of violence within a familial matrix. Thus, we cannot limit consideration of this act's motivations and ramifications to two individuals. Interestingly enough, however, just as the basic mythemic act (man raping woman) robs the woman of identity, so too the mythemic interact; dependent upon familial roles for personal verification ("mother of," "sister of," "wife of"[7]) the female must fear a loss of identity as the family loses its boundaries—or, more accurately, as the male transgresses these boundaries.

Having noted the most important structural elements in Philomela's story, we cross an ocean, several centuries and countless historical, racial, and class lines before coming to the story of Pecola. Despite obvious contextual differences between the two stories, structural similarities abound. Individual my themes from Philomela's story appear, without distortion, in that of Pecola. First, in various ways and at various costs, the female figure suffers violation: by Mr. Yacobowski, Junior, Bay Boy and friends, Cholly, Soaphead. Second, with this violation a man asserts his presence as "master," "man-in-control," or "god" at the expense of a young woman who exists only as someone to "impress upon." Third, following the violation/assertion, this woman suffers an enclosure or undesirable transformation; she cowers, shrinks, or resides behind walls of madness. Finally, the most characteristic example of violation/assertion/destruction occurs within the family matrix; Cholly Breedlove rapes his own daughter, violating a standard code of familial relations. We now might look more closely at individual instances of mythemes structuring the Pecola story.

An early, and paradigmatic, example of male transgression and subsequent female silence occurs in the "See the Cat" section. Junior, a tyrannical, unloving black boy, invites a rather credulous Pecola into his house, ostensibly to show her some kittens; like Philomela, Pecola has no idea of the dangers involved in trusting herself to a male guide. Once inside, engrossed in admiration of the furnishings, she forgets about Junior until he insists that she acknowledge him:

> She was deep in admiration of the flowers when Junior said, "Here!" Pecola turned. "Here is your kitten!" he screeched. And he threw a big black cat right in her face.[8]

Pecola immediately responds to this unexpected penetration by sucking in her breath; metaphorically she draws herself inward. She then attempts to flee, but just as Tereus confines Philomela behind stone walls, Junior confines Pecola behind the wall of his will:

> Junior leaped in front of her. "You can't get out. You're my prisoner," he said. His eyes were merry but hard.... He pushed her down, ran out the door that separated the rooms, and held it shut with his hands. (pp. 73–74)

Male realms expand as those of the female suffer an almost fatal contraction.

Junior does not actually rape Pecola, Morrison, however, duplicates the dynamics of the scene between Junior and Pecola in a scene between Cholly and Pecola, where rape *does* occur. Eleven-year-old Pecola stands at the sink, scraping away at dirty dishes, when her father, drunk, staggers into the kitchen. Unlike Tereus and Junior, Cholly does not carry his victim into foreign territories; rather, Pecola's rape occurs within her own house, and this fact increases its raw horror (Morrison denies us the cover of metaphor and confronts us directly with a father's violation of his daughter). As Morrison explains, several factors motivate Cholly, but the two thoughts floating through his besotted brain immediately prior to his penetration of Pecola point, once more, to his desire for confirmation of his presence. First, a gesture of Pecola's, a scratching of the leg, reminds him of a similar gesture of Pauline's—or, more accurately, reminds him of *his own* response to this gesture. He repeats his response, catching Pecola's foot in his hand, nibbling on the flesh of her leg, just as he had done with Pauline, so many years before. Of consequence here is not Pecola's gesture, but Cholly's belief that he can regain an earlier perception of himself as young, carefree and whimsical by using this girl/woman as medium. When Pecola, however, unlike the laughing Pauline, remains stiff and silent, Cholly shifts to a second train of thought, a second stimulus to self-assertion: "The rigidness of her shocked body, the silence of her stunned throat, was better than Pauline's easy laughter had been. The confused mixture of his memories of Pauline and the doing of a wild and forbidden thing excited him, and a bolt of desire ran down his genitals, giving it length" (p. 128). Thus, on a literal level, Cholly expands as Pecola contracts:

> The tightness of her vagina was more than he could bear. His soul seemed to slip down to his guts and fly out into her, and the gigantic thrust he made into her then provoked the only sound she made a hollow suck of air in the back of her throat. Like the rapid loss of air from a circus balloon. (p. 128)

As in the episode with Junior, Pecola sucks inward, but without positive effect; like a deflating circus balloon, she *loses* the benefits of lifegiving oxygen and the power of speech.

To enforce this silence, Cholly need not cut off Pecola's tongue or imprison her behind stone walls. The depresencing of Pecola Breedlove takes a different form from that of Philomela. Upon regaining consciousness following the rape, Pecola *is* able to speak; she tells Mrs. Breedlove what has happened. But as Mrs. Breedlove does not want to hear and does not want to believe, Pecola must recognize the futility of attempted communication. Thus when Cholly, like Tereus, rapes a second time, Pecola keeps the story to herself; in silence this eleven-year-old girl steps across commonly accepted borders of reason and speech to enter her own personal world of silence and madness. Pecola's "self" becomes so crazed, so fragmented, that it conducts conversations with itself—and with no one else:

> "How come you don't talk to anybody?"
> "I talk to you."
> "Besides me."
> "I don't like anybody besides you...."
> "You don't talk to anybody. You don't go to school. And nobody talks to you." (p. 153)

Of course, when Pecola comments that her mirror image does not engage other people in conversation, she engages in self-commentary; "I" and "you" are one and the same. Tragically, even when combined, this "I" and "you" do not compose one whole being. Claudia's description of the mutilated Pecola leaves no doubt that she no longer exists as a reasonable human being; like Philomela-turned-nightingale, the "little-girl-gone-to-woman" undergoes a transformation:

> The damage done was total.... Elbows bent, hands on shoulders, she flailed her arms like a bird in an eternal, grotesquely futile effort to fly. Beating the air, a winged but grounded bird, intent on the blue void it could not reach—could not even see—but which filled the valleys of the mind. (p. 158)

Silent, isolated, insane: Pecola cannot escape.

In depicting the effects of rape on one young woman, Morrison sets into motion a series of associations that take their cue from gender. Men, potential rapists, assume presence, language, and reason as their particular province. Women, potential victims, fall prey to absence, silence, and madness.[9] An understanding of the powerful dynamics behind this allotment of presence/absence, language/silence, reason/madness along sexual lines contributes to an understanding of the painful truths contained in Philomela's story, in Pecola's story, and in the story of yet another rape victim: Persephone. While clearly related to the Philomela myth, that of Persephone differs in certain details which, when brought to *The Bluest Eye*, prompt an even richer reading of the novel. Before engaging in an application of Persephone's story to that of Pecola, however, we might look at three different renditions of the Persephone myth, each of which may advance our understanding of the way Persephone's and Pecola's stories intersect mythopoetically.

Homer sets a springtime mood of warmth, gaiety, youthfulness, and beauty as he begins his rendition of Persephone's story:

> Now I will sing/of golden-haired Demeter,
> the awe-inspiring goddess,
> and of her trim-ankled daughter,
> Persephone,
> who was frolicking in a grassy meadow.[10]

When Pluto, god of the underworld, abducts the "trim-ankled" young woman (and surely it is not mere coincidence that Morrison specifies Pecola's ankles as a stimulant to Cholly's desire) this mood changes abruptly; in terror, the virgin shrieks for her father, Zeus. While noting that Persephone directs her shrieks to her father, Homer also comments on the virgin's hopes relative to her mother:

Still *glimpsing* the earth,
the brilliant sky,
the billowing, fish-filled sea
and the rays of the sun,
Persephone vainly hoped *to see* her mother again.[11]

Homer establishes a causal connection between rape and the loss of a particular *vision*. He further substantiates this connection in Demeter's response to her daughter's rape, a punitive response which involves Demeter's changing the world so that its occupants will no longer see fruits and flowers:

She made that year
most shocking and frightening
for mortals who lived on the nourishing earth.
The soil did not yield a single seed.
Demeter kept them all underground.[12]

The goddess imposes a sensual deprivation on mortals parallel to the sensual deprivation suffered by her daughter (note that *The Bluest Eye* opens with a statement of similar deprivation: "Quiet as it's kept, there were no marigolds in the fall of 1941"). By the end of the hymn, Demeter and Pluto reach a compromise; half of the year Persephone resides with her mother and the flowers grow; during the other half, Persephone remains with Pluto and the earth produces no fruits.

James Frazer, in *The Golden Bough*, relates another version of the Persephone story. In substance, Frazer comes very close to Homer; in detail, however, the two diverge, and Frazer's details reverberate in *The Bluest Eye*. First, Frazer provides more specifies about Persephone's "frolic"; the young woman gathers "roses and lilies, crocuses and violets, hyacinths and narcissuses in a lush meadow."[13] Individual flowers in Frazer's catalog call forth associations of importance to *The Bluest Eye*: the virginal lily, bloody hyacinth (taking its color from the slain youth, Hyacinthus, beloved of Apollo) and narcotic Narcissus (taking its name from the self-enclosed youth, Narcissus, capable of seeing only himself).[14] The mythic situation itself, flower picking, finds an analog in the novel as Pecola, on her way to the candy store, peers into the heads of yellow dandelions. Second, Frazer's more detailed description of Persephone's abduction and underworld residence might serve as metaphoric description of Pecola's state of mind following her rape: "the earth gaped and Pluto, Lord of the Dead, issuing from the *abyss*, carried her off ... to be his bride and queen in the *gloomy subterranean world.*[15] Finally, when Frazer concludes the story, he notes that although the "grim Lord of the Dead" obeys Zeus's command to restore Persephone to Demeter, this Lord first gives his mistress the seed of a pomegranate to eat, which ensures that she will return to him. Tereus and Cholly also "give seeds" to women, thereby ensuring that the women never will be able to reassume their previously experienced wholeness.

In a very recent reworking of the Persephone story, Phyllis Chesler focuses most intently on the fate of this myth's female characters. Because she places women's experiences at the center of her version, Chesler begins with a chapter of the story which does not appear in Homer and Frazer: Persephone menstruates. Further, Chesler specifies the nature of certain acts and relationships that her male counterparts choose to obscure; she identifies rape as rape, fathers as fathers:

> One morning Persephone menstruated. That afternoon, Demeter's daughters gathered flowers to celebrate the loveliness of the event. A chariot thundered, then clattered into their midst. It was Hades, the middle aged god of death, come to *rape* Persephone, come to carry her off to be his queen, to sit beside him in the realm of *non-being* below the earth, come to commit the first act of violence earth's children had ever known. Afterwards, the three sisters agreed that he was old enough to be Persephone's *father.* Perhaps he was; who else could he be? There were no known male parents ... and thus they discovered that in shame and sorrow childhood ends, and that nothing remains the same.[16]

Morrison, like Chesler, pays attention to female rites of passage; she includes a description of Pecola's first menstruation, an experience which bonds Pecola to her adopted sisters, Claudia and Frieda. Also like Chesler, Morrison insists on the paternal identity of the rapist (Pecola need not shriek the name of father as Philomela and Persephone do; father is right there) and emphasizes that the rape act brings one entire way of life to a close ("nothing remains the same"). This rapport between Chesler's Persephone and Morrison's Pecola surfaces in conclusions to the stories as well. Chesler writes:

> Persephone still had to visit her husband once each year (in winter, when no crops could grow), but her union with him

remained a barren one. Persephone was childless. Neither husband nor child—no stranger would ever claim her as his own.[17]

Pecola's fate runs along strikingly parallel lines. Despite the offerings and incantations of Claudia and Frieda, Pecola miscarries and remains childless. Grown people turn away, children laugh, and no stranger attempts to share Pecola's world.

Structurally, the stories of Philomela, Persephone, and Pecola share the same blueprint: violated by a male relative, a young virgin suffers sensual loss of such an extreme that her very identity is called into question. In one brutally explicit scene Ovid conveys the terror of Philomela's sensual loss— Tereus severs his sister-in-law's tongue and deprives her of speech. As chroniclers of this same basic female experience, Homer, Frazer, and Chesler also must convey the terror of sensual loss. In their versions, however, *sight* rather than speech assumes priority, and they convey the terror of deprivation not in one explicit scene, but by depicting the ramifications of an altered vision. Of course, this particular emphasis encourages yet further consideration of the Persephone myth and Morrison's novel, the very title of which suggests an interest in the way vision structures our world. This interest, reflected in the novel's title (what does it mean to see through "the bluest eye"?) and in sectional titles (how does one "see mother," "see father"?) springs naturally from Morrison's more fundamental interests: how does the world see a young black girl? how does a young black girl see a world? and finally, what are the correspondences between presence/absence, vision/nonvision, male/female?

As described by various psychologists and psychoanalysts,[18] the processes of identity construction and personal integration involve an extremely sensitive and constantly shifting balance between seeing and being seen—so that, for example, only after an infant sees itself reflected in the mother's eyes (that is, given a presence) can the infant, through its own eyes, bestow a presence on others. Throughout *The Bluest Eye*, Morrison provides several examples of the ways sex and race may prompt a dangerous distortion of this visual balance. An early instance of this distortion, and subsequent personal disintegration, occurs during an exchange between Pecola and Mr. Yacobowski, white male proprietor of a candy store on Garden Avenue.[19] Pecola enjoys her walk to Mr. Yacobowski's store. Many times she has seen that crack in the walk, this clump of dandelions. Having seen them, she grants them a reality, a reality which redounds to include Pecola herself:

These and other inanimate things she saw and experienced. They
were real to her. She knew them.... She owned the crack ... she
owned the clump of dandelions.... And owning them made her
part of the world, and the world part of her. (p. 41)

Such a happy rapport between viewer and vision is short-lived,
however. When Pecola enters the candy store and comes under Mr.
Yacobowski's eyes, her existence, as well as the existence of her world,
become matters of doubt. Mr. Yacobowski *does not see* her:

Somewhere between retina and object, between vision and view,
his eyes draw back, hesitate, and hover. At some fixed point in
time and space he senses that he need not waste the effort of a
glance. He does not see her, because for him there is *nothing to
see.* (pp. 41–42;, my italics)

In effect, this scene parallels previously described rape scenes in the novel:
male denies presence to female. Pecola cannot defend herself against this
denial: "she looks up at him and sees the vacuum where curiosity ought to
lodge. And something more. The total absence of human recognition—the
glazed separateness" (p. 42). Nor can she defend her world; walking home,
she rejects dandelions she formerly has favored. They, like Pecola herself,
certainly will not satisfy standards that the blue eyes of a Mr. Yacobowski may
impose:

Dandelions. A dart of affection leaps out from her to them. But
they do not look at her and do not send love back. She thinks
"They are ugly. They are weeds." (p. 43)

Before contact with this white male, Pecola creates belief in both a world and
a self; following contact with Yacobowski, her conjuring powers impaired,
she abandons the effort.

A second example of visual distortion finds Pecola face to face with
Geraldine, one of those "brown girls from Mobile and Aiken" able to
construct inviolable worlds by imposing strict boundaries between the
acceptable and the unacceptable, the seen and the unseen. Unlike Mr.
Yacobowski, Geraldine does *look* at Pecola, but, like Yacobowski, Geraldine
does not *see* Pecola; she sees only a series of signs, a symbolic configuration.
Thus, when Geraldine returns home and discovers a shrieking son, a frying
feline on the radiator, and an unfamiliar black girl in her living room, she

responds by distancing herself from Pecola. With no qualms whatsoever she relegates the young girl to the general category of "black female who is an embarrassment to us all", or, "black female whom we would prefer to keep out of sight":

> She looked at Pecola. Saw the dirty torn dress, the plaits sticking out of her head, hair matted where the plaits had come undone, the muddy shoes with the wad of gum peeking out from between the cheap soles, the soiled socks, one of which had been walked down into the heel of the shoe. She saw the safety pin holding the hem of the dress up.... She had seen this little girl all of her life. (p. 75)

Pecola, for Geraldine, serves as symbol of everything ugly, dirty, and degrading. Physically as well as symbolically, Geraldine must negate Pecola, must deny the ragged eleven-year-old access to her world. The woman who does not sweat in her armpits or thighs, who smells of wood and vanilla (pp. 70–71) says to Pecola, *quietly* says to Pecola: "'Get out.... You nasty little black bitch. Get out of my house!'" (p. 75). In other words, get out of my world, out of the vision I construct before and about me. Pecola leaves. As she leaves, she hangs her head. lowers her eyes: incapable of defending herself against visual distortion, Pecola attempts to deny vision altogether. But, even here, she fails: "she could not hold it [her head] low enough to avoid seeing the snowflakes falling and dying on the pavement" (p. 76). These snowflakes, falling and dying, suggest the visual perimeters of Pecola's world. In an earlier comment, Morrison generalizes as to the nature of these perimeters: "She would see only what there was to see: the eyes of other people" (p. 40). As these eyes do not see her, or see her only as a sign of something other, Pecola loses sight of herself.

Although Pecola's encounters with Mr. Yacobowski and Geraldine serve as the most complete and sensitively drawn examples of visual imbalance, they merely reenforce a pattern of imbalance begun much earlier in Pecola's life—for that matter, begun even before Pecola sees the light of day, while she is in Pauline's womb. During the nine months of pregnancy, Pauline spends most afternoons at the movies, picking up an education in white values of beauty and ugliness. Morrison describes this education as yet another violation of male on female, white on black. There, in a darkened theater, images come together, "all projected through the ray of light from above and behind" (p. 97). This ray of light resembles a gigantic eyeball (apologies to Emerson) which defines the boundaries of existence and which, of necessity, projects a white male vision. Having absorbed these silverscreen values, Pauline conjures up "a mind's eye view" of her soon-to-be-born child more in keeping with white fantasy than black reality. Upon birth, Pecola gives the lie to this view, and Pauline expresses her disappointment:

> So when I seed it, it was like looking at a picture of your mama when she was a girl. You know who she is, but she don't look the same.... Head full of pretty hair, but Lord she was ugly. (p. 99)

As various psychologists attest, the mother's gaze is of primary importance in generating a child's sense of self. Tragically, Pauline looks at her infant daughter and then looks away.

Morrison's novel contains repeated instances of Pecola's negation as other characters refuse to see her. *The Bluest Eye* also provides numerous instances of Pecola's desire to hide her own eyes, thereby refusing to acknowledge certain aspects of her world. Morrison articulates this desire for self-abnegation most explicitly in a postscript to her description of a typical fight between family members in the Breedlove home. Mrs. Breedlove hits Cholly with a dishpan, Cholly returns the blow with his fists, Sammy strikes at Cholly while shouting "you naked fuck," and Pecola covers her head with a quilt. The quilt of course cannot completely block out this scene, so Pecola prays that God will make her disappear. Receiving no response from the man in the sky, she does her best on her own:

> She squeezed her eyes shut. Little parts of her body faded away. Now slowly, now with a rush. Slowly again. Her fingers went, one by one; then her arms disappeared all the way to the elbow. Her feet now. Yes, that was good. The legs all at once. It was hardest above the thighs. She had to be real still and pull. Her stomach would not go. But finally it, too, went away. Then her chest, her neck. The face was hard too. Almost done, almost. Only her tight, tight eyes were left. They were always left.
>
> Try as she might, she could never get her eyes to disappear. So what was the point? They were everything. Everything was there, in them. (p. 39)

These paragraphs forcefully convey Pecola's desire and her notion of how she might realize it. If Pecola were to *see* things differently, she might *be seen* differently; if her eyes were different, her world might be different too.[20] As Morrison deals out one ugly jigsaw piece after another, as she fits the pieces together to construct Pecola's world, we come to understand the impulse behind Pecola's desire, as well as its ultimate futility. When boys shout at her, "'Black e mo Black e mo Ya daddy sleeps nekked'" (p. 55), Pecola drops her head and covers her eyes; when Maureen accuses her of having seen her father naked, Pecola maintains her innocence by disclaiming, "'I wouldn't even look at him, even if I did see him'" (p. 59); when Maureen attacks her yet again Pecola tucks her head in "a funny, sad, helpless movement. A kind of hunching of the shoulders, pulling in of the neck, as though she wanted to cover her ears" (p. 60). By covering ears, eyes, and nose Pecola attempts to shut out the testimony of her senses. Reminded of her own ugliness or that of her world, she repeatedly resorts to an elemental self-denial.

Pecola quavers when Mr. Yacobowski and Geraldine refuse to acknowledge her. She shrinks in fear when Maureen and Bay Boy insist on acknowledging her ugliness. Quavering and shaking, Pecola *does* maintain a hold on her world and herself—until Cholly smashes her illusions about the possibility of unambivalent love in this world. Throughout the novel, Pecola ponders the nature of love, pursues it as a potentially miraculous phenomenon. On the evening of her first menstruation, for example, she asks, "'How do you do that? I mean, how do you get somebody to love you'" (p. 29). And, after a visit to Marie, Poland, and China, Pecola ponders, "What did love feel like? ... How do grownups act when they love each other? Eat fish together?" (p. 48). When Cholly rapes his daughter, he commits a sacrilege—not only against Pecola, but against her vision of love and its potential. Following the rape, Pecola, an unattractive eleven-year-old black girl, knows that for her, even love is bound to be dirty, ugly, of a piece with the fabric of her world. Desperate, determined to unwind the threads that compose this fabric, Pecola falls back on an early notion: the world changes as the eyes which see it change. To effect this recreation, Pecola seeks out the only magician she knows, Soaphead Church, and presents him with the only plan she can conceive. She asks that he make her eyes different, make them blue—blue because in Pecola's experience only those with blue eyes receive love: Shirley Temple, Geraldine's cat, the Fisher girl.

In its emotional complications, Soaphead's response to Pecola's request resembles Cholly's response to Pecola's defeated stance; both men move through misdirected feelings of love, tenderness, and anger.[21] Soaphead perceives Pecola's need and knows that he must direct the anger he feels not at her, but rather at the God who has encased her within black skin and behind brown eyes. But finally, when Soaphead decides to "look at that ugly black girl" and love her (p. 143), he violates her integrity in much the same way Cholly violates her body when he forces open her thighs. Prompted by the desire to play God and to make this performance a convincing one, Soaphead casts Pecola in the role of believer. Thus, although he *sees* Pecola more accurately than other characters do, he subordinates his vision of her to his vision of self-as-God. He later boasts in his letter "To He Who Greatly Ennobled Human Nature by Creating It":

> I did what you did not, could not, would not do. I looked at that ugly little black girl, and I loved her. I played You. And it was a very good show! (p. 143)

Of course, the script for this show sends Pecola into realms of madness. Even Soaphead acknowledges that "No one else will see her blue eyes" (p. 143), but Soaphead justifies himself first on the grounds that "she will love happily ever after" and then, more honestly, on the grounds that "I, I have found it meet and right to do so" (p. 143). In other words, Soaphead's creation of false belief is not necessarily right for Pecola, but for himself. Morrison substantiates this assessment of Soaphead's creation a few pages later, when she portrays its effect on Pecola. Imprisoned now behind blue eyes, the schizophrenic little girl can talk only to herself. Obviously, this instance of male-female interaction parallels earlier scenes from the novel: "rape" occurs as Soaphead elevates himself at the expense of Pecola.

In *The Raw and the Cooked* Lévi-Strauss observes: "There exists no veritable end or term to mythical analysis, no secret unity which could be grasped at the end of the work of decomposition. The themes duplicate themselves to infinity."[22] Although the stories of Philomela, Persephone, and Pecola do not form a composite whole, each of them, with its varied and individual emphases, contributes to a much larger woman's myth, which tells of denial and disintegration, which unveils the off-concealed connections between male reason, speech, presence and female madness, silence, absence. As a young black woman, Pecola assumes an especially poignant position in this growing complex of mythic representations; she is absent (and absenced) in relation to the norms of male culture and in relation to the norms of white culture. Ultimately, I read Pecola's story as a tragic version of the myth; this twentieth-century black woman remains behind blue eyes, an inarticulate, arm-fluttering bird. But I cannot read *The Bluest Eye* as tragedy; Claudia, our sometimes-narrator, *speaks*, as does Morrison, our full-time novelist. Thus, although the novel documents the sacrifice of one black woman, it attests to the survival of two others—a survival akin to that of Philomela or Persephone—filled with hardship, but also with hope.

NOTES

1. Robert Stepto, " 'Intimate Things in Place': A Conversation with Toni Morrison," in *The Third Woman*, ed. Dexter Fisher (Boston: Houghton Mifflin, 1979), p. 167.

2. A.E. Watts, trans., *The Metamorphoses of Ovid* (Berkeley: University of California Press, 1954), p. 131.

3. Watts, p. 133.

4. Ibid., p. 133.

5. Ibid., p. 133.

6. I take this term from Claude Lévi-Strauss. For an explanation of Lévi-Strauss's *modus operandi* see Robert Scholes, *Structuralism in Literature* (New Haven: Yale University Press, 1974), pp. 68–74.

7. "From her initial family upbringing throughout her subsequent development, the social role assigned to the women is that of serving an image, authoritative and central, of man: a woman is first and foremost a daughter/a mother/a wife." Shoshana Felman, "Women and Madness: The Critical Phallacy," *Diacritics* 5 (1975), p. 2.

8. Toni Morrison, *The Bluest Eye* (New York: Pocket Books, 1979), p. 73. I will include all further page citations from Morrison's novel within the body of my text.

9. An observation from Shoshana Felman about Balzac's short story "Adieu" condenses many of the associations described. Felman notes: "the dichotomy Reason/Madness, as well as Speech/Silence, exactly coincides in this text with the dichotomy Men/Women. Women as such are associated both with madness and with silence, whereas men appear not only as the possessors, but also as the dispensers, of reason, which they can at will mete out to—or take away from—others.... Masculine reason thus constitutes a scheme to capture and master, indeed, metaphorically RAPE the woman" (p. 7).

10. Penelope Proddow, trans., *Demeter and Persephone, Homeric Hymn Number Two* (Garden City, N.Y.: Doubleday, 1972), n.p.

11. Ibid., my italics.

12. Ibid., n.p.

13. Sir James George Frazer, *The Golden Bough* (New York: Macmillan and Company, 1950), p. 456.

14. According to Frazer, in the original Homeric myth Persephone, drawn by the sight of narcissuses, moves beyond the reach of help. The choice of this particular plant as lure is of interest not only because of the Narcissus myth, but also because of recent psychoanalytic readings of this myth. These readings stress the importance of a child's progression through a stage of narcissistic self-love and suggest that this progression can occur only with the help of a mother-figure who assures the child of external love.

15. Frazer, p. 456.

16. Phyllis Chesler, *Women and Madness* (New York: Avon Books, 1973), p. xiv.

17. Ibid., p. xv.

18. See, for example, D.W. Winnicott, "Mirror-role of Mother and Family in Child Development," in *The Predicament of the Family*, ed. Peter Lomas (New York: International University Press, 1967), pp. 26–33; Heinz Lichtenstein, "The Role of Narcissism in the Emergence and Maintenance of a Primary Identity," *International Journal of Psychoanlysis* 45 (1964), pp. 49–56.

19. Why specify "Garden Avenue"? Perhaps Morrison wants to suggest that Pecola's experience is the twentieth-century urban counterpart to Persephone's experience in an actual garden?

20. "If she looked different, beautiful, maybe Cholly would be different, and Mrs. Breedlove too. Maybe they'd say, 'Why look at pretty-eyed Pecola. We mustn't do bad things in front of these pretty eyes' " (p. 40).

21. Compare, for example, Cholly's response (pp. 127–28) to that of Soaphead (p. 137).

22. Lévi-Strauss, *The Raw and the Cooked* (New York: Harpers, 1969), p.5.

MELVIN DIXON

Like an Eagle in the Air:
Toni Morrison

In recent interviews Toni Morrison has talked about her mid-western, Ohio background and the possibilities it presents for new settings in Afro-American fiction. "It's an interesting state from the point of view of black people because it is right there by the Ohio River, in the south, and at its northern tip is Canada. And there were these fantastic abolitionists there, and also the Ku Klux Klan lived there.... So I loved writing about that because it was so wide open" (*Chant*, 215). On another occasion she remarked, "Ohio offers an escape from stereotyped black settings. It is neither plantation nor ghetto" (Tate, 119). From a home that is neither typically North nor South, Morrison, like Ellison, who comes from Oklahoma, freely explores new physical and metaphorical landscapes in her fiction. She envisions space with fewer historically or politically fixed boundaries and endows her characters with considerable mobility. Her play of language upon and from within the land creates areas of symbolic activity for both author and protagonists: house and yard become scenes of psychological dislocation in *The Bluest Eye* (1970); land gradations and moral codes have inverted meaning in *Sula* (1973); mountain, farm, and island emerge as stages for enacting dramas of self-creation, racial visibility, and cultural performance in *Song of Solomon* (1977) and in *Tar Baby* (1981). Starting with her birthplace in Lorain, Ohio, and subsequent

From *Ride Out the Wilderness: Geography and Identity in Afro-American Literature*. © 1987 by the Board of Trustees of the University of Illinois.

23

transformations of that place into several charged fields in fiction, Toni Morrison has imagined a complex and multitextured world.

The symbolic geography in Morrison's fiction emerges from the precise physical details that give her black neighborhoods so much startling character and presence. Medallion, Ohio, or Shalimar, Virginia, fixes firmly in the imagination and shapes either terrestrial or celestial images through which Morrison initiates a dialogue with earlier texts discussed in this study, most notably with Ralph Ellison's *Invisible Man*. In the three novels that have earned Morrison an indisputable prominence in contemporary American letters, the author enlarges and completes many previous attempts to show the importance of both place and person in the development of Afro-American culture. From the songs her characters sing to transform otherwise dreary households into spiritual havens, and from the journeys they undertake through history and myth as in the early slave narratives (as the author revealed, "You know, I go sometimes and, just for sustenance, I read those slave narratives—there are sometimes three or four sentences or half a page, each one of which could be developed in an art form, marvelous" [*Chant*, 229]) comes the achievement of form and art in Morrison's fiction.

Attentive to the physical and cultural geography of the small black towns that have shaped her and her characters, Morrison constructs familiar yet new dialectical oppositions between enclosed and open spaces, between the fluid horizontality of neighborhoods (shifting, migrating populations, a profusion of character types and changing morals) and the fixed verticality, hence presumed stability, of the house. Morrison calls for an end to Ellisonian inertia and a delight in the free fall. These oppositions produce various exciting results that propel characters and readers toward the principal movement in Morrison's fiction: the leap from land into sky. Pecola Breedlove, for one, ventures to the "cave" of Elihue's mind (the cerebral force, readers will recall, that pushed Ellison's protagonist to consider ending his underground hibernation. "Because, damn it, there's the mind, the *mind*. It wouldn't let me rest" [433]) and its reservoir of conjure and magic. Pecola comes away with the cherished blue eyes that she alone can see (a blindness that completes the invisibility she had suffered from others). She wears a vision of the sky but never gains its reward of flight (is the name Pecola a variant of peacock?). For Pecola's aesthetic choice sinks her evermore into the mire of self-hatred that had initially created her desire. Sula, on the other hand, longs for flight and song but gets no farther than the upper rooms of Eva's house of death. The house opposes the space of Ellison's cellar, but it is filled with the same inertia (the stunted growth of the eternally juvenile Deweys is one example). The one character who eventually learns to resist the gravitational pull of social conformity and to grasp what his newly stretched imagination can reach is Milkman Dead. He earns the authority to sing his real name, for he not only has discovered the long-sought-for-ancestor Solomon, he becomes him when he tries the air. That test of the air—the risk, the ultimate surrender to it, and the strengthening *ride*—culminates Morrison's metaphorical triumph over conventional terrestrial frontiers or boundaries to identity, moving up into the celestial infinity of its achievement. Milkman's journey from No Mercy Hospital to the cave in Danville, Pennsylvania, and from a wilderness hunt to a mountaintop discovery in Shalimar, Virginia, offers a more satisfying solution to black homelessness than the reflective yet artificial hibernation Ellison had proposed.

The Bluest Eye. "When the land kills of its own volition"

Claudia MacTeer, the occasional and maturing narrator in Morrison's first novel, discovers one of the earth's peculiar traits that may mitigate the guilt she feels for the failure of her marigold seeds to grow: *"For years I thought my sister was right: it was my fault. I had planted* [our seeds] *too far down in the earth. It never occurred to either of us that the earth itself might have been unyielding"* (3). This revelation brings only partial relief. It offers one explanation of the novel's theme: the loss of innocence. The underlying question concerns the earth's role in bringing on misfortune, in creating a climate for Pecola's suffering and insanity as well as confusing the parameters of moral responsibility. The actual telling of the story, the sharing of narration among several voices, including Pauline's interior monologues, leads Claudia to confess too late the community's and her own complicity in acquiescing to hostility by taking life's misery too much for granted. "We acquiesce and say the victim had no right to live. We are wrong, of course, but it doesn't matter. It's too late" (164). The victim here is not only Pecola's premature and dead baby, sired by Pecola's own father, but also Pecola herself. The loss of Claudia's and Frieda's innocence, as they witness and report Pecola's decline, makes them victims as well.

The Bluest Eye is Morrison's study of a community out of touch with the land and the history that might have saved them. The displacement of blacks had begun long before Claudia's retrospective narration about the failed marigolds. The distance between their lives and the ideal American home or family, depicted in the passage from the grade-school reader that opens the novel, is also measured by the increasingly distorted passage, parts of which later introduce the subject of each subsequent chapter. This technique reveals the pervasive trauma of dislocation suffered by Pecola, Claudia, Soaphead Church, and the entire community.

The grade-school text is designed primarily to teach language skills by describing supposedly familiar situations lodged in social myths of education and upward mobility. The environment evoked by Mother, Father, Dick, and Jane in their neat little house and yard with the requisite cat and dog juxtaposes starkly against the lives of the pupils who are learning to read. They do learn their position outside the text as readers, but, more important, their place outside the "home" and "neighborhood" depicted here. Pecola's distance from the text and from society increases greatly when her most intimate spaces—the home and parts of the body—are violated when she is raped by her father. Pecola's deteriorating emotional balance and the trouble witnessed by Frieda and Claudia that forces their early maturation appear first in a gradual compression of print in the passage until the words jumble together. The distortion represents the girls' actual education. The syntactical and typographical disorder reveals the increasing violation of physical, social, and personal space. The position of the words and set of type on the page as well as that of reader to the text have been altered not only by the difference between ideal and actual settings, but also by those forces in society that constantly displace individuals by offering negative refuge. Morrison returns us once again to the prototypical nameless, homeless, landless situation of black Americans in literature and in society. The myth of recovery and replacement and the false hope Pecola constructs—having blue eyes—are more damaging.

The concern for place and home hinted at by the grade-school text is developed further in Claudia's description of her neighborhood and the difference between her house and Pecola's storefront residence. Their respective homes indicate more than a difference in social class; they set the stage for Morrison's view of the ambivalent attraction and repulsion of the middle class for lower-class vitality. In Morrison's later novels, the prissy Nel is drawn to Sula's "woolly house" (29) and bourgeois Milkman Dead finds vibrant life in the disorder at Pilate's ramshackle cabin. Morrison is less concerned with class conflict, however, than with the spontaneous affirmation of cultural and spiritual well-being that exists outside the borders of middle-class respectability.

"Our house is old, cold, and green" (5), says Claudia, bringing to mind a variation of the "green and white" house in the grade-school text. Claudia's assessment of place and house introduces her perception of black homelessness and wilderness that motivates an almost desperate urge to own property and secure refuge. Cholly Breedlove violates the primacy of the home in an affront to middle-class aspirations by burning his storefront dwelling and putting his family out. He incurs Claudia's wrath and exposes her insecurity as well as her fear of homelessness and the uncertain outdoors (a wilderness of sorts): "If you are put out, you go somewhere else, if you are outdoors, there is no place to go" (11). Outdoors becomes the real terror of the middle class, a grim reminder of their political and economic vulnerability. To relieve this insecurity, people buy property with a vengeance. Cholly Breedlove, however, a "renting black" (12), exists apart from this class concern. His violent behavior turns his son Sammy into a perennial runaway and his daughter Pecola into a welfare "case" (11), which is how she enters the MacTeer family temporarily and begins a precarious friendship with Frieda and Claudia. Breedlove, in his disdain for property (burning his residence) and family (putting them out*doors*) is seen as part of the moral as well as physical wilderness: "having put his family outdoors [he] had catapulted himself beyond the reaches of human consideration. He had joined the animals, was, indeed, an old dog, a snake, a ratty nigger" (12). He lands in jail. Until her family is reunited, Pecola has more than a taste of the comfortable life: she drinks three quarts of milk a day from a Shirley Temple glass.

The Breedloves' storefront residence is a "box of peeling gray" (25) on the top floor of which live several prostitutes: China, Poland, and the Maginot Line (Miss Marie), named for landscapes they would neither visit nor represent. The whores become a surrogate family to Pecola, for they are comfortable in their profession, their self-chosen place. They offer Pecola a social education her more-displaced mother refuses to give. Pauline, who "never felt at home anywhere, or that she belonged anyplace" (86), finds a world where her sense of order, arrangement, and privacy can have full reign, working, ironically, as a maid for the white Fisher family. They not only allow Pauline this private, self-defined space, but also give her a nickname so place-specific that it signifies both the "illusion" of privacy and its invasion each time she is called Polly. More devastating is Pauline's proprietary selfishness; she refuses to share the kitchen with her own children: "Pauline kept this order, this beauty, for herself, a private world, and never introduced it into her storefront, or to her children" (100). Given such maternal neglect, it is small wonder that Pecola would also seek an illusion of beauty in wanting blue eyes.

Morrison's further explorations into the relation between person and place, between identity (visible or invisible) and land center in the lives of Pecola and Cholly and inform all of her fiction. Invisibility is foisted upon Pecola not only because she is black and female, but also because she is ugly. She suffers "the total absence of human recognition—the glazed separateness" (36), alienating her from others. Cholly, when young, mired himself in ugly behavior and self-hatred when he started to see himself as negatively as whites viewed him. On the night following his Great-Aunt Jimmy's funeral, Cholly was caught in the act of making love in the woods by white hunters. The flashlight they shone on his nakedness also illuminated their view of him: "Get on wid it, nigger.... An' make it good" (116). Turning his rage inward and onto Darlene instead of at the whites, Cholly experiences the self-hatred he will later inspire in Pauline and Pecola. Furthermore, the physical ugliness that makes Cholly and Pecola so visible that they are invisible also makes them, in Claudia's view, willful prisoners of their shabby storefront: "They lived there because they were poor and black, and they stayed there because they believed they were ugly" (28).

What might have redeemed Cholly in his own eyes and have prevented the internalization of ugliness was his search for his estranged father. Cholly's journey when young had led him not to the "green and white" (1) house of social myth, nor to the "old, cold, and green" (5) house of the black middle class, but to the folded greenbacks poking from the fists of city gamblers. Among them he finds his father, who is more interested in scoring a hit than recognizing his son. Crushed by this rejection, Cholly loses control of himself (indeed, his very bowels) and retreats into the woods. There by the Ocmulgee River, he washes himself and his clothes in a kind of purification ritual, which is complete only when pent-up tears of grief and loneliness finally cascade down his face. Cholly had been prepared to show his grief (a form of recognition itself) by nesting in the woods ("the dark, the warmth, the quiet, enclosed Cholly like the skin and flesh of an elderberry protecting its own seed" [124]), undressing, and feeling about on his hands and knees for the cleansing edge of water. When he cries, he becomes the "new young boy" (125) who will be received back in town by three women offering him lemonade and his manhood through sex. But the freedom Cholly experiences so briefly needs connections to be fully meaningful, even to Cholly, and he longs for a song to sing to activate his new identity. Lacking the music, his transformation and self-confidence are all too brief:

> The pieces of Cholly's life could become coherent only in the head of a musician. Only those who talk their talk through the gold of curved metal, or in the touch of black-and-white rectangles and taut skins and strings echoing from wooden corridors, could give true form to his life. Only they would know how to connect the heart of a red watermelon to the asafetida bag to the muscadine to the flashlight on his behind to the fists of

money to the lemonade in a Mason jar to a man called Blue and come up with what all of that meant in joy, in pain, in anger, in love, and give it its final and pervading ache of freedom. Only a musician would sense, know, without even knowing that he knew, that Cholly was free.
(125)

Without music, Cholly's freedom has no voice, no meaningful or cohering performance to tie together the loose tangling strands of his life thus far. His failure to act upon or act with the identity he has discovered renders his freedom tenuous, his virility inadequate. Cholly's one effort to make connections to the past and present through love results in his rape of Pecola. Cholly had perceived Pecola's unconscious and innocent scratching of her leg with the opposite foot as a reminder of the moment he had fallen in love with Pauline, who was leaning against a road fence—like Hurston's Janie— "scratching herself with a broken foot" (126). Cholly's warped confusion of time and place becomes his odd performance. His one effort to heal displacement ends up sending Pecola and Pauline more out *doors* than before, right to "the edge of town."

Pecola's rape neither begins nor completes her emotional disintegration. That deed is left to Soaphead Church, another figure alienated from the land ("Dear God: ... Once upon a time I lived greenly and youngish on one of your islands" [140]), who had accepted the nickname in exchange for his false conjure and magic. He grants Pecola's wish for blue eyes. His appearance and act in the novel as a *deus ex machina* borrowed from drama are more diabolical than Cholly's deed, which at least offered Pecola a kind of love and recognition, however perverted. Soaphead offers insanity. Both men keep Pecola grounded—if not pinned bodily—to the kitchen floor until she loses consciousness or becomes mired in schizophrenia and delusion. Both family and community, loved ones and landscape, have banished Pecola. A devastating inertia prevents her from achieving the flight she thought would come with the blue eyes. Pecola wears a vision of the sky (like Cholly's search for transcendent, cohering music) but fails to achieve its reward of flight: "The damage done was total. She spent her days, her tendril sap-green days, walking up and down, up and down, her head jerking to the beat of a drummer so distant only she could hear. Elbows bent, hands on shoulders, she flailed her arms like a bird in an eternal, grotesquely futile effort to fly. Beating the air, a winged but grounded bird, intent on the blue void it could not reach—could not even see—but which filled the valleys of the mind" (162).

As Pecola scavenges through garbage, her birdlike gestures diminish "to a mere picking and plucking her way between the tire rims and the sunflowers, between Coke bottles and milkweed, among all the waste and beauty of the world" (162), and Claudia realizes the extent to which Pecola had absorbed the waste she and others had dumped on her. In return Pecola simply gave the only beauty she had: her innocence. Claudia, now mature, realizes that the failure of marigold seeds to grow that year was not only the fault of "the earth, the land, of our town" (164), but hers as well. Having acquiesced to the easy victimization of Pecola, Claudia had failed to acknowledge the earth's own will to kill and the readiness of humans to accomplish the deed.

Sula. "It's the bottom of heaven—best land there is"

A more complex figuration of land and identity emerges in *Sula*. Beyond the psychological boundaries that imprison Pecola and allow the MacTeer sisters to bear witness to the loss of sexual and mental place, *Sula* tells the story of two women who renegotiate the pressures of place and person through their long friendship, which is not without moments of rupture and discord. The growing bond between Nel Wright and Sula Mae Peace as well as their complementary personalities are first revealed to us by the contrasting features of the land.

Two key terrestrial images frame the novel: the hillside signifying the creation of the black community of Medallion, Ohio, known as the Bottom (through the chicanery of a white planter unwilling to fulfill his promise of valley land to an industrious and newly emancipated slave), and a tunnel under construction at New River Road that collapses upon participants in Shadrack's last march to commemorate National Suicide Day. At first glance, the hillside and the tunnel appear dichotomous. The hillside, or the Bottom, is named ironically, and it is viewed through a passing of time: "there was once a neighborhood." The phrase introduces a narrative about an entire community, but also prophesies its destruction, the hell of mutability alluded to by Nel: "Hell ain't things lasting forever. Hell is change" (108).

One reading of these two regions suggests they have male and female characteristics: the phallic hillside and the vaginal tunnel, particularly when one recalls that the Bottom was established as a black community through a barter between two men. But Morrison gives the two regions feminine traits and infuses them with a preponderance of female properties, in the dual sense. One then suspects a different personification at work. Irene's Palace of Cosmetology, Reba's Grill, the dance of a "dark woman in a flowered dress doing a bit of catwalk, a bit of black bottom, a bit of 'messing around' to the lively notes of a mouth organ" (4), all depict a procreative, female environment. The hillside is nurturing; it is a veritable breast of the earth. Within a feminine figuration (accompanying the narrative of a nurturing friendship between Nel and Sula) the hillside complements rather than contrasts with the womblike tunnel, which upon "breaking water" becomes a haunting, unsuspecting grave when several Bottom luminaries drown. This "abortion" of life occurs right at the time Medallion is undergoing a kind of rebirth through urban renewal. Whites and blacks are changing geographical spaces: the former moving to the cooler hills, the latter descending to the crowded valley floor. This change and death reverse the notion of economic upward mobility for Medallion blacks, who have only a promise of work on New River Road, and foreshadow the further decline, or bottoming *out*, of the community. The nurture-destruction tension in Morrison's figuration of the land this early in the novel more than prepares us for the complementary relationship, shifting moral dualism, and irony between Sula Mae Peace, who makes and unmakes peace in the community, and Nel Wright, who is never fully as right or as morally stalwart as she would like to appear.

The double figuration of the land as a framing device also foreshadows the novel's curiously double closure. One ending, effected by Shadrack's haunting, successful celebration of death, culminates his search for a "place for fear" as a way of "controlling it" (14) and brings his social marginality to a shocking conclusion. A second ending, however, forces the reader to revise this reading of the novel. Nel's visit to the elderly Eva, now in a nursing home, picks up the unfinished business between Nel and Sula (here represented by Eva) with shattering results: Nel is forced to acknowledge the guilt she shares with Sula for the accidental drowning of Chicken Little, who had slipped from Sula's swinging hands and had entered the "closed place of the water" (61). The scene also foreshadows the tunnel's sudden collapse. Nel must also acknowledge the grief for Sula she had tried to suppress, only to discover in her solitary walk home that grief like guilt has no prescribed boundaries; it demands open public expression. When she realizes the extent of her accountability to Sula's friendship—"We was girls together"—Nel lets loose the emotion she had artificially held in check all these years: the cry without "bottom" or "top," but "circles and circles of sorrow" (174). The ever-spiraling geometry of Nel's grief returns readers to the scene of Chicken Little's death and forces us to rethink and replace the event. Sula's "evil" now appears innocuous and Nel's guilt more calculating and malevolent. We must also reconsider Nel's [W] rightness, for her cry admits a moral responsibility for wrongdoing that was not Sula's alone. Riding the spiral of Nel's grief back through the novel, we encounter other geometrical and geographical images that clearly establish the theme of moral dualism and double meaning in society and in nature. *Sula* then becomes as much a novel about the shifting patterns of accountability in Sula and Nel's friendship as it concerns a community's acceptance of moral relativism.

The boomerang effect of the shifting moral and physical geography of Medallion, Ohio, can be seen, for example, in the medallion Sula wears, the birthmark above her eye, the meaning of which changes according to who reads it. Morrison's novel is as much about interpretation as it is about art. How members of the community *read* Sula tells us a great deal about their relation to the land, to themselves, and to the meaning they create. The first indication of this theme is the novel's epigraph, taken from *The Rose Tattoo*, which implicates an entire community, a "they," in the speaker's nonconformist assertion of self: *"Nobody knew my rose of the world but me.... I had too much glory. They don't want glory like that in nobody's heart."* No one really knows Sula or why she sets about—as she tells Eva—to "make herself." But nearly everyone has an opinion about Sula's medallion: a sign they believe of her "evil," her *"too much glory"* in flaunting her disregard of social conventions. At first Sula's birthmark is described as a "stemmed rose" (52); as she matures, it becomes a "stem and rose" (74), suggesting the duality in nature as well as Sula's developing thorny yet attractive personality. With age, the mark becomes "the scary black thing over her eye" (97–98). When Jude begins to see the mark as a "copperhead" (103) and a "rattlesnake" (104), he is seduced by Sula. And as Sula becomes the evil the community fears yet abides, her mark indicates either "Hannah's ashes" (114) or, as Shadrack sees it, "a tadpole" (156). No one, not even Nel, knows Sula's heart. Indeed, Sula's closest kin, in terms of the community's social and moral landscape, is none other than Shadrack, whose madness makes him at once both an outsider and insider: "Once the people understood the boundaries and nature of his madness, they could fit him, so to speak, into the scheme of things" (15). His shack in the woods or wilderness, halfway between the order of the town and the disorder of the lake where Chicken Little drowned, becomes Sula's refuge, a more useful shelter after the accident than Nel's calculated silence. When Shadrack answers "always" (62) to the distraught Sula's unvoiced question, he seals the doubling of their characters in one word of recognition.

The shifting geometry of Sula's birthmark also shapes her actions throughout the novel and identifies the forces directing her. Readers will recall that we know nothing of Sula's life away from Medallion—her time spent in college, in New York, and in other parts of the country—because

Sula's real character, however enigmatic, comes from this community, this Medallion. It is her home and, as suggested above, her landmark. When Sula returns home after an absence of ten years, she fully claims the territory as hers by dispossessing Eva of the house. Sula then occupies Eva's third floor bedroom. Her hibernation behind the boarded window seals her fate in the family and in the community. Sula's appropriation of height in the upper room does not, however, bring the desired refuge or elevation. Nor does it become the place of performance where the creation of character, the "making of oneself" can take place. Although she repossesses a space, Sula, like Cholly Breedlove, fails to find therein a voice for her identity. The self she finds in the house where she was born is still incomplete, as fragile and infantile as her uncle Plum. When Eva descended the stairs on her one leg— the only time she actually went down those stairs—she found Plum in a stupor of drug addiction, trying to return to her womb. Childlike, he clearly needed a new identity, a new birth, but one that Eva could neither provide nor accommodate. She set fire to him. Plum's vision before he burned to death may offer a clue to Sula's fate: "He opened his eyes and saw what he imagined was the great wing of an eagle pouring a wet lightness over him. Some kind of baptism, some kind of blessing, he thought" (47). Plum succumbs to the "bright hole of sleep" (47) without achieving flight on the eagle's wing. Sula, who had returned to Medallion during a plague of robins, also yearns for flight as the fulfillment of the self-creation she thought she had achieved. In the upper room, now the setting for her ardent lovemaking with Ajax, Sula discovers her human frailty (sexual possessiveness and emotional vulnerability). It is also the place where she dies.

Flight appears in Morrison's oeuvre as early as *The Bluest Eye*. Pecola, enticed into Junior's house, encounters his black cat with fascinating blue eyes, suggesting the probability that a black person can also have blue eyes. Junior ruthlessly snatches the cat from Pecola and begins to "swing it around his head in a circle." Defying Pecola's cries for him to stop, Junior lets the cat go "in midmotion" (71), throwing it against the window; it falls dead behind the radiator, its fur singeing. In a similar geometrical gesture, "Sula picked [Chicken Little] up by his hands and swung him outward then around and around," until he slips "from her hands and sailed away out over the water," still laughing in delight (60–61). When he lands in the "closed place in the water" (61), his flight, like that of the blue-eyed cat, is aborted in death. But the height and sense of the free fall he achieves brings him to the cutting edge of the kind of freedom and transcendence Sula herself seeks.

Sula's own quest for height and power through performance occurs in Eva's third floor bedroom. Mounted *on top of* Ajax in their lovemaking, Sula "rocked there, swayed there, like a Georgia pine on its knees, high above the slipping, falling smile, high above the golden eyes and the velvet helmet of hair, rocking, swaying.... She looked down, down from what seemed an awful height at the head of the man whose lemon-yellow gabardines had been the first sexual excitement she'd known. Letting her thoughts dwell on his face in order to confine, for just a while longer, the drift of her flesh toward the high silence of orgasm" (129–30). Sula's discovery of height and freedom confirming her self-centered identity and place is only partially realized because the milk-bearing Ajax, in a gesture of sexual nurture, counters her contrived image of flight with a more realistic, attainable one of his own. When Sula experiences the human frailty of love and possessiveness that ultimately destroys her at the same time that it brings her closer to Nel, she becomes just domestic enough to make the adventuresome Ajax lose interest: "when Ajax came that evening ... the bathroom was gleaming, the bed was made, and the table was set for two" (131–32). Ajax's compelling desire, however, is to attend an air show in Dayton. Sula has indeed met her match.

Moreover, Ajax shows how trivial, self-indulgent, and incomplete is Sula's notion of the "free fall" (120), which she felt made her different from Nel, whose imagination had been driven "underground" by her repressive mother, and from the other women of Medallion. Ajax's presence heightens Sula's self-contradictions as he effectively matches her false, showy nonconformity with his more authentic eccentricity: he is the son of a conjurer mother, and his knowledge of magic and lore surpasses Sula's allure. Here Morrison's prevailing metaphor of flight begins with a leap, or free fall, and offers a rectifying alternative to Ellison's idea of hibernation. As Sula hibernates on the upper floor at 7 Carpenter Road, not in an underground cellar, she longs for the kind of performance that would complete her discovery of self-mastery and complete control. This metaphor is hinted at in *The Bluest Eye*, sketched out and challenged by Ajax in *Sula*, and finds its fullest, if not most conclusive statement in *Song of Solomon*.

The relation between Sula and Nel ruptures when Sula interprets Nel's possessiveness of her husband, Jude, to mean that Nel is one of *them*, the conventional housewives of Medallion. Nel had earlier shared Sula's vision of "the slant of life that makes it possible to stretch [life] to its limits." Becoming the clichéd wronged wife, outraged at Jude and Sula's adultery, Nel is too quickly linked with other women in the community who had "interpreted" Sula as incarnating some kind of evil. They had measured themselves morally and socially by abiding "evil"—as Pauline Breedlove did with Cholly in *The Bluest Eye*—and garnering a false dignity, even heroism, by tolerating it: "The purpose of evil was to survive it" (90). When Nel shows her natural jealousy and hurt, she begins to belong, in Sula's view, "to the town and all of its ways" (120). Nel also begins to oppose Sula's notion of invention and free fall on which Sula had based her ascendant self-mastery and their complementary friendship: "But the free fall, oh no, that required—demanded—invention: a thing to do with the wings, a way of holding the legs and most of all a full surrender to the downward flight if they wished to taste their tongues or stay alive. But alive was what they, and now Nel, did not want to be. Too dangerous" (120).

"Dangerous" more than evil is an accurate description of Sula. As an "artist with no art form" (121) Sula is vulnerable to the shifting interpretations of the only form she carries in her very being: her birthmark. Like Hannah, Sula's art lay in lovemaking, in her enjoyment of the sheer abandon of sex. This clearly is how Sula makes the leap from sexual conventions that lead to marriage and braves the outer limits of promiscuity, the ultimate breach of which is to have sex with white men. It was through carefree sex, nonetheless, that Sula found the cutting edge and the leap of free fall, her performance:

> During the lovemaking she found and needed to find the cutting edge. When she left off cooperating with her body and began to assert herself in the act, particles of strength gathered in her like steel shavings drawn to a spacious magnetic center, forming a tight cluster that nothing, it seemed, could break. And there was utmost irony and outrage in lying *under* someone, in a position of surrender, feeling her own abiding strength and limitless power. But the cluster did break, fall apart, and in her panic to hold it together she *leaped* from the edge into soundlessness and went down howling, howling in a stinging awareness of the endings of things: an eye of sorrow in the midst of all that hurricane rage of joy. There, in the center of that silence was not eternity but the death of time and a loneliness so profound the word itself had no meaning. (122–23, emphasis mine)

In an interview published in *Nimrod*, Morrison once discussed the importance of venturing to the cutting edge and experiencing the leap. What is needed, she said, is complete self-control, divesting oneself of the vanities that weigh people down. This surrender is a triumph and results in a stark change of territory: from land to sky, from the confining boundaries of conventional morality and selfishness to the thrill of self-creation, a riding of the air. "Suppose it were literally so, what would it take to fly?" Morrison speculated. "But suppose you could just move one step up and fly? What would you have to be, and feel, and know, and do, in order to do that?" *Sula* begins to answer Morrison's own question. The author, however, asks for more: "You would have to be able to surrender, give up all of the weights, all of the vanities, all of the ignorances. And you'd have to trust and have faith in the harmony of your body. You would also have to have perfect control" (49). Sula indeed wishes for power, control, and the reward of flight. Ajax, the aviation-dreaming lover, brings her milk in blue, sky-colored glass bottles: "Ajax looked at her through the blue glass and held the milk aloft like a trophy" (127). Perhaps it is Ajax who can lift Sula from the ground, or perhaps she will lift him up into the flight and transcendence he also seeks. The only uncertainty is Sula's ability to let herself go and to release Ajax from the confining domesticity of housebound sex.

Sula fails. Her wish for total freedom, for flight, becomes as much a delusion as Pecola's blue eyes. Even the unobstructed mobility or license granted by Sula's land/birthmark is illusory because Sula is both ostracized and nourished by the same community, the same land; her mobility is limited by the interpretative needs of the community, shown by Medallion's quick regression into antagonistic behavior once the "threat" of Sula passes with her death and just prior to the parade into the tunnel. The illusory nature of Sula's desire is revealed in the contrast between her and Ajax, who, like Bigger Thomas in *Native Son* or Buster and Riley in Ellison's story "That I Had The Wings," yearns for freedom through aviation. Although Ajax's dream is realized only in his frequent trips to airports, he establishes a degree of realism against Sula's illusion of control and flight through sex. (It is he who requests that she mount him.) He thinks equally about his conjurer mother and airplanes: "when he was not sitting enchanted listening to his mother's words, he thought of airplanes, and pilots, and the deep sky that held them both" (126). The blue bottle of milk offered to Sula as a trophy connects her to the blue sky and the maternal milk. Flight and aviation as the exercise of creativity, the fulfillment of perfect control, hold both Sula and Ajax in its cobalt blue glow.

Yet the moment that Sula falls in love with Ajax and discovers possessiveness, both she and Ajax are more grounded than either desires. Ajax escapes this confinement by losing interest in Sula, but she remains trapped, totally overwhelmed by feeling human and vulnerable. When she takes Ajax through her newly cleaned house—"the spotless bathroom where dust had been swept from underneath the claw-foot tub"—she shows him her nest, a space for her hibernation, nurture, and fulfillment of sexual desire. Ajax makes love to her in the more conventional position, but he thinks less about Sula than "the date of the air show in Dayton" (134). Sula is "under" him now, and he moves "with the steadiness and the intensity of a man about to leave for Dayton" (134).

In his stunning absence, Sula tries to come to terms with her love for Ajax, for the flight of fancy he represented, for the adventuresome love, not the self-gratifying control that grounds her. Like Pecola, Sula is weighed down by the human, emotional vulnerability she succumbs to, particularly the self-willed grief she hibernates in, shut away in Eva's room. Like Cholly Breedlove, Sula reaches a momentary height of self-awareness in her admission of loneliness and possessiveness of Ajax (particularly when she realizes she never really possessed him, for she never knew his name), but she fails to give full voice to this spark of self-recognition. Hence, her freedom is never fully realized. Her flight is not only aborted, but Sula also dies. The song she wanted to sing might have saved her by providing a different kind of performance and presentation of self, as Milkman's song performance will. But the right lyrics elude her; she can only mouth repeated nonsense words. Sula, then, like Cholly, is a failed "person"-of-words, left dreaming, like Pecola, of "cobalt blue" (137) without even an air show in Dayton to claim her: "When she awoke, there was a melody in her head she could not identify or recall ever hearing before.... Then it came to her—the name of the song and all its lyrics just as she had heard it many times before.... She lay down again on the bed and sang a little wandering tune made up of the words *I have sung all the songs all the songs I have sung all the songs there are* until, touched by her own lullaby, she grew drowsy, and in the hollow of near-sleep she tasted the acridness of gold, left the chill of alabaster and smelled the dark, sweet stench of loam" (137). Sula succumbs to the "hollow," as Plum did at the "hole" of sleep, because she could not give adequate voice and action to her vision. Instead of flying, she descends to the loam of the very land that had marked her from birth.

Sula's death offers no "invention," only descent; it is neither a free fall nor the redeeming flight she had longed for. One clue to her decline lies in Morrison's verbal design of Sula's place of hibernation, Eva's room with its blind window, boarded up indirectly by Sula herself. Sula's paralyzing interest in watching her mother Hannah burn necessitated Eva's leap of rescue out of that window. When Sula subsequently dispossesses Eva of that room, she puts herself in the physical, but not the emotional, space for the reconciliation Eva had attempted in her failed rescue of Hannah, and, paradoxically, in her mercy killing of Plum—to keep him from descending further into the stupor of drugs, or reducing his already fragile maturity to the helpless state of an infant wanting a return to the womb. Instead of a womb, Eva offered Plum the scent and vision of the eagle's wings. Instead of flight, Eva's upper room offers Sula the best setting for the only performance she is then capable of; her foetal plunge down an imaginary birth canal or tunnel (prefiguring the town's later disaster) is a perversion of the rebirth in death that Eva had granted Plum: "The sealed window soothed her with its sturdy termination, its unassailable finality.... It would be here, only here, held by this blind window high above the elm tree, that she might draw her legs up to her chest, close her eyes, put her thumb in her mouth and float over and down the tunnels, just missing the dark walls, down, down until she met a rain scent and would know the water was near, and she would curl into its heavy softness and it would envelop her, carry her, and wash her tired flesh always. Always" (148–49).

Sula's plunge into the tunnel following a period of willful hibernation completes the solitude she had always wanted. This hibernation, however, had rendered her immobile, incapacitated (except in death), for Ajax's departure and Sula's recognition of her human vulnerability stun her into physical and emotional paralysis. This backfire, or boomerang, reverses the moment of moral strength Eva felt in her husband BoyBoy's desertion, and now Eva, as a discerning, combative ancestor, cannot help Sula, for Eva has been safely locked away.

Neither Sula's solitude nor tunnel plunge is a fate left to her alone. Being a product of the land, a mark of the community, she reflects the fate of others. In the collapse of the half-finished tunnel at New River Road to the clanging tune of Sula's brother in marginality, Shadrack's pied-piper parade, the town, which had made Sula both person and pariah and a source of their negatively realized pride, meets its end. Both Sula and Shadrack have presided over figurations of the land that reveal underground refuge or hibernation to be the simple burial it is, which is what Wright's Fred Daniels discovered. Hibernation, despite the subversive bravura of Ellison's invisible man, does not lead to the effective overt activity or self-assertion he had promised. Morrison's more complex rendering of place and person in the collapse of the tunnel and the spirals of grief that bind Nel to repetitions of guilt, necessitates an end to hibernation, whether underground or three floors up. In *Song of Solomon*, Morrison offers the corrective reach of the mountaintop and a triumphant surrender to the air.

Song of Solomon. *"You see?" the farm said to them. "See?*
See what you can do?"

Whereas the framing images in *Sula* are terrestrial enclosures, those in *Song of Solomon* are celestial flights. The novel opens with Robert Smith's aborted takeoff that brings about his planned suicide, and it ends with the violent reunion between Milkman and Guitar as one of them leaps from the mountain and into the "killing" arms of the other. The difference between the flights, how their angles of ascent exceed or grasp the long-sought-for family treasure, the home and name initially giving these characters wings, is the novel's main concern.

The novel encompasses three principal organizing structures that enlarge the orbit of cultural performances suggested thus far by several key texts, including Morrison's earlier fiction. These organizational structures include the relationship between Milkman and Guitar as the problematic moral center of the novel, the conflict between family and property ties that fuels tension between Pilate and her brother Macon Dead, and finally Milkman's initiatory "errand" into and out of the wilderness. By discovering his name and performing the song that redeems him and helps him to fly, Milkman completes the unrealized gestures and dreams of Morrison's earlier characters: Pecola, Cholly, Sula, and Ajax. *Song of Solomon* is Morrison's carefully drawn map of ancestral landscape that reclaims and resurrects moribund (the family name is Dead) or hibernating personalities.

Robert Smith, insurance salesman by day and by night a member of the "underground" radical group, the Seven Days, occupies enemy territory when he climbs to the roof of No Mercy Hospital, so called because it had never admitted black patients. Smith appears to act out the words of one Negro spiritual that describes the kind of release he desires:

> Some o' dese mornin's bright an' fair,
> Way in de middle of de air
> Goin' hitch on my wings an' try de air
> Way in de middle of de air.

Both the foreign, outer terrain of the hospital roof and the artifice involved in the "hitching" on of wings—"his wide blue silk wings curved forward around his chest" (5)—are ominous. Instead of a smooth and graceful death, Smith loses his balance, reaches for a triangle of wood jutting from the hospital's cupola, and goes "splat" (as one observer described the scene). Robert Smith's "leap" is an undignified, clumsy fall.

Smith's death sends another witness, the pregnant Ruth Foster Dead, into labor. Her son Milkman, the "little bird," whose hour of birth was accurately predicted by his aunt Pilate, who had earlier helped in his conception, becomes the first black child to be born in No Mercy. Milkman now has a more legitimate claim to the space Robert Smith had usurped. As a real "bird," a descendant of the Byrds in Shalimar, Virginia, revealed in the ending, Milkman will not need the artifice of Robert Smith's "blue silk," Ajax's cobalt blue bottles, or Pecola's "blue" eyes. Milkman's maturation in his midwestern hometown and his departure South to discover the land of his ancestors and to sing the song of Solomon—the core subject of the novel—teach him to use his own wings. Milkman's *leap* at the novel's close is a redeeming *flight*. His journey is not an easy one; nor is the novel's moral center in the magnetic friendship between Milkman and Guitar without a healthy dose of ambiguity and role reversal. Before Pilate takes over as Milkman's veritable pilot, his first navigator through a difficult childhood and adolescence is Guitar, who as a child had also witnessed Robert Smith's fall. Guitar is best suited to be the kind of friend and adversary who can enlarge the reach of Milkman's leap "way in de middle of de air."

Guitar and Milkman do not have the same complementary personalities that make Sula and Nel appear to be one character. Although from different backgrounds, they manage to build a friendship upon mutual interests and a pendular sway of dominant and submissive roles between them as Guitar then Milkman then Guitar takes the upper hand. Older than Milkman, Guitar has the lead at first; he introduces Milkman to Pilate, whose folk conjure aided his conception and birth. Her conjure of a successful aphrodisiac had encouraged Macon and Ruth to conceive after many years of uninterest and celibacy. Pilate, who helped make Milkman's "egg," later teaches Milkman and Guitar how to make the perfect three-minute soft-boiled egg. The recipe indirectly reveals the ambiguity of love and power in their friendship and how a growing estrangement between them will be reconciled, even if in battle. "Now, the water and the egg," Pilate instructs the boys, "have to meet each other on a kind of equal standing. One can't get the upper hand over the other. So the temperature has to be the same for both" (39). In the folk logic of this equation, Milkman is the egg. What about the water? Guitar's last name is Bains, which in French means "bath" or "watering place" or both. Pilate's foolproof recipe thus becomes a formula for reconciliation; Guitar and Milkman need equal matching for either of them to assume the "perfect" control of the leap, which is the only way, as shown in *Sula*, the free fall becomes flight.

Throughout most of the novel, however, Guitar does have the upper hand. In addition to introducing Milkman to Pilate, Guitar is the one who initially guides Milkman away from his stifling, bourgeois upbringing—summers at St. Honoré Island, collecting rents for his slumlord father—and Guitar teaches Milkman the novel's core lesson: "Wanna fly, you got to give up the shit that weighs you down" (179). Until Guitar's participation in the Seven Days weakens him morally and psychologically (as had happened to mild-mannered Robert Smith) to the point where he assumes the "greed for gold" that Milkman has outgrown, Guitar, as his name suggests, is as instrumental in Milkman's development of character and cultural awareness as McKay's *Banjo* was for the aspiring writer Ray. That is, until Milkman finds his own voice.

The attraction of opposite social classes that initially brings Milkman and Guitar together is similar to the magnetism between Sula and Nel or the delicate class comforts that barely distinguish Pecola from Frieda and Claudia, yet allow the sisters to take Pecola under their wings. Morrison's characters appear to find stability in kinship ties and bonds of friendship that cut across class barriers and generational differences. Note the strong matrilinear network linking Eva-Hannah-Sula, for example, or the generational patterning among Pilate-Reba-Hagar. These sets of historical relationships anchor Sula and Pilate in a culture and family they use for support, particularly when the larger society rejects them as pariahs. Their hearths are comforting and inviting to Nel and Milkman, who are fleeing the stultifying middle-class repression that renders them marginal and homeless. Morrison's use of class differences as one element of mutual attraction suggests that economic conditions alone do not alienate lower or middle classes from a common culture. In *Song of Solomon* this idea is explored further when members of two different social classes represent the same family.

Macon and Pilate are brother and sister, separated after their father's murder; each inherits something different from him. Macon turns his father's love of the land and talent for farming into an obsessive ownership of property, reducing land and people to mere commodities. He advises his son Milkman: "Own things. And let the things you own own other things. Then you'll own yourself and other people too" (55). Pilate, just the opposite, already owns herself—the physical evidence of her self-possession and self-creation is her stomach without a navel. She interprets the one word uttered by her father's ghost, a regular visitor, as an admonition for performance: "Sing." Instead of acquiring property, Pilate creates song, transmitting the family lore unconsciously. The history and culture voiced here first draws Macon, then Milkman and Guitar into the charged orbit of Pilate's single-story house on Darling Street, "whose basement seemed to be rising from rather than settling into the ground" (27). Pilate's home thus moves us up out of the underground and to the mountaintop. The wings of her song first attract, then encourage full surrender to that upward motion, even for Macon, who listens surreptitiously:

They were singing some melody that Pilate was leading. A phrase that the other two were taking up and building on. Her powerful contralto, Reba's piercing soprano in counterpoint, and the soft voice of the girl, Hagar, who must be about ten or eleven now, pulled him like a carpet tack under the influence of a magnet.

Surrendering to the sound, Macon moved closer. He wanted no conversation, no witness, only to listen and perhaps to see the three of them, the source of that music that made him think of fields and wild turkey and calico. (29)

As Macon peers unseen into the lives of these women, he becomes a version of Wright's man who lived underground or of Ellison's invisible man. Lacking Daniels's cynicism, Macon secretly yearns to come out of hibernation and to accept fully the family he had denied in his "drive for wealth" (28): "Near the window, hidden by the dark, he felt the irritability of the day drain from him and relished the effortless beauty of the women singing in the candlelight.... As Macon felt himself softening under the weight of memory and music, the song died down. The air was quiet and yet Macon Dead could not leave. He liked looking at them freely this way" (29–30).

Macon is the kind of invisible man Milkman refuses to be. Without ever learning all that his nickname means (the prolonged "sexual" nursing from his mother and the demands of nurture he places on other women), Milkman will develop any trait, any *device*, to differentiate himself from his father, even to the point of affecting a limp. "Milkman feared his father, respected him, but knew, because of the leg, that he could never emulate him. So he differed from him as much as he dared" (63). Unlike Macon, who listens from outside, Milkman penetrates Pilate's house and there learns the magic in the perfect meeting of egg and water.

Macon and Pilate vie for a controlling influence over Milkman. They also compete over their relation to the dead father and to the farmland that was as fertile as it was generous, "See? See what you can do?" The father had made it the best farming in Montour County, earning him the adoration of blacks and the enmity of the whites who eventually killed him. The land and the family heritage become battlegrounds for the continuing struggle between Pilate and Macon. While Macon is an owner of land and of people (his assistant Sonny, his tenant Porter), or so he thinks, Pilate, like Cholly Breedlove, is a "renting" black. Their different relation to the land inversely determines how they function in the novel to help or hinder Milkman. Macon remains dead to the past, which is celebrated and *possessed* unselfconsciously by Pilate. Macon, defeated by his father's murder, has leased his identity to fluctuations in the real estate market and in the whims of bank lenders out of desperation to prove his worth. Pilate, on the other hand, a restless wanderer, owns only those objects that implicitly direct her search for place (and for refuge from pariah status): rocks, a sack of human bones, and a geography book—her only legacy until she nurtures Milkman. Instead of washing her hands free of the past, she fills them with such common objects, burdens really, until Milkman's discovery shows them to be the family treasure they always were. By identifying the invisible ancestor in Pilate's song—"reading and re-reading" Pilate's oral poetry—Milkman lifts the burden of those bones from Pilate's shoulders and allows her to experience a surrender to the air that prefigures his more complete flight.

Cursed with endless wandering because the lack of a navel relegates her to pariah status in whatever community she finds herself, Pilate and her smooth stomach, like Sula and her birthmark, are objects of interpretation. Unlike Sula's artistic formlessness, Pilate has her bootlegging business, her conjure, and most importantly, her song—the same song that announced Robert Smith's presence on the hospital roof and that cushioned his awkward, suicidal descent; the same song that drew Macon to her part of town and partially out of his preferred invisibility. It is also the song neither Sula nor Cholly could sing. Like the Negro spiritual encoding messages for escape or resistance, it contains the riddle and the answer to the question of survival; it is a mystery to be unraveled, like the enigmatic advice of the grandfather in *Invisible Man*. This is the poem Milkman will hear again and again until he recites it by heart; his performance in the land of his ancestors reveals the hidden family name:

O Sugarman done fly away
Sugarman done gone
Sugarman cut across the sky
Sugarman gone home.... (6)

When Milkman learns the full text of the song and the history transmitted through it—"Jake the only son of Solomon"—he recognizes the ancestor and the homeland Pilate perhaps had been reading about in her frayed geography book. She can now let go of the burden of bones. She buries them and her earring locket, containing her name written by her father, in a mountaintop grave. The interment of the bones also signals Pilate's end, for she is killed by a bullet intended for Milkman. Once again, she gives him life, if only for the time it takes Guitar to exchange his gun for his fists. More important, however, Pilate's death concludes her terrestrial wandering. When a bird, attracted by the glittering earring near her crumpled body, swoops down and soars away with the locket, Pilate achieves symbolic flight. She experiences the full meaning of her ancestry among the Flying Africans and of her name, no longer Pilate but *Pilot* (a fulfillment that eludes LeRoi Jones's Air Force gunner and Ellison's flight trainee). The meaning of the novel's epigraph also comes clear: *"The fathers may soar / And the children may know their names."* In addition to wholeness of identity, Pilate achieves at last her rightful, celestial place.

Macon Dead, on the other hand, remains grounded in his lust for gold and in his accumulation of property. He has misread the lesson his father had learned from the land and its harvest, as heard in Morrison's thrilling rendition of the sermon the land itself delivers:

> "You see?" the farm said to them. "See? See what you can do?...
> Here, this here, is what a man can do if he puts his mind to it and
> his back in it. Stop sniveling," it said. "Stop picking around the
> edges of the world. Take advantage, and if you can't take
> advantage, take disadvantage. We live here. On this planet, in this
> nation, in this country right here. *No* where else! We got a home
> in this rock, don't you see! Nobody starving in my home; nobody
> crying in my home, and if I got a home you got one too! Grab it.
> Grab this land! Take it, hold it, my brothers, make it, my
> brothers, shake it, squeeze it, turn it, twist it, beat it, kick it, kiss
> it, whip it, stomp it ... own it, build it, multiply it, and pass it on—
> can you hear me? Pass it on!" (235)

This land, its voice full of the language and cadence of Negro spirituals and rich with sources of identity, should offer prosperity to any family willing to use it in the ways suggested above, not merely acquire more and more of it. The land is to be used for procreation and harvest, not hibernation and greed. Thus, in many respects, Macon remains invisible to the land, to the community, to his family, and finally, to the culture that commands him to perform, not just to listen secretively. In the conflict between Macon and Pilate over the land, over history, and over Milkman, Pilate wins because she has shown Milkman a way out of the hibernation advocated by Macon's inertia. In this way, too, Milkman's struggle enlarges the orbit of geography for Afro-American identity and cultural performance beyond the cave of hibernation promoted in Ellison's *Invisible Man*.

Song of Solomon signals a major break from Ellison's territoriality in Afro-American letters, yet Morrison's thematic and imagistic challenge to Ellison begins with interesting points of comparison to his novel. These common areas of concern suggest Morrison's careful reading of Ellison and the detour she takes from his "highway," and from the theme, setting, language, and literary form he enshrined. Morrison's break becomes all the more bold, startling, and significant because the comparisons suggest that she has explored Ellison's terrain and found it lacking in the kind of cultural mobility her characters and their experiences demand.

Morrison completes the groping for avian imagery and the search for redemptive flight first articulated in slave songs and narratives and then imagined more existentially in texts by Wright, Ellison, and LeRoi Jones. Morrison's aviators, the Air Force men who frequent a local bar, inspire Milkman's envy only until he discovers that he can fly without the encumbrance of military obligations. She also manipulates and enlarges the conventions of surrealism and the *bildungsroman*, which Ellison viewed as granting the writer freedom from the sociological predilections and realistic persuasions most readers impose upon black American fiction. This was Ellison's main criticism of Wright, but his injunction stops there. Morrison undercuts the hegemony of Ellison's preferred narrative strategy, what Robert Stepto has called "the narrative of hibernation" (193), by enlarging the structure to encompass multiple lives and points of view as her characters aim for motion, not stasis. The multiplicity of perspectives and situations in Morrison's fiction requires protagonists writ large; her novels are *bildungsromans* of entire communities and racial idioms rather than the voice of a single individual. What central protagonist exists develops only through the interplay between the community and the individual. Even Milkman is admonished by his father to "know the whole story" before taking sides. "And if you want to be a whole man, you have to deal with the whole truth" (70). Morrison's novels require us to read the life of a community as the text and context of an individual's articulation of voice. Milkman needs the play of the children of Shalimar to help him hear Jake's "narrative" in the song and to "close" the story of his own self-possession. Milkman's cultural performance when he sings the song of Solomon makes him a successful man-of-words.

Other parallels are at work and play between Morrison and Ellison. Both their protagonists struggle against an identity imposed by others. The nameless invisible man must end his passivity and willingness to be named by others, from the letters sent by Bledsoe to the slip of paper revealing the Brotherhood's name for him. Morrison's protagonist must come to terms with a nickname whose origin he never knows and with people who want to "use" him: "Somehow everybody was using him for something or as something. Working out some scheme of their own on him, making him the subject of their dreams of wealth, or love, or martyrdom" (165). Sonny, when he discovers Ruth's prolonged nursing of her son, announces, "A natural milkman if ever I seen one. Look out womens. Here he come" (15). Milkman feels his name to be "dirty, intimate, and hot" (15) as he grows up to fulfill, unwittingly, Sonny's double-edged prophecy: he will take from women, but he will also be a passive, bleached, colorless (invisible?) personality until he takes charge of himself, shares himself with others. When Milkman learns through his journey to the South that names can bear witness, indeed "had meaning," he can give up his old self more easily (he loses his fine clothes and jewelry and car while on his journey) and reciprocate in lovemaking with Sweet more than he had done with any other woman ("He washed her hair.... He made up the bed.... He washed the dishes.... She kissed his mouth. He touched her face. She said please come back. He said I'll see you tonight" [285]). Milkman's increased awareness of the mutual responsibilities in love and self-discovery brings about his visibility.

Both novels also share a figuration of geography that shapes the protagonists' journeys. Ellison's narrative (apart from the frame) moves from the South to the North; Morrison moves from the North to the South. She alters the direction of cultural history away from simple chronology and toward a single, charged moment of multiple discoveries by emphasizing Milkman's embrace of cultural and familial geography. He arrives at the ancestral ground to become rooted in it as deep and as high as Pilate's father's bones. The protagonists in both novels also confront a riddle that invites interpretation and subversion of the nameless condition of Afro-Americans: one proffered by Ellison's protagonist's grandfather, the other by Morrison's "Sugarman" or Milkman's great-great-great grandfather, whose identity could save his life. Both narratives or novels are framed or enclosed; one by the static posture of *telling* a story through the device of prologue and epilogue, the other by dual *actions* that are dynamic performances: Smith's suicide is revised in Milkman's flight.

Although Ellison's protagonist's writing of *Invisible Man* in his underground retreat can be seen as an active deed (since it creates the space and action of the novel), Morrison offers an effective contrast: She replaces the cellar-basement environment for the invisible man's *written* performance with the mountaintop height of Milkman's *oral* performance. Also significant is their different treatment of flight. Ellison offers the folk rhyme "They picked poor robin clean" as a warning about the protagonist's grounded predicament. Morrison counteracts with the myth of the Flying Africans to show Milkman the reach and promise of the air, *if* he can ride it. Milkman becomes a true descendant of Jake, the only son of Solomon, whereas Ellison's protagonist fails to become a true blood following Trueblood's example of storytelling and rhetorical flourish. When Milkman actually sings the song of Solomon, he assumes the name that had been denied the invisible man, without which Milkman would be colorless and the land of his culture invisible to all. Milkman can now nurture others: Pilate, Ruth, Sweet, Jake, and himself. From that exchange of emotional commitment, Milkman gains the strength he needs to meet his adversary Guitar and gain an equal if not *upper* hand.

Above and beyond these various points of comparison between *Song of Solomon* and *Invisible Man* lies Morrison's most significant achievement. She extends the geographical imagery and enriches the acts of deliverance established so far in Afro-American letters. Her novel encompasses the three principal landscapes of retreat and regeneration already present in black American culture: the wilderness, the underground, and the mountain-top. Taken as part of Morrison's assessment of geography and identity in fiction, they exceed earlier attempts to fix or promote one region over another. *Song of Solomon* not only returns us to landscapes suggested in the slave songs and narratives, it also plays upon the fundamental contrast between underground and mountain stages of self-achievement, thus exposing the limits of a Wright-Ellison geography and moving us forward to other heights of self-awareness through action.

Macon and Pilate Dead, for all their successes and failures, are still connected to figures of spatial enclosures, even the imminent grave suggested by their unfortunate family name. They are also prisoners of a haunting guilt in having killed a miner at the mouth of a cave in the wilderness through which they wandered aimlessly after their father's death. Once overcoming the menacing miner—a digger of undergrounds probing for hidden treasures below—the two children are prepared to conquer other spaces, such as houses, later on. Pilate's single-story dwelling appears to rise from the basement or underground, and Macon's acquisition of property represents his rise in society. Yet both are still tied to either material goods or to the alternative meaning they can convey, which is how Fred Daniels reacted to the bank notes and diamonds in his cave. It is Milkman who eventually develops a more effective relation to the land when he confronts the wilderness. There he not only searches for the cave where the miner's gold is presumably hidden, but he is prepared for the strenuous encounter with the Shalimar woods during the nighttime hunt of the bobcat with Calvin and

King Walker and the other men of the town. They hate him at first ("They looked with hatred at the city Negro who could buy a car as if it were a bottle of whiskey because the one he had was broken" [266]), but Milkman's participation in the hunt gains their fraternity and friendship. He secures his own place in the ancestral territory apart from the claims of Pilate or Macon.

It is not enough, however, for Milkman simply to arrive in Shalimar, or to lose his material possessions while there (the vanities that weigh him down). He has to walk that lonesome valley, as the slave songs required, by himself:

> There was nothing here to help him—not his money, his car, his father's reputation, his suit, or his shoes. In fact, they hampered him. Except for his broken watch, and his wallet with about two hundred dollars, all he had started out with on his journey was gone.... His watch and his two hundred dollars would be of no help out here, where all a man had was what he was born with, or had learned to use. And endurance. Eyes, ears, nose, taste, touch—and some other sense that he knew he did not have: an ability to separate out, of all the things there were to sense, the one that life itself might depend on. (277)

Milkman has to earn kinship by enduring the woods, the wilderness. Like the fugitive in slave narratives, he has to renew his covenant with nature to secure passage out of the wilderness that had invited him in. Only through this initiatory trial in the woods of Blue Ridge County will he encounter those figures of the landscape that will give definite meaning to the otherwise confusing names and places in the children's song:

> *Jay the only son of Solomon*
> *Come booba yale, come booba tambee*
> *Whirl about and touch the sun*
> *Come booba yalle, come booba tambee ... (264)*

Each step of his way puts Milkman "on land that sloped upward" (274). Only by surviving the wilderness—which is not a foregone conclusion since he is caught off-guard by the now crazed, nightseeing, cat-eyed Guitar, who, with this unfair advantage, cannot "kill" Milkman yet because the water and egg need equal matching—does Milkman learn the historical meaning associated with two figures of landscape that lie beyond the vision and experience of Macon or Pilate: Ryna's Gulch and Solomon's Leap, a valley and a mountaintop. These contrasting, gender-related spaces extend from Morrison's earlier survey of cultural territory used as the framing images in *Sula:* the hilltop Bottom leading to the collapsing tunnel. Here the movement is reversed. Ryna's Gulch (as well as the bodies of the women Milkman has exploited through sexual conquest) points him to Solomon's Leap, but only after Milkman has bent his ear to the ground to hear the land's sermon or "anything the earth had to say" (279). Milkman's discovery of these new spaces and new territories, makes him the pilot to guide Pilate to the resting place for her father's bones.

In this wilderness, Milkman earns friendship with the men of Shalimar, with himself, and with the earth. Milkman discovers that he can be his own man, based on his proven skills of survival. Walking on the earth like he belonged to it, Milkman no longer needs the artificial device, the dutchman, of his limp to distinguish himself from his father. Nor does he need material possessions to differentiate himself from the kinsmen of Shalimar. Sharing at last a good-hearted laugh with them, Milkman becomes exhilarated "by simply walking the earth. Walking it like he belonged on it; like his legs were stalks, tree trunks, a part of his body that extended down down down into the rock and soil, and were comfortable there—on the earth and on the place where he walked. And he did not limp" (281). Here Milkman becomes rooted. "Back home he had never felt that way, as though he belonged to anyplace or anybody" (293). This belonging enables him to decode the children's rhyme that gives meaning to the landscape and to Milkman's ancestry. Caught without pencil or paper, Milkman cannot write the song down, as Ellison's protagonist could do with his narrative. Milkman "would just have to listen and memorize it" (303), internalize it.

When Milkman leads Pilate to Shalimar, he brings her similar homelessness to an end: she "blended into the population like a stick of butter in a churn" (335). Together they advance to the higher ground of Solomon's Leap, both to bury the bones and to meet their separate fates. Pilate will fly without ever leaving the ground, comforted by Milkman's rendition of the song, which Morrison leaves unindented and without italics on the page to suggest that it has been refashioned in Milkman's voice and fused into the uninterrupted flow of the narrative: "Sugargirl don't leave me here / Cotton balls to choke me / Sugargirl don't leave me here / Buckra's arms to yoke me" (336). Now Milkman can ride the air. His leap of surrender is his ultimate performance, a flight he has earned by doffing his vanities and passing the test of the wilderness. His leap transcends the rootedness and the freedom he has gained. Milkman and Morrison's flight, their ride out of the wilderness, demonstrates self-mastery and perfect control.

DEBORAH E. McDOWELL*

"The Self and the Other": Reading Toni Morrison's Sula and the Black Female Text

What shall we call our "self"? Where does it begin? Where does it end? It overflows into everything that belongs to us.

—Henry James, *Portrait of a Lady*

She had clung to Nel as the closest thing to both an other and a self, only to discover that she and Nel were not one and the same thing.

—Toni Morrison, *Sula*[1]

In "Negro Art," an essay published in the *Crisis* in 1921, W. E. B. DuBois described the desire of blacks for idealized literary representation. "We want everything said about us to tell of the best and highest and noblest in us ... we fear that the evil in us will be called racial, while in others, it is viewed as individual."[2] A few years later, in 1926, DuBois seemed himself to want to see the "best and highest and noblest" image of the black SELF in literature. Concerned because blacks were being "continually painted at their worst and judged by the public as they [were] painted," DuBois organized a write-in symposium called "The Negro in Art: How Shall He Be Portrayed?" that ran from March-December in the *Crisis* magazine. The subject of intense debate, the symposium elicited applause and critiques from its respondents. Though not written directly in response to the symposium, one famous critique of its concerns was Langston Hughes's famous manifesto, published in the same year, "The Negro Artist and the Racial Mountain," in which he blasted the

From *Critical Essays on Toni Morrison* by Nellie Y. McKay. © 1988 by Nellie Y. McKay.

"Nordicized Negro intelligentsia" for demanding that black artists "be respectable, write about nice people, [and] show how good [black people] are."[3]

Roughly fifty years later, those in the vanguard of the Black Aesthetic movement described and called for black writers to inscribe the "positive" racial self in literature. In his 1977 essay "Blueprint for Black Criticism," for example, Addison Gayle appealed specifically for literary characters modeled upon such men and women as Sojourner Truth, Harriet Tubman, Martin Delaney, H. Rap Brown, and Fannie Lou Hamer—a kind of Plutarch's *Lives* of the black race. In that they offer images of "heroism, beauty, and courage," Gayle continues, "these men and women are positive" characters, functional "alternatives to the stereotypes of Blacks," and thus warriors in the "struggle against American racism."[4]

In the ten years since Gayle issued his blueprint, Afro-American literary criticism has finally seen the beginnings of a paradigm shift, one that has extended the boundaries and altered the terms of its inquiry. Falling in step with recent developments in contemporary critical theory, some critics of Afro-American literature have complicated some of our most common assumptions about the SELF, and about race as a meaningful category in literary study and critical theory.[5] These recent developments have made it difficult, if not impossible, to posit, with any assurance, a "positive" black SELF, always already unified, coherent, stable, and known.

And yet, despite these important and sophisticated developments, Afro-American critics of Afro-American literature, in both the popular media and academic journals, continue to resist any work that does not satisfy the nebulous demand for the "positive" racial SELF. And perhaps at no time has such resistance been more determined and judgments been more harsh than now, when diehard critics, reducing contemporary black women writers to a homogenized bloc, have alleged that their portryal of black male characters is uniformly "negative."

A full inquiry into this debate, which has escaped the pages of literary journals and essay collections, and spilled over into the privileged organs of the literary establishment—the *New York Times Book Review* and the *New York Review of Books*—is not possible here, although it is in urgent need of address. But allow me to use Mel Watkins's comments from his June 1986 essay, "Sexism, Racism, and Black Women Writers," published in the *New York Times Book Review* to represent the insistent refrain. Watkins argues that in the great majority of their novels, black women indicate that "sexism is more oppressive than racism." In these works, black males are portrayed in an "unflinchingly candid and often negative manner," almost without exception, "thieves, sadists, rapists, and ne'er-do-wells." In choosing "Black men as a target," Watkins continues, "these writers have set themselves outside a tradition, devoted to "establishing humane, positive images of Blacks" (36).[6]

It is useful here to pause and extrapolate the interlocking assumptions of Watkins's essay most relevant to my concerns. These assumptions are the struts of the dominant Afro-American critical paradigm in which 1) the world is neatly divided into black and white; 2) race is the sole determinant of being and identity, subsuming sexual difference; 3) identity is preexistent, coherent, and known; and 4) literature has the power to unify and liberate the race. This paradigm pivots on a set of oppositions—black/white, positive/negative, self/other—among an interchangeable field. The overarching preoccupation with "positive" racial representation has worked side by side with a static view of the nature of identification in the act of reading. Further, when accepted and upheld, it has resulted in substantial figurations of myth akin to Alice Walker's description: "I am Black, beautiful, and strong, and almost always right."[7] *This* is the SELF, with which our hypothetical Afro-American critic, desperately seeking flattery, is likely to identify. It is uniformly "positive" and "good" and defined in contradistinction to its OTHER, uniformly "negative" and "bad."

Easily recognizable here is the classic condition of "otherness," a subject that is itself fast becoming an industry in current critical theory and practice. And, as feminist theorists consistently and emphatically point out, the opposition of "self" to "other," and all those analogous to it, relate hierarchically and reproduce the more fundamental opposition between male and female. Man is SELF, and woman, other.[8] And in this configuration, as Shoshana Felman puts it eloquently, echoing the dutiful terms of the dominant Afro-American paradigm, woman is "the negative of the positive."[9] We face here an exponential expression of what Henry Gates has observed about Afro-American narrative more generally. He notes astutely that the irony of the Afro-American writers' "attempt to posit a 'black self' in the very Western languages in which blackness [multiply femaleness] itself is a figure of absence [is] a negation."[10]

While these observations are commonplace in feminist discourse, their usefulness to students of Afro-American literary history has not been fully interrogated. Preventing such interrogation is an almost exclusive focus on race in Afro-American literary discourse, which is often tantamount to a focus on maleness. Further preventing such investigation is what might be called an orthodoxy of victimage that unifies and homogenizes black men. In reducing their relationship to white male power and privilege as exclusively one of victimization, this orthodoxy ignores the extent to which black men share in the ideologies and practices of male privilege. The subordination (if not the absolute erasure) of black women in discourses on blackness is well known. The black SELF has been assumed male historically, of which Gloria Hull, Patricia Bell-Scott, and Barbara Smith are well aware. They do not engage in cheap and idle rhetoric in entitling their landmark anthology: *All the Women Are White, All the Blacks Are Men*, for we are all too familiar with the fact that, in significant periods of their history, black women saw black men as the privileged centers of the race. While that pattern is widely evident, it stands out in noticeable relief both in Afro-American critical inquiry and in the Afro-American literary canon.[11] There, the "face" of the race, the "speaking subject," is male.[12]

While these issues need to be exposed, it will no longer suffice to leave the discourse at the point of simple descriptive exposure to which we are all inured. The next stage in the development of feminist criticism on Afro-American women writers must lead us beyond the descriptions that keep us locked in opposition and antagonism. Toni Morrison's novel, *Sula* (1973), is rife with liberating possibilities in that it transgresses all deterministic structures of opposition.

The novel invokes oppositions of good/evil, virgin/whore, self/other, but moves beyond them, avoiding the false choices they imply and dictate. As Hortense Spillers puts it eloquently, when we read *Sula*, "No Manichean analysis demanding a polarity of interest—black/white, male/female, good/bad [and I might add, positive/negative, self/other]—will do."[13] The narrative insistently blurs and confuses these and other binary oppositions. It glories in paradox and ambiguity beginning with the prologue that describes the setting, the Bottom, situated spatially in the top. We enter a new world here, a world where we never get to the "bottom" of things, a world that demands a shift from an either/or orientation to one that is both/and, full of shifts and contradictions.

In these, as well as other particulars, *Sula* opens up new literary and critical options, not only for the study of texts by Afro-American women, but for Afro-American literary study more generally. The novel certainly helps to set a new agenda for black women's social and narrative possiblities. Coming significantly on the heels of the Black Power Movement that rendered black women prone or the "queens" of the male warrior—an updated version of a familiar script—the narrative invites the reader to imagine a different script for women that transcends the boundaries of social and linguistic convention. Further, it offers a useful model of self, of identity and identification in the reading process, a model that springs the traditional Afro-American critic from the rhetoric of opposition that has kept the discourse in arrest.

2

Day and night are mingled in our gazes ... If we divide light from night, we give up the lightness of our mixture ... We put ourselves into watertight compartments, break ourselves up into parts, cut ourselves in two ... we are always one and the other, at the same time.

—Luce Irigaray[14]

To posit that we are always one and the other at the same time is to challenge effectively a fundamental assumption of Western metaphysics that has operated historically, in Afro-American literature and criticism: "the unity of the ego-centered individual self"[15] defined in opposition to an other. In *Sula*, Toni Morrison complicates and questions that assumption, evoking the very oppositions on which it has tended to rest. She transgresses and blurs the boundaries these oppositions create, boundaries separating us from others and rendering us "others" to ourselves.

Morrison's transgression begins with questioning traditional notions of SELF as they have been translated into narrative. She implicitly critiques such concepts as "protagonist," "hero," and "major character" by emphatically decentering and deferring the presence of Sula, the title character. Bearing *her* name, the narrative suggests that she is the protagonist, the privileged center, but her presence is constantly deferred. We are first introduced to a caravan of characters: Shadrack, Nel, Helene, Eva, the Deweys, Tar Baby, Hannah, and Plum before we get any sustained treatment of Sula. Economical to begin with, the novel is roughly one-third over when Sula is introduced and it continues almost that long after her death.

Not only does the narrative deny the reader a "central" character, but it also denies the whole notion of character as static *essence*, replacing it with the idea of character as *process*.[16] Whereas the former is based on the assumption that the self is knowable, centered, and unified, the latter is based on the assumption that the self is multiple, fluid, relational, and in a perpetual state of becoming. Significantly, Sula, whose eyes are "as steady and clear as rain," is associated throughout with water, fluidity. Her birthmark, which shifts in meaning depending on the viewer's perspective, acts as metaphor for her figurative "selves," her multiple identity. To Nel, it is a "stemmed rose"; to her children, a "scary black thing," a "black mark"; to Jude, a "copperhead" and a "rattlesnake"; to Shadrack, a "tadpole." The image of the tadpole reinforces this notion of SELF as perpetually in process. Sula never achieves completeness of being. She dies in the fetal position welcoming this "sleep of water," in a passage that clearly suggests, she is dying yet aborning (149). Morrison's reconceptualization of character has clear and direct implications for Afro-American literature and critical study, for if the self is perceived as perpetually in process, rather than a static entity always already formed, it is thereby difficult to posit its ideal or "positive" representation.

Appropriate to this conception of character as process, the narrative employs the double, a technique related, as Baruch Hoffman has observed, to the "rupturing of coherence in character."[17] It positions its doubles, Nel and Sula, in adolescence, a state of becoming when they are "unshaped, formless things" (53) "us[ing] each other to grow on," finding "in each other's eyes the intimacy they were looking for" (52). As doubles, Sula and Nel complement and flow into each other, their closeness evoked throughout the narrative in physical metaphors. Sula's return to the Bottom, after a ten-year absence is, for Nel, "like getting the use of an eye back, having a cataract removed" (95). The two are likened to "two throats and one eye" (147).

But while Sula and Nel are represented as two parts of a self, those parts are distinct; they are complementary, not identical. Although Sula and Nel might share a common vision (suggested by "one eye"), their needs and desires are distinct (they have "two throats").[18] Sula comes to understand the fact of their difference, as the epigraph to this essay suggests: "She clung to Nel as the closest thing to an *other* and a *self* only to discover that she and Nel were not one and the same thing." The relationship of other to self in this passage, and throughout the narrative, must be seen as "different but connected rather than separate and opposed," to borrow from Carole Gilligan.[19]

Sula's understanding of her relationship to Nel results from self-understanding and self-intimacy, a process that Nel's marriage to Jude interrupts. Like so many women writers, Morrison equates marriage with the death of the female self and imagination. Nel would be the "someone sweet, industrious, and loyal, to shore him up ... the two of them would make one Jude" (83). After marriage she freezes into her wifely role, becoming one of the women who had "folded themselves into starched coffins" (122). Her definition of self becomes based on the community's "absolute" moral categories about "good" and "bad" women, categories that result in her separation from and opposition to Sula.

The narrative anticipates that opposition in one of its early descriptions of Nel and Sula. Nel is the color of "wet sandpaper," Sula is the "heavy brown" (52), a distinction that can be read as patriarchy's conventional fair lady/dark woman, virgin/whore dichotomy, one reflected in Sula's and Nel's separate matrilineages.

Sula's female heritage is an unbroken line of "manloving" women who exist as sexually desiring subjects rather than as objects of male desire. Her mother, Hannah, "ripple[s] with sex" (42), exasperating the "good" women of the community who call her "nasty." But that does not prevent her taking her lovers into the pantry for "some touching every day" (44). In contrast, Nel's is a split heritage. On one side is her grandmother, the whore of the Sundown House, and on the other her great-grandmother, who worshipped the Virgin Mary and counseled Helene "to be constantly on guard for any sign of her mother's wild blood" (17). Nel takes her great-grandmother's counsel to heart, spending her life warding off being "turn[ed] to jelly" and "custard" (22). Jelly and pudding here are metaphors of sexuality characteristic in classic blues lyrics.

Nel's sexuality is not expressed in itself and for her own pleasure, but rather, for the pleasure of her husband and in obedience to a system of ethical judgment and moral virtue, her "only mooring" (139). Because Nel's sexuality is harnessed to and only enacted within the institutions that sanction sexuality for women—marriage and family—she does not own it.[20] It is impossible for her to imagine sex without Jude. After she finds him and Sula in the sex act she describes her thighs—the metaphor for her sexuality—as "empty and dead ... and it was Sula who had taken the life from them." She concludes that "the both of them ... left her with no thighs and no heart, just her brain raveling away" (110).

Without Jude, Nel thinks her thighs are useless. Her sexuality is harnessed to duty and virtue in a simple cause/effect relationship as is clear from the plaintive questions she puts to an imaginary God after Jude leaves:

> even if I sew up those old pillow cases and rinse down the porch and feed my children and beat the rugs and haul the coal up out of the bin even then nobody.... I could be a mule or plow the furrows with my hands if need be or hold these rickety walls up with my back if I knew that somewhere in this world in the pocket of some night I could open my legs to some cowboy lean hips but you are trying to tell me no and O my sweet Jesus, what kind of cross is that? (111)

Sula, on the other hand, "went to bed with men as frequently as she could" (122) and assumed responsibility for her own pleasure. In her first sexual experience with Ajax, significantly a reenactment of Hannah's sexual rituals in the pantry, Sula "stood wide-legged against the wall and pulled from his track-lean hips all the pleasure her thighs could hold" (125). This is not to suggest that Sula's sexual expression is uncomplicated or unproblematic, but rather that unlike Nel's, it is not attached to anything outside herself, especially not to social definitions of female sexuality and conventions of duty. Although initially she "liked the sootiness of sex," liked "to think of it as wicked" (122), she comes to realize that it was not wicked. Further, apart from bringing her "a special kind of joy," it brought her "misery and the ability to feel deep sorrow" and "a stinging awareness of the endings of things" (122, 123), a feeling of "her own abiding strength and limitless power" (123). In other words, Sula's sexuality is neither located in the realm of "moral" abstractions nor expressed within the institution of marriage that legitimates it for women. Rather it is in the realm of sensory experience and in the service of the self-exploration that leads to self-intimacy. After sex, Sula enters that "post-coital privateness in which she met herself, welcomed herself, and joined herself in matchless harmony" (123). Unlike Nel, Sula has no ego and therefore feels "no compulsion ... to be consistent with herself" (119). In describing her, Morrison notes that Sula "examines herself ... is experimental with herself [and] perfectly willing to think the unthinkable thing."[21] To Sula "there was only her own mood and whim" enabling her to explore "that version of herself which she sought to reach out to and touch with an ungloved hand," "to discover it and let others become as intimate with their own selves as she was" (121).

Not only is sexual expression an act of self-exploration, but it is also associated throughout the narrative with creativity as seen in the long prose poem she creates while making love to Ajax. But significantly that creativity is without sufficient outlet within her community. According to Morrison, "If Sula had any sense she'd go somewhere and sing or get into show business," implying that her "strangeness," her "lawlessness" can only be sanctioned in a world like the theater.[22] Because of her community's rigid norms for women, Sula's impulses cannot be absorbed. Without an "art form," her "tremendous curiosity and gift for metaphor" become destructive (121). Without art forms, Sula is the artist become her own work of art.[23] As she responds defiantly to Eva's injunction that she make babies to settle herself, "I don't want to make somebody else. I want to make myself" (92).

Because she resists self-exploration, such creativity is closed to Nel. She has no "sparkle or splutter," just a "dull glow" (83). Her imagination has been driven "underground" from years of obeying the normative female script. She "belonged to the town and all of its ways" (120). The narrative strongly suggests that one cannot belong to the community and preserve the imagination, for the orthodox vocations for women—marriage and motherhood—restrict if not preclude imaginative expression.

Obedience to community also precludes intimacy with self for women.

Nel rejects this intimacy that involves confronting what both Sula and Shadrack have confronted: the unknown parts of themselves. In turning her back on the unknown, Nel fails to grow, to change, or to learn anything about herself until the last page of the novel. She thinks that "hell is change" (108). "One of the last true pedestrians" in the Bottom, Nel walks on the road's shoulder (on its edge, not on the road), "allowing herself to accept rides only when the weather required it" (166).

Nel fits Docherty's description of the type of character who is "fixed and centered up on one locatable ego," blocking "the possibility of authentic response, genuine sentiment." According to this ego-centered schema, "the self can only act in accord with a determined and limited 'characteristic' response" (80). Whereas Sula is an ambiguous character with a repertoire of responses along a continuum and thus cannot be defined as either totally "good" or "bad," Nel's is a limited response: "goodness," "rightness," as her name "Wright" suggests. As it is classically defined for women "goodness" is sexual faithfulness, self-abnegation, and the idealization of marriage and motherhood.

After years of nursing the belief that Sula has irreparably wronged her and violated their friendship, Nel goes to visit Sula on her deathbed as any "good woman" would do. Virtue, "her only mooring," has hidden "from her the true motives for her charity" (139). Their conversation, after years of estrangement, is peppered with references to good and evil, right and wrong. Nel protests, "I was good to you, Sula, why don't that matter?" And Sula responds in her characteristically defiant way "Being good to somebody is just like being mean to somebody. Risky. You don't get nothing for it." Exasperated because "talking to [Sula] about right and wrong" (144–45) was impossible, Nel leaves but not before Sula has the last word. And significantly, that last word takes the form of a question, an uncertainty, not an unambiguous statement of fact or truth:

> "How you know?" Sula asked.
> "Know what?" Nel still wouldn't look at her.
> "About who was good. How you know it was you?"
> "What you mean?"
> "I mean maybe it wasn't you. Maybe it was me."

In the space of the narrative Nel has another twenty-five years to deflect the contemplation of Sula's question through desperate acts of goodness: visits to "the sick and shut in," the category on the back page of black church bulletins that pull on the chords of duty. But on one such mission to visit Eva, Nel is confronted with not only the question but the more *unsettling* suggestion of guilt.

> "Tell me how you killed that little boy."
> "What? What little boy?"
> "The one you threw in the water ..."
> "I didn't throw no little boy in the river. That was Sula."
> "You, Sula. What's the difference?"

After years of repression, Nel must own her complicity in Chicken Little's drowning, a complicity that is both sign and symbol of the disowned piece of herself. She recalls the incident in its fullness, remembering "the good feeling she had had when Chicken's hands slipped" (170) and "the tranquillity that follow[ed] [that] joyful stimulation" (170). That remembrance makes space for Nel's psychic reconnection with Sula as a friend as well as symbol of that disowned self. Significantly, that reconnection occurs in the cemetery, a metaphor for Nel's buried shadow. The "circles and circles of sorrow" she cried at the narrative's end prepare her for what Sula strained to experience throughout her life: the process of mourning and remembering that leads to intimacy with the self, which is all that makes intimacy with others possible.

And the reader must mourn as Nel mourns, must undergo the process of development that Nel undergoes.[24] And as with Nel, that process begins with releasing the static and coherent conception of SELF and embracing what Sula represents: the self as process and fluid possibility. That embrace makes possible an altered understanding of the nature of identification in the reading process.

III

Recent theories of the act of reading have enriched and complicated—for the good—our understanding of what takes place in the act of reading. They have described the reading process as dialogical, as an interaction between a reader (a SELF) and an OTHER, an interaction in which neither remains the same.[25] In light of this information, we can conceive the act of reading as a process of self-exploration that the narrative strategies of Sula compel. What strategies does the narrative employ to generate that process? It deliberately miscues the reader, disappointing the very expectations the narrative arouses, forcing the reader to shift gears, to change perspective. Though these strategies might well apply to all readers, they have specific implications for Afro-American critics.

Sula threatens the readers' assumptions and disappoints their expectations at every turn. It begins by disappointing the reader's expectations of a "realistic" and unified narrative documenting black/white confrontation. Although the novel's prologue, which describes a community's destruction by white greed and deception, gestures toward "realistic" documentation, leads the reader to expect "realistic" documentation of a black community's confrontation with an oppressive white world, that familiar and expected plot is in the background. In the foreground are the characters whose lives transcend their social circumstances. They laugh, they dance, they sing, and are "mightily preoccupied with earthly things—and each other" (6). The narrative retreats from linearity privileged in the realist mode. Though dates entitle the novel's chapters, they relate only indirectly to its central concerns and do not permit the reader to use chronology in order to intepret its events in any cause/effect fashion. In other words, the story's forward movement in time is deliberately nonsequential and without explicit reference to "real" time. It roves lightly over historical events, dates, and details as seen in the first chapter. Titled "1919," the chapter begins with a reference to World War II, then refers, in quick and, paradoxically, regressive succession, to National Suicide Day, instituted in 1920, then backwards to Shadrack running across a battlefield in France in World War I.

In addition, the narrative forces us to question our readings, to hold our judgment in check, and to continually revise it. Susan Blake is on the mark when she says that "the reader never knows quite what to think" of characters and events in *Sula*: "whether to applaud Eva's self-sacrifice or deplore her tyranny, whether to admire Sula's freedom or condemn her heartlessness."[26] The narrative is neither an apology for Sula's destruction nor an unsympathetic critique of Nel's smug conformity. It does not reduce a complex set of dynamics to a simple opposition or choice between two "pure" alternatives.

Among the strategies Morrison uses to complicate choice and block judgment are the dots within dots (....) in the narrative that mark time breaks and function as stop signs. They compel the reader to pause, think back, evaluate the narrative's events, and formulate new expectations in light of them, expectations that are never quite fulfilled.[27] The Afro-American critic, wanting a world cleansed of uncertainty and contradictions and based on the rhetorical polarities—positive and negative—might ask in frustration, "Can we ever determine the right judgment?" The narrative implies that that answer can only come from within, from exploring all parts of the SELF. As Nel asks Eva in the scene mentioned earlier, "You think I'm guilty?" Eva whispers, "Who would know that better than you?" (169).

Not only does the narrative disappoint the reader's expectations of correct answers and appropriate judgment, but it also prevents a stable and unified reading of the text, though I have fabricated one here by tracing a dominant thread in the narrative: the relationship between self and other. But in exploring this relationship, Morrison deliberately provides echoing passages that cancel each other out, that thwart the reader's desire for stability and consistency:

> "She clung to Nel as the closest thing to both an other and a self, only to discover that she and Nel were not one and the same thing."

But the following passage, which comes much later in the narrative, effectively cancels this passage out: Sula learned that

> "there was no other that you could count on ... [and] there was no *self* to count on either."

The novel's fragmentary, episodic, elliptical quality helps to thwart textual unity, to prevent a totalized interpretation. An early reviewer described the text as a series of scenes and glimpses, each "written ... from scratch." Since none of them has anything much to do with the ones that preceded them, "we can never piece the glimpses into a coherent picture."[28] Whatever coherence and meaning resides in the narrative, the reader must struggle to create.

The gaps in the text allow for the reader's participation in the creation of meaning in the text. Morrison has commented on the importance of the "affective and participatory relationship between the artist and the audience," and her desire "to have the reader work *with* the author in the construction of the book." She adds, "What is left out is as important as what is there."[29] The reader must fill in the narrative's many gaps, for instance: Why is there no funeral for either Plum or Hannah? What happens to Jude? Where *was* Eva during her eighteen-month absence from the Bottom? What really happened to her leg? How does Sula support herself after she returns from her ten-year absence?

The reader's participation in the meaning-making process helps to fill in the gaps in the text, as well as to bridge the gaps separating the reader *from* the text. This returns us full circle to the beginning of this essay: the boundary separating some Afro-American readers from the black text that opposes a single unified image of the black SELF.

As Norman Holland and others have noted, each reader has a vision of the world arising from her/his identity theme. In the act of reading, the reader tries to re-create the text according to that identity theme. Holland continues, as we read, we use the "literary work to symbolize and finally to replicate ourselves,"[30] to reflect ourselves, to affirm ourselves by denying or demeaning the other. But, writing in a different context, Holland usefully suggests that, "one of literature's adaptive functions ... is that it allows us to loosen boundaries between self and not self."[31]

Transgressing that boundary and viewing identity and the self in relation, rather than coherent, separate, and opposed, permits an analogous view of identification in the reading process. Just as the self is fluid, dynamic, and formed in relation, so is identification a process involving a relationship between the SELF and the "otherness" of writers, texts, and literary characters.

If we would approach that "unified" black community splintered, many argue, by black women writers' imaginative daring, those boundaries and the rigid identity themes and fantasies holding them up must be crossed. After all, as *Sula* playfully suggests, our conceptions of who we are never include all that we are anyway. One answer, then, to the epigraph: "What shall we call our 'self?'" is we shall call ourselves by many names. Our metaphors of self cannot then rest in stasis, but will glory in difference and overflow into everything that belongs to us.

NOTES

* This essay was written specifically for this volume and is published here for the first time by permission of the author.

1. Toni Morrison, *Sula* (New York: New American Library, 1973), 119. Subsequent references are to this edition and will be indicated parenthetically in the text.

2. W.E.B. DuBois, "Negro Art," *Crisis* (June 1921): 55–56.

3. Langston Hughes, "The Negro Artist and the Racial Mountain," in *Five Black Writers*, ed. Donald B. Gibson (New York: New York University Press, 1970), 227–28.

4. Addison Gayle, "Blueprint for Black Criticism," *First World* (January/February 1977): 44.

5. See three essays by Henry Louis Gates: "Preface to Blackness: Text and Pretext," in *Afro-American Literature: The Reconstruction of Instruction*, ed. Dexter Fischer and Robert Stepto (New York: MLA, 1979), 44–69; "Criticism in the Jungle," in *Black Literature and Literary Theory*, ed. Henry Gates (New York: Methuen, 1984), 1–24; and "Writing 'Race' and the Difference it Makes," *Critical Inquiry* 12 (Autumn 1985): 1–20. For critiques of the issue on "'Race,' Writing and Difference," in which the last essay appears, see *Critical Inquiry* 13 (Autumn 1986).

6. Mel Watkins, "Sexism, Racism, and Black Women Writers," *New York Times Book Review* (June 1986): 36. For similar discussions see Darryl Pinckney, "Black Victims, Black

Villains," *New York Review of Books* 34 (29 January 1987): 17–20 and Richard Barksdale, "Castration Symbolism in Recent Black American Fiction," *College Language Association Journal* 29 (June 1986): 400–13.

7. Alice Walker, "The Unglamorous But Worthwhile Duties of the Black Revolutionary Artist, or of the Black Writer Who Simply Works and Writes," in *In Search of Our Mother's Gardens* (New York: Harcourt Brace Jovanovich, 1983), 137.

8. Although a whole field of binary oppositions can be viewed as analogous to the male/female opposition, Cary Nelson rightly cautions against so rigid a reading. He argues persuasively that when such dualities are considered in cultural and historical context, the basic male/female opposition breaks down and the qualities associated with each side are often reversed. See "Envoys of Otherness: Difference and Continuity in Feminist Criticism," in *For Alma Mater: Theory and Practice in Feminist Scholarship*, ed. Paula Treichler et al. (Urbana: University of Illinois Press, 1985), 91–118.

9. Shoshana Felman, "Women and Madness: The Critical Phallacy," *Diacritics* 5 (Winter 1975): 3.

10. See Gates, "Criticism in the Jungle," 7.

11. The historical equation of blackness with maleness in discourses on blackness and in the development of the Afro-American literary canon is an issue calling urgently for examination. Although I cannot address it here in any detail it is the subject of my essay-in-progress forthcoming in *Black American Literature Forum*. For a discussion of how this equation has worked out in discourses on slavery see Deborah Gray White, *Ar'n't I a Woman: Female Slaves in the Plantation South* (New York: Norton, 1985). White examines slave women whose experiences are neglected, more often than not, from scholarship on slavery. According to White, the pattern began with the publication of Stanley Elkins's *Slavery, A Problem in American Institutional and Intellectual Life* (Chicago: University of Chicago Press, 1959) in which he posited his controversial "Sambo" thesis of male infantilism and incompetence which historians have since focussed their energies on negating. That focus has effectively eclipsed black women from view.

12. See Robert Stepto, *From Behind the Veil: A Study of Afro-American Narrative* (Urbana: University of Illinois Press, 1979), who defines the Afro-American narrative tradition in almost exclusively male terms. See also Henry Gates's preface to the special issue of *Critical Inquiry*, "'Race,' Writing, and Difference," in which he describes the beginning of that tradition: the writings of John Gronniosaw, John Marrant, Olaudah Equiano, Ottabah Cugoano, and John Jea, all male. They, he argues, posited both "the individual 'I' of the Black author as well as the collective 'I' of the race. Text created author; and Black authors, it was hoped would create or re-create the image of the race in European discourse" (11).

13. Hortense Spillers, "A Hateful Passion, A Lost Love," *Feminist Studies* 9 (Summer 1983): 296.

14. Luce Irigaray, *This Sex Which Is Not One* (Ithaca: Cornell University Press, 1985), 217.

15. Thomas Docherty, *Reading (Absent) Character: Toward a Theory of Characterization in Fiction* (Oxford: Clarendon Press, 1983), 265.

16. I am adapting Docherty's distinction between "character as a 'becoming' rather than as an 'essence.'" See Docherty, *Reading (Absent) Character*, 268.

17. Baruch Hoffman, *Character in Literature* (Ithaca: Cornell University Press, 1985), 79.

18. I borrow this point from Judith Kegan Gardiner, "The (US)es of (I)dentity: A Response to Abel on '(E)Merging Identities,'" *Signs* 6 (Spring 1981): 439.

19. Carole Gilligan, *In a Different Voice* (Cambridge: Harvard University Press, 1982), 147.

20. In *The Bluest Eye* Morrison is similarly concerned with those women who view sex as a marital duty rather than a source of their own pleasure. Called the Mobile women, they try to rid themselves of the "dreadful funkiness of passion," give their "bod[ies] sparingly and partially," and hope that they will "remain dry between [their] legs" (68–69).

21. Toni Morrison, "Intimate Things in Place," *Massachusetts Review* (Autumn 1977): 477.

22. See Bettye J. Parker, "Complexity: Toni Morrison's Women—An Interview Essay in *Sturdy Black Bridges: Visions of Black Women in Literature*, ed. Roseann P. Bell, Bettye J. Parker and Beverly Guy-Sheftall (New York: Anchor/Doubleday, 1979), 256.

23. For a discussion of this theme in other Morrison novels see Renita Weems, "'Artists Without Art Form': A Look At One Black Woman's World of Unrevered Black Women," *Conditions: Five* 2 (Autumn 1979): 46–58.

24. *Sula* is an intensely elegiac novel about loss, grieving, and the release of pain. The epigraph signals the concern. "It is sheer good fortune to miss somebody long before they leave you." It implies that leave-taking and loss are inevitable. At the end of the book Shadrack gives over to his grief for Sula, and when he does, he ceases to fill his life with compulsive activity. At Chicken Little's funeral, the women grieve for their own painful childhoods, the "most devastating pain there is" (65). The narrator grieves for a community that has become increasingly atomistic with the passage of time. Barbara Christian also sees these qualities in the novel, reading the epilogue as "a eulogy to the Bottom." See "Community and Nature: The Novels of Toni Morrison," *Journal of Ethnic Studies* 7 (Winter 1980): 64–78.

25. Wolfgang Iser, for example, discusses the two "selves" that interact in the reading process: one, the reader's own self or "disposition"; the other, that offered by the text. See *The Act of Reading* (Baltimore: Johns Hopkins, 1978), 37. For a thorough overview and synthesis of theories of reading see Susan R. Suleiman, "Introduction: Varieties of Audience-Oriented Criticism," in *The Reader in the Text*, ed. Susan Suleiman and Inge Crosman (Princeton: Princeton University Press, 1980), 3–45.

26. Susan Blake, "Toni Morrison," in *Dictionary of Literary Biography* (Detroit: Gale Research Co., 1984), 191.

27. I am indebted here to Jerome Beaty's afterward to *Sula* in *The Norton Introduction to the Short Novel*, 2d ed. (1987), 699.

28. Christopher Lehman-Haupt, Review of *Sula*, *New York Times* 123 (7 January 1974): 29.

29. "Rootedness: The Ancestor as Foundation," in *Black Women Writers: A Critical Evaluation*, ed. Mari Evans (New York: Anchor/Doubleday, 1984), 341.

30. "UNITY IDENTITY TEXT SELF" *PMLA* 90 (1975): 816. See also Jean Kennard, "Ourself Behind Ourself: A Theory for Lesbian Readers," in *Gender and Reading*, ed. Elizabeth Flynn and Patrocinio Schweikart (Baltimore: Johns Hopkins, 1986), 63–80.

31. See *Dynamics of Literary Response* (New York: Oxford University Press, 1968), 101.

MARILYN SANDERS MOBLEY

A Different Remembering:
Memory, History and Meaning
in Toni Morrison's Beloved

The slave woman ought not to be judged by the same standards as others.
—Harriet Jacobs, *Incidents in the Life of a Slave Girl*

... when we get a little farther away from the conflict, some brave and truth-loving man, with all the facts before him ... will gather ... the scattered fragments ... and give to those who shall come after us an impartial history of this the grandest moral conflict of the century. {For} Truth is patient and time is just.

—Frederick Douglass[1]

Every age re-accentuates in its own way the works of its most immediate past.

— Mikhail Bahtin, "Discourse in the Novel"

In 1974 Toni Morrison edited an often overlooked publication called *The Black Book*.[2] This collection of memorabilia represents 300 years of black history, and not only records the material conditions of black life from slavery to freedom, but also exhibits the black cultural production that grew out of and in spite of these conditions. Compiled in scrapbook fashion, it contains everything from bills of sale for slaves to jazz and poetry. Through diverse images of black life presented in such items as photos of lynchings, share-cropping families and slave-made quilts, and encoded in excerpts from such sources as slave narratives, folk sayings and black newspapers, *The Black Book* tells a complex story of oppression, resistance and survival. More

From *Toni Morrison*, edited by Harold Bloom. © 1990 by Chelsea House Publishers.

importantly, it was published at a moment in American history when many feared that the Black Power movement of the 1960s and early 1970s would be reduced to faddish rhetoric and mere image rather than understood for its cultural and political implications. Morrison herself feared the movement propounded a kind of historical erasure or denial of those aspects of the past which could not be easily assimilated into its rhetorical discourse or into the collective consciousness of black people as a group. She feared, for example, that the rhetoric of the movement, in its desire to create a new version of history that would affirm the African past and the heroic deeds of a few great men, had inadvertently bypassed the equally heroic deeds of ordinary African-Americans who had resisted and survived the painful traumas of slavery. In other words, she questioned what she perceived to be a romanticization of both the African past and the American past that threatened to devalue 300 years of black life on American soil before it was fully recorded, examined or understood for its complexity and significance. Thus, *The Black Book* was a literary intervention in the historical dialogue of the period to attest to "Black life as lived" experience.[3]

What is particularly pertinent, however, is that in the process of editing *The Black Book*, Morrison discovered the story that would become the basis of her fifth novel, *Beloved*.[4] Indeed, on the tenth page of *The Black Book* is a copy of a news article, "A Visit to the Slave Mother Who Killed Her Child," that documents the historical basis for what would later become Morrison's most challenging fictional project.[5] Although the relevance of history informs all her novels from *The Bluest Eye* to *Tar Baby*, it is in *Beloved* that history simultaneously becomes both theme and narrative process.[6] In other words, *Beloved* dramatizes the complex relationship between history and memory by shifting from lived experience as documented in *The Black Book* to remembered experience as represented in the novel.

Yet the intertextual relationship between *The Black Book* and *Beloved* is not the only one that can illuminate the compelling intricacies of this novel. Several reviewers place it in the American literary tradition with intertextual connections to Harriet Beecher Stowe's *Uncle Tom's Cabin* (1852). Others compare Morrison's narrative strategies to those of William Faulkner, who incidentally, along with Virginia Woolf, was the subject of her master's thesis. Certainly, the thematics of guilt and the complex fragmentation of time that shape Morrison's fiction are inherent in Faulkner's writing, as well as in the work of many other white authors of the American literary tradition. Yet Morrison's own expressed suspicions of critical efforts to place her in a white literary tradition are instructive. She explains:

> Most criticism ... justifies itself by identifying black writers with some already accepted white writer ... I find such criticism dishonest because it never goes into the work on its own terms. It comes from some other place and finds content outside of the work and wholly irrelevant to it to support the work ... It's merely trying to place the book into an already established literary tradition.[7]

With Morrison's own comments in mind, I would like to suggest that the intertextual relationship between *Beloved* and the slave narratives—the genre that began the African-American literary tradition in prose—offers significant interpretative possibilities for entering the hermeneutic circle of this novel. More specifically, I would like to argue that Morrison uses the trope of memory to revise the genre of the slave narrative and thereby to make the slave experience it inscribes more accessible to contemporary readers. In other words, she uses memory as the metaphorical sign of the interior life to explore and represent dimensions of slave life that the classic slave narrative omitted. By so doing, she seeks to make slavery accessible to readers for whom slavery is not a memory, but a remote historical fact to be ignored, repressed or forgotten. Thus, just as the slave narratives were a form of narrative intervention designed to disrupt the system of slavery, *Beloved* can be read as a narrative intervention that disrupts the cultural notion that the untold story of the black slave mother is, in the words of the novel, "the past something to leave behind."[8]

One of the first observations often made about the slave narratives is the striking similarities that exist among the hundreds of them that were written. In the "Introduction" to *The Classic Slave Narratives*, Henry Louis Gates, Jr., accounts for this phenomenon by reminding us that

> when the ex-slave author decided to write his or her story, he or she did so only after reading and rereading the telling stories of other slave authors who preceded them.[9]

While we cannot know exactly which narratives Morrison read, it is certain that she read widely in the genre and that she is familiar with the two most popular classics—Frederick Douglass's *Narrative* (1845) and Harriet Jacobs's *Incidents in the Life of a Slave Girl* (1861).[10] As prototypical examples of the genre, they adhere to the narrative conventions carefully delineated and described by James Olney. According to him, the vast majority of narratives begin with the three words "I was born" and proceed to provide information about parents, siblings, the cruelty of masters, mistresses and overseers, barriers to literacy, slave auctions, attempts, failures and successes at escaping, name changes, and general reflections on the peculiar institution of slavery.[11] As Valerie Smith points out, however, the important distinction between the narratives of Douglass and Jacobs is that while his narrative not only concerns "the journey from slavery to freedom but also the journey from slavery to manhood," her narrative describes the sexual exploitation that challenged the womanhood of slave women and tells the story of their resistance to that exploitation.[12] *Beloved* contains all these characteristics with several signifying differences. While the classic slave narrative draws on memory as though it is a monologic, mechanical conduit for facts and incidents, Morrison's text foregrounds the dialogic characteristics of memory along with its imaginative capacity to construct and reconstruct the significance of the past. Thus, while the slave narrative characteristically moves in a chronological, linear narrative fashion, *Beloved* meanders through time, sometimes circling back, other times moving vertically, spirally out of time and down into space. Indeed, Morrison's text challenges the Western notion of linear time that informs American history and the slave narratives. It engages the reader not just with the physical, material consequences of slavery, but with the psychological consequences as well. Through the trope of memory, Morrison moves into the psychic consequences of slavery for women, who, by their very existence, were both the means and the source of production. In the words of the text, the slave woman was "property that reproduced itself without cost" (228). Moreover, by exploring this dimension of slavery, Morrison produces a text that is at once very different from and similar to its literary antecedent with its intervention in the cultural, political and social order of black people in general and of black women in particular. What the reader encounters in this text is Morrison as both writer and reader, for inscribed in her writing of the novel is her own "reading"—a revisionary rereading—of the slave's narrative plot of the journey from bondage to freedom. In the process of entering the old text of slavery from "a new critical direction," Morrison discovers what Adrienne Rich refers to as a "whole new psychic geography to be explored," and what Morrison herself identifies as the "interior life of black people under those circumstances."[13] Ultimately, *Beloved* responds to Fredric Jameson's dictum to "always historicize" by illustrating the dynamics of the act of interpretation that memory performs on a regular basis at any given historical moment.[14]

Unlike the slave narratives which sought to be all-inclusive eyewitness accounts of the material conditions of slavery, Morrison's novel exposes the unsaid of the narratives, the psychic subtexts that lie within and beneath the historical facts. In the author's words, she attempts to leave "spaces so the reader can come into it."[15] Critic Steven Mallioux refers to such hermeneutic gaps as places where the text must be "supplemented by its readers before its meaning can be discovered."[16] By examining the use of memory in *Beloved*, we can not only discover to what extent she revises the slave narrative, but also explore how her narrative poetics operate through memory and history to create meaning.

The actual story upon which the novel is based is an 1855 newspaper account of a runaway slave from Kentucky named Margaret Garner. When she realizes she is about to be recaptured in accordance with the Fugitive Slave Law, she kills her child rather than allow it to return to a "future of servitude."[17] Indeed, the story itself involves a conflation of past, present and future in a single act. In the novel, Margaret Garner becomes Sethe, a fugitive slave whose killing of her two-year-old daughter, Beloved, haunts her first as a ghost and later as a physical reincarnation. But time is not so much conflated as fragmented in the fictional rendering of the tale. Moreover, the text contains not only Sethe's story or version of the past, but those of her friend and eventual lover, Paul D, her mother-in-law, Baby Suggs, her remaining child, a daughter named Denver, and later, Beloved herself. Each of their fragments amplifies or modifies Sethe's narrative for the reader. In that the fragments constitute voices which speak to and comment on one another, the text illustrates the call and response pattern of the African-American oral tradition.[18]

The setting of the novel is 1873 in Cincinnati, Ohio, where Sethe resides in a small house with her daughter, Denver. Her mother-in-law, Baby Suggs, has recently died and her two sons, Howard and Buglar, have left home, unable to live any longer in a ghost-haunted house with a mother who seems oblivious or indifferent to the disturbing, disruptive presence. Sethe seems locked in memories of her escape from slavery, the failure of her husband, Halle, to show up at the planned time of escape, her murder of her child, and the Kentucky plantation referred to by its benevolent white slave owner as Sweet Home. One of the Sweet Home men, Paul D, inadvertently arrives on her porch after years of wandering, locked in his own guilt, alienation and shame from the psychic scars of slavery. They become lovers, but more importantly, his arrival initiates the painful plunge into the past through the sharing of their individual stories, memories and experiences. Unable to tolerate the presence of the ghost, however, he drives it away, only to be driven away himself by his inability to cope with Sethe's obsession with Denver, whom he calls a "room-and-board witch" (165). A bond of affection unites Sethe, Denver and Beloved until Denver realizes that her mother has become oblivious to her and has begun to devote her attention exclusively to Beloved. As she watches her mother deterioriate physically and mentally in the grips of overwhelming guilt and consuming love, Denver realizes she must abandon the security of home to get help for her mother and to rid their lives of Beloved once and for all. With the help of the black community, she eventually rescues her mother and Beloved vanishes.

What this cursory synopsis of the plot cannot account for is the ways in which Sethe modifies, amplifies and subverts her own memory of the murder that serves as the locus of the narrative. In fact, even in freedom she lives in a kind of psychic bondage to the task of "keeping the past at bay" (43). While she had murdered Beloved to save her from the future, she raises Denver by "keeping her from the past" (43). The two different manifestations of maternal love are just one source of the novel's narrative tension that evolves from Sethe's response to slavery. The more compelling source of tension lies in the complexity Morrison brings to the normal property of literature Frank Kermode refers to as the "secrecy of narrative."[19] While all texts develop to a certain extent by secrecy or by what information they withhold and gradually release to the reader, the text of *Beloved* moves through a series of narrative starts and stops that are complicated by Sethe's desire to forget or "disremember" the past (118). Thus, at the same time that the reader seeks to know "the how and why" (120) of Sethe's infanticide, Sethe seeks to withhold that information not only from everyone else, but even from herself. Thus, the early sections of the novel reveal the complex ways in which memories of the past disrupt Sethe's concerted attempt to forget.

The first sign of this tension between remembering and forgetting occurs on the second page of the text in a scene where Denver and Sethe attempt to call the ghost forth. When Denver grows impatient with the seeming reluctance of the ghost to make its presence felt, Sethe cautions her by saying: "You forgetting how little it is ... She wasn't even two years old when she died" (4). Denver's expression of surprise that a baby can throw such a "powerful spell" is countered in the following passage:

'No more powerful than the way I loved her,' Sethe answered and there it was again. The welcoming cool of unchiseled headstones; the one she selected to lean against on tiptoe, her knees wide open as any grave. Pink as a fingernail it was, and sprinkled with glittering chips ... Counting on the stillness of her own soul, she had forgotten the other one: the soul of her baby girl. (5)

In this passage we have several things occurring at once. First, Sethe's verbalization of love triggers her memory of selecting a tombstone for the baby she murdered. The phrase "there it was again" signals that this is a memory that recurs and that brings the ambivalent emotions of consolation and anguish. Second, the memory of the tombstone triggers her memory of the shameful circumstances of getting it engraved. In this memory, the reality of gender and oppression converge, for the engraver offers to place seven letters—the name "Beloved"—on the headstone in exchange for sex. She also remembers that for ten more minutes, she could have gotten the word "dearly" added. Thirdly, this memory raises the issue around which the entire novel is constructed and which is the consequence and/or responsibility that she must carry for her actions.

Throughout the novel there are similar passages that signal the narrative tension between remembering and forgetting. At various points in the text, a single phrase, a look or the most trivial incident rivets Sethe's attention to the very details of the past she is least ready to confront. In the words of the text, "she worked hard to remember as close to nothing as was safe" (6). In another place the text refers to the "serious work of beating back the past" (73). Moreover, a mindless task such as folding clothes takes on grave significance, as the following passage suggests: "She had to do something with her hands because she was remembering something she had forgotten she knew. Something privately shameful that had seeped into a slit in her mind" (61). Morrison even includes vernacular versions of words to suggest the slaves' own preoccupation with mnemonic processes. For example, at one point "rememory" is used as a noun, when Sethe refers to what Paul D stirs up with his romantic attention to her. Later, the same word is used as a verb, when Sethe begins to come to terms with the past through her relationship with Beloved. She allows her mind to be "busy with the things she could forget" and thinks to herself: "Thank God I don't have to rememory or say a thing" (191). Even the vernacular word for forgetting, "disremember" (118), calls our attention to its binary opposite of remembering.

When Paul D arrives at Sethe's home on 124 Bluestone, Denver seeks to frighten this unwanted guest away by telling him they have a "lonely and rebuked" ghost on the premises (13). The obsolete meaning of rebuked— repressed—not only suggests that the ghost represents repressed memory, but that, as with anything that is repressed, it eventually resurfaces or returns on one form or another. 'Paul D's arrival is a return of sorts in that he is reunited with Sethe, his friend from Mr. Garner's Sweet Home plantation. His presence signals an opportunity to share both the positive and negative memories of life there. On the one hand, he and Sethe talk fondly of the "headless bride back behind Sweet Home" and thus share a harmless ghost story of a haunted house. On the other hand, when they remember Sweet Home as a place, they regard it with ambivalence and admit that "it wasn't sweet and it sure wasn't home" (14). Sethe warns against a total dismissal of it, however, by saying: "But it's where we were [and it] comes back whether we want it to or not" (14).

What also comes back through the stories Paul D shares are fragments of history Sethe is unprepared for such as the fact that years ago her husband had witnessed the white boys forcibly take milk from her breasts, but had been powerless to come to her rescue or stop them. Furthermore, his personal stories of enduring a "bit" (69) in his mouth—the barbaric symbol of silence and oppression that Morrison says created a perfect "labor force"—along with numerous other atrocities, such as working on the chain gang, introduce elements of the classic slave narrative into the text. Perhaps more importantly, these elements comprise the signs of history that punctuate the text and that disrupt the text of the mind which is both historical and ahistorical at the same time.

I believe the meaning of Morrison's complex use of the trope of memory becomes most clear in what many readers regard as the most poetic passages in the text. These passages appear in sections two through five of Part Two, where we have a series of interior monologues that become a dialogue among the three central female characters. The first is Sethe's, the second is Denver's, the third is Beloved's and the last one is a merging of all three. Beloved's is the most intriguing, for the text of her monologue contains no punctuation. Instead, there are literal spaces between groups of words that signal the timelessness of her presence as well as the unlived spaces of her life. Earlier in the novel, Sethe even refers to Beloved as "her daughter [who had] ... come back home from the timeless place" (182). Samples of phrases from Beloved's monologue reveal the meaning of her presence: "[H]ow can I say things that are pictures I am not separate from her—there is no place where I stop ... her face is my own ... all of it is now ... it is always now" (210). These words suggest not only the seamlessness of time, but the inextricability of the past and present, of ancestors and their progeny. In the last interior "dialogue," the voices of Sethe, Denver and Beloved blend to suggest not only that it is always now, but to suggest that the past, present and future are all one and the same.

In an article entitled "Rediscovering Black History," written on the occasion of the publication of the *The Black Book*, Toni Morrison speaks of the "complicated psychic power one had to exercise to resist devastation."[20]

She was speaking, of course, not just of slavery, but of the Black existence in America after slavery as well. *Beloved* and all her novels, to a certain extent, bear witness to this psychic power. It must be stated as I conclude, however, that my intertextual reading of this novel as a revision of the slave narrative should not be construed as an attempt to diminish the form and content of the slave narratives themselves in any way. It is, instead, a recognition of the truth that Gates offers in the introduction to *The Slave's Narrative:*

> Once slavery was abolished, no need existed for the slave to write himself {or herself} into the human community through the action of first-person narration. As Frederick Douglass in 1855 succinctly put the matter, the free human being "cannot see things in the same light with the slave, because he does not and cannot look from the same point from which the slave does" ... The nature of the narratives, and their rhetorical strategies and import, changed once slavery no longer existed.[21]

Beloved is a complex, contemporary manifestation of this shift. In a larger sense, however, it is what Mikhail Bakhtin calls a "reaccentuation" of the past (in this case, the past of slavery) to discover newer aspects of meaning embedded in the classic slave narrative.[22] Morrison's purpose is not to convince white readers of the slave's humanity, but to address black readers by inviting us to return to the very part of our past that many have repressed, forgotten or ignored. At the end of the novel, after the community has helped Denver rescue her mother from Beloved's ferocious spell by driving her out of town, Paul D returns to Sethe "to put his story next to hers" (273). Despite the psychic healing that Sethe undergoes, however, the community's response to her healing is encoded in the choruslike declaration on the last two pages of the text, that this was "not a story to pass on" (274). Yet, as readers, if we understand Toni Morrison's ironic and subversive vision at all, we know that our response to the text's apparent final call for silence and forgetting is not that at all. Instead, it is an ironic reminder that the process of consciously remembering not only empowers us to tell the difficult stories that must be passed on, but it also empowers us to make meaning of our individual and collective lives as well.

NOTES

1. Quoted in the opening epigraph of Charles T. Davis and Henry Louis Gates, Jr., eds., *The Slave's Narrative* (New York: Oxford University Press, 1985).

2. Middleton A. Harris, comp., *The Black Book* (New York: Random House, 1974). A

shorter version of the text of this essay was presented at the annual convention of the Modern Language Association of America on December 29, 1988, in New Orleans, Louisiana. I am grateful to my colleagues of the First Draft Club—Carolyn Brown, Evelyn Hawthorne, Ann Kelly and especially, Claudia Tate—for their generous response to this essay.

3. Toni Morrison, "Behind the Making of *The Black Book*," *Black World* 23 (February 1974): 86–90. Compiled by Middleton A. Harris, *The Black Book* does not identify Morrison as its editor. In this article, however, she not only discusses her role as editor, but describes the project of producing the book as an act of professional service and personal mission: "I was scared that the world would fall away before somebody put together a thing that got close to the way we really were" (90). Ironically, although *The Black Book* omits any mention of Morrison as its editor, it names her parents, Ramah Wofford and George Carl Wofford, in the acknowledgments, as two of the people who contributed to the text "with stories, pictures, recollections and general aid."

4. See Amanda Smith, "Toni Morrison," *Publishers Weekly*, 21 August 1987, 51. This article is a report on an interview with Morrison a month before the publication of *Beloved*.

5. See Harris, *Black Book*, 10.

6. Toni Morrison, *The Bluest Eye* (New York: Holt, Rinehart and Winston, 1970); *Sula* (New York: Knopf, 1973); *Song of Solomon* (New York: Knopf, 1977) and *Tar Baby* (New York: Knopf, 1981). Of the first four novels, *Song of Solomon* is most clearly engaged with the subject of history. Specifically, it connects the African past with the lived life of African-Americans from slavery to the recent past of the 1960s.

7. Claudia Tate, ed., *Black Women Writers at Work* (New York: Continuum, 1984), 122.

8. Toni Morrison, *Beloved* (New York: Knopf, 1988), 256. All subsequent references to this novel are cited in the text parenthetically. The term "narrative intervention" is one I borrow from Hazel Carby's analysis of the uses of fiction in moments of historical crisis. See Hazel Carby, *Reconstructing Womanhood: The Emergence of the Afro-American Woman Novelist* (New York: Oxford University Press, 1987), 121–44.

9. Henry Louis Gates, Jr., ed., *The Classic Slave Narratives* (New York: New American Library, 1987), x.

10. Frederick Douglass, *The Narrative of the Life of Frederick Douglass* (New York: Signet, 1968); Harriet Jacobs, *Incidents in the Life of a Slave Girl*, ed. Jean Fagan Yellin (Cambridge: Harvard University Press, 1987).

11. See James Olney, "'I Was Born': Slave Narratives, Their Status as Autobiography and as Literature," *Callaloo* 7 (Winter 1984): 46–73. Reprinted in Davis and Gates, *The Slave's Narrative*, 148–75.

12. Valerie Smith, *Self-Discovery and Authority in Afro-American Narrative* (Cambridge: Harvard University Press, 1987), 34. See also Mary Helen Washington, ed., *Invented Lives: Narratives of Black Women 1860–1960* (Garden City: Doubleday/Anchor, 1987), 3–15.

13. Adrienne Rich, "When We Dead Awaken: Writing as Re-Vision," *College English* 34 (October 1972): 18–26; Morrison's words are quoted in Smith, *Publishers Weekly*, 51.

14. Fredric Jameson, *The Political Unconscious: Narrative as a Socially Symbolic Act* (Ithaca: Cornell University Press, 1981), 9.

15. Tate, *Black Women Writers*, 125.

16. Steven Mallioux, *Interpretive Conventions: The Reader in the Study of American Fiction* (Ithaca: Cornell University Press, 1982), 170.

17. See Helen Dudar, "Toni Morrison: Finally Just a Writer," *The Wall Street Journal*, 30 September 1987, 34. This is one of several newspaper articles to appear around the time of *Beloved's* publication in which Morrison discussed the actual story upon which the novel is based.

18. See Sherley Anne Williams, "The Blues Roots of Contemporary Afro-American Poetry," in Dexter Fisher and Robert Stepto, eds., *Afro-American Literature: The Reconstruction of Instruction* (New York: Modern Language Association of America), 73. In the novel, the statements of individual characters shape the "call" to which other characters offer a "response" by sharing their versions of the past. This pattern of call and reponse then shapes the collective story of slavery that binds the members of the community together. This pattern resonates with similar patterns found in the blues and other forms of African-American oral expression.

19. Frank Kermode, *The Genesis of Secrecy: On the Interpretation of Narrative* (Cambridge: Harvard University Press, 1979), 144.

20. Toni Morrison, "Rediscovering Black History," *New York Times Magazine*, 11 August 1974, 18.

21. Davis and Gates, *The Slave's Narrative*, xiii.

22. Mikhail Bakhtin, "Discourse in the Novel," *The Dialogic Imagination*, Michael Holquist, ed., Caryl Emerson and Michael Holquist, trs. (Austin: University of Texas Press, 1981), 421.

TRUDIER HARRIS

Sula: *Within and Beyond the African-American Folk Tradition*

*T*he *Bluest Eye* (1970), with its grounding in Lorain, Ohio, provides at least geographical identification with events in the world as we know it. What the people do to each other there might be cruel and insensitive, but those characters approximate many we have seen. There is a verisimilitude in the cruelty of the children who reject Pecola, and we can easily visualize the likes of Pauline Breedlove in her adherence to a loyalty and love for the white family in preference for her own. With the creation of the Bottom in *Sula* (New York: Knopf, 1974), Toni Morrison removes that grounding in a known place and locates her characters in a territory that invites the fantastic and the mythical as easily as the realistic. In the political-racial-economic confrontation surrounding its creation, the Bottom differs from other fictional communities; it was concocted out of hope, belief, and the power of dreams to transcend the harshness of the real world. It lends itself, therefore, much more readily to occurrences that are strange or fantastic and to characters who are at times more nether creatures than flesh and blood.

Toni Morrison has asserted that she writes the kind of books she wants to read.[1] We might conclude, therefore, that in her use of folklore she is fascinated by the magic of fairy tales and intrigued with the horrors to be found in monsters, or at least in monstrous behavior. In *Sula*, Morrison continues her creation of literary folklore by drawing upon and expanding historical patterns.

From *Fiction and Folklore: The Novels of Toni Morrison.* © 1991 by Trudier Harris.

Morrison may begin with structural components of tales or peculiar traits of characters with which we may be superficially familiar, but she quickly embroiders upon these patterns. Her familiarity with African-American folk communities and with other oral traditions enables her to touch base with them in the outline of her materials, but to differ in the details. What Morrison does might be compared with what Charles Waddell Chesnutt did in *The Conjure Woman* (1899); beginning with the outlines of tales he had heard in North Carolina, he expanded details to shape political statements disguised as seemingly innocuous stories. Chesnutt's tales seem so true to black folk tradition that many students of his work have searched for exact parallels in published collections of folklore. Although Morrison surrounds her novel with an aura of unreality that discourages seeking exact parallels, her lore is further fictionalized beyond the mere germ of a traditional idea. Though we can see those basic inspirations in the ideas that shape the structure of the novel, delineate the characters, and develop the themes, it is also clear where Morrison has created something else.

Three oral sources are helpful in illuminating the structure of *Sula*. First of all, the structure evokes the formulaic opening of fairy tales from European cultures; secondly, it evokes a pattern of joking in African-American communities and, thirdly, it evokes the form of the ballad, which, in its incremental development, in turn reminds us of jazz composition. In the first paragraph of the novel, Morrison establishes an almost mythical status for the Bottom, claiming kinship for it with the many places in which strange, almost supernatural, incidents have occurred. "In that place, where they tore the nightshade and blackberry patches from their roots to make room for the Medallion City Golf Course, there was once a neighborhood" (3) deviates little from the "Once upon a time" formula for fairy tales; the fictional reality of the Bottom is thus juxtaposed with the lack of reality of some of those never-never lands.[2] The formula establishes distance, a perspective from which to view the incidents about to be related. It is a signal that we can sit back and read of marvelous events, or at least that is what the formula usually conveys.

As we begin our journey into that other world Morrison has created, we quickly discover a series of reversals: the fantastic events are disturbingly real, and the formula promising wondrous occurrences moves them from the realm of imagination to commonplaces such as war, poverty, and murder. The expected distance collapses, but it does not collapse thoroughly enough for us, without reservations, to accept Shadrack as the guy next door or Sula as the girl next door. Expected dragonslayers become frightened young soldiers afraid of their own hands, afraid that war has taught them not only to kill others but to kill themselves. Ogres are alcohol and drugs, and those strong enough to kill, such as Eva, cannot separate evil from the innocent victims it inhabits. Fires that save Hansel and Gretel or the three little pigs become scars upon the soul of a mother who kills her only son and upon a daughter who quietly watches her mother burn to death.

In another classic Morrison reversal, *Sula* is antithetical to the basic premise of the fairy tale—that the heroine is a helpless, passive creature who must depend upon some man, preferably a stranger, to save her from whatever "fate worse than death" she has innocently or stupidly managed to get herself into.[3] There is little passivity in *Sula*, and innocence is not treasured; indeed, as is typical of Morrison's girl/women, Sula and Nel seem to blossom into adolescence with more knowledge than is comfortable for either of them. In fact, as the experimenter with life, the Ethan Brand type who explores the limits of sin, Sula is an active, destructive artist who, in the absence of "paints, or clay" or a knowledge of "dance, or strings" (121) makes human beings her adventure in life. She is as active as Jack the giant killer and as amoral as Brer Rabbit the trickster.

In this literary folklore, therefore, there is a marked gap between expectation and outcome, between what the familiar leads us to anticipate and what Morrison's changing of the familiar actually provides. She undercuts any potential fairy tale outcomes by making Sula, her princess, a despicable user who needs rescue from no one; by making Eva, her fairy godmother, impotent at the most crucial moment of her life (Hannah's burning); and by making Shadrack, her potential prince, an outcast from the world where his services are most needed. None of these characters portends the "happily ever after" dimension of the formula. By novel's end, the princess is dead, the prince has unwittingly led many of her adversaries to their deaths, the twin sister is almost crazy with grief, and the kingdom is slowly being destroyed.

Its destruction has been foreshadowed in the second structural pattern underlying the novel, the "nigger joke" about the origin of the Bottom. The story fits a classic tale cycle of the black man being duped by the white man:

> A good white farmer promised freedom and a piece of bottom land to his slave if he would perform some very difficult chores. When the slave completed the work, he asked the farmer to keep his end of the bargain. Freedom was easy—the farmer had no objection to that. But he didn't want to give up any land. So he told the slave that he was very sorry that he had to give him valley land. He had hoped to give him a piece of the Bottom. The

slave blinked and said he thought valley land was bottom land. The master said, "Oh, no! See those hills? That's bottom land, rich and fertile."

"But it's high up in the hills," said the slave.

"High up from us," said the master, "but when God looks down, it's the bottom. That's why we call it so. It's the bottom of heaven—best land there is."

So the slave pressed his master to try to get him some. He preferred it to the valley. And it was done. The nigger got the hilly land, where planting was backbreaking, where the soil slid down and washed away the seeds, and where the wind lingered all through the winter.

Which accounted for the fact that white people lived on the rich valley floor in that little river town in Ohio, and the blacks populated the hills above it, taking small consolation in the fact that every day they could literally look down on the white folks. (5)

The tale presents two archetypes of African-American folklore: the white man of means and the "blinking," almost minstrel black man who learns too late the true nature of the bargain he has made. The basic discrepancy inherent in such interactions is also apparent: power (including the language skills to control or create reality) versus the absence of power. The twist in the tale is that the white farmer is the trickster, the figure who dupes instead of being duped.

The story is an etiological one, in that it serves to explain how the current state of affairs came to be. In a world in which the black man is destined to lose, because of or in spite of his labor, the slave here fares no better. The rules of the games will always be changed, as Daryl C. Dance astutely observes in her discussion of etiological tales in *Shuckin' and Jivin'* (1978) and elsewhere; the black man will always receive the reward of lesser value.[4] But Morrison turns the joke around; it is difficult to grow things there, but it is "lovely up in the Bottom" (5), and the trees are so "wonderful to see" (6) that whites speculate on the Bottom indeed being "the bottom of heaven" (6). In spite of their ancestors having been shortchanged, the black folks create reasonably happy lives for themselves in a place almost animate in its influence upon them.

Reminiscent of the storefront, communal, interactive culture that Zora Neale Hurston describes in *Mules and Men* (1935) and other works,[5] the Bottom is a joke where the tables are turned, for a time, back on the joker.

For that portion of the novel where the Bottom is vibrant—despite its occasional strangenesses—the last laugh is really on the whites, because they have not been able to destroy the will to survive of those blacks up in the Bottom. Indeed, the philosophy exemplified in the Bottom is one of survival at all costs, of making all mountains, built by whites or blacks, into mole hills. The black folks in the Bottom place white folks like the man in the tale in the large category of evil that will later contain Sula, and they resolve to withstand all of it. "The purpose of evil was to survive it and they determined (without ever knowing they had made up their minds to do it) to survive floods, white people, tuberculosis, famine and ignorance" (90).

Morrison allows them to invert the stereotype of their existence (that they deserve and should be resigned to content themselves with less) for almost a hundred years. Ultimately, the structure imposed by the "nigger joke"—that outcomes will always fall short of expectations—reigns in the novel. Blacks who moved to the Bottom and expected to be left in peace are not. Eventually, the whites decide that the Bottom is ideal for suburbs and a golf course, so the blacks who have not voluntarily moved away are displaced once again. Although slight variations have occurred over the years, the basic structure is retained: whites get what they consider the best, and blacks must settle for what is left.

This structure also provides a backdrop against which to view the actions of the characters, especially those of Sula. In a world in which expectations are invariably short-circuited, it is not surprising to find Sula's actions a series of expectations that she measures against some invisible yardstick and finds wanting. Life is in many ways the "nigger joke" that has been played on her. From her twelve-year-old discovery that her mother "loved" rather than "liked" her, to her twenty-seven-year-old Weltschmerz, Sula learns that life holds few genuine adventures for her and even fewer pleasures. The cards dealt out to her are all marked with the notation that she is black and female; therefore, winning hands must be kept from her. Paralleling the structure that defines the fate of the Bottom, the fate of Sula's existence is similarly determined.

Sula's personality, along with the snake-like birthmark that so intrigues those who encounter her, makes her the closest thing to a witch that the Bottom will ever have. Yet, in its ability to contain contradictions, the community provides for her, as Morrison has noted on several occasions, the only place that will accept her and the only home she will ever know.[6] Her wanderings away from the Bottom can only bring her full circle, like Eva, back to it, for it is able to absorb if not to condone her "otherness," and it gives her the identity that locks her both inside and outside the community's folk traditions. People in the community grant to her the power she has, and she accommodates them by living out their fantasies of otherness.

The third structural pattern in *Sula* evokes the ballad tradition, in which a "leaping and lingering" method of storytelling pauses on significant events in each character's life. In the ballad "Lord Rendal," for example, we are not told of Lord Rendal's birthplace or his growing up; we meet him as a young man who has gone into the woods and been poisoned by his "true love"—for some inexplicable reason.[7] The murder, the encounter with his mother asking what has happened, and his request that his mother make his deathbed "soon" are the three significant points in his life. The whys and wherefores are less important than the consequences of the bloody confrontation. Thus Rendal's life is reduced to the three incidents that lead to his death; perhaps the ballad, over years of telling, has lost some of its detail, but probably not much. The form of the genre demands brevity and heightened scenes, the tableau scenes, as Axel Olrik calls them in reference to the major incidents recorded in folktales.[8]

We can see a similar sparse depiction in the ballad of Barbara Allan, in which Sir John Graeme's failure to toast her is less central than the consequences of that action.[9] As a result, he pines and dies; then Barbara, sensing that he has indeed cherished her, anticipates her own death. The deaths here, like the murder and anticipated death in "Lord Rendal," keep the listener's attention. The same is true of traditional African-American ballads, such as "Stagolee." The "central event" is the gun battle between Stagolee and the other man, who has various names, the most common of which is Billy Lyons. Background on the two men is not particularly important; indeed, Billy Lyons exists only to allow Stagolee to act out his fate as a bad man. Some versions of the ballad include Stagolee's early encounters with his father or law officers (individual will versus authority in any form), but the ballad is basically stripped to its essential details.[10]

In an oral tradition, where memory could be subject to error, such standout scenes insured the singer a better chance of recalling what the audience was most interested in—the criminal activity surrounding rape, death, murder, hanging, and infanticide, and the pathos surrounding unrequited love. If there are valleys and peaks in an individual's life, then the peaks consistently receive attention ("peak" is used here to refer to emotional intensity, either good or bad, and not exclusively to pleasure or happiness). In relating her tale of passions, burnings, drownings, and witchery, Morrison, too, is interested in the highlights, the peaks, rather than the ordinariness represented by the valleys.

Morrison does not purport to be realistic to the minutiae of following characters on a day-to-day, year-by-year basis; her very labeling of the years she does dwell on (1919, 1920, 1921, 1922, 1923, 1927, 1937, 1939, 1940, 1941, 1965) indicates the leaping and lingering tradition. She selects the most impressive events and concentrates upon them for each of her most impressionable characters. The effects of the war upon Shadrack are finally more important than physically depicting him in battle, although the one scene he does recall is a striking one in which a soldier whose head has been blown off continues to run in spite of that catastrophe. The bloody images of the war lead to Shadrack's perennial celebration of National Suicide Day, and the visit from Sula, the other tableau scene in his life, serves as his last untainted tie to humanity.

Eva's life is crystallized in several scenes: pushing lard up Plum's rectum in the midst of unbearable poverty, knowing that hating BoyBoy after his return will give her peace, trying to save Hannah from a burning death, and being carted off to the old folks' home. The loss of her leg is certainly important, but we are left to speculate about the circumstances under which that occurred; what that loss enabled her to do is more significant. Nel and Sula's friendship solidifies on the day Sula hears Hannah's frank, but destructive, comment on her motherly feelings—which is also the day Sula accidentally kills Chicken Little. Nel's marriage collapses into the few minutes she finds Jude and Sula together, and her grief careens off the tombstones on the day, after her visit to Eva in the old folks' home, that she realizes the extent of her love for Sula. Perhaps the bits and pieces of these lives, as Morrison said about Cholly Breedlove, would make more sense in a musician's head, but they also make sense in the tradition that does not expect fairy tale completeness. Leaping and lingering, frequently with the bloody, or at least the violent, consequences of the ballad tradition, Morrison tells her story in sketches, in vignettes that encourage us to feel that we know her characters, but that really point out the facility with which their complexity is kept before us—and sometimes just beyond our reach.

The leaping and lingering of the ballad tradition suggests the jazz structuring of the novel, where the theme of death has many variations and improvisations upon it as Morrison manifests its meaning for various of the characters. Death is the stable point of this jazz composition, the center to which each year returns in spite of its individual departure. This allowance for individuality within an overall structure contrasts sharply with what is possible for Sula in the Bottom; the community would prefer that she play the straight refrain of the blues rather than the creative deviation allowable with the jazz comparison.[11]

While these structural patterns are illuminating, they do not explain all that happens in the organization of the novel (we could also talk about the structure of a journey, in which Shadrack moves from innocence to experience to innocence, or where Nel moves from innocence to an almost unbearable knowledge); nor do they in any way confine Morrison to identification with these forms. Instead, they show how Morrison has used folk traditions to expand our expectations of what a novel should be and do. That expansion adds a richness and complexity to her work that is frequently absent in the works of other authors who draw upon oral traditions.

Within the structures Morrison devises for her novel, she creates many characters who echo either specific or general concepts from folk tradition. Local characters, such as Sula, and anecdotes about them, are particularly inspiring for Morrison. From Shadrack, who acts as a chorus to open and close this human drama, to the three deweys, Morrison's characters elicit comparison to those from other folk communities and various wonderlands. Communities that designate some of their inhabitants "weirdos," "crazies," and "loonies" have usually observed several traits in them. They are unusual in appearance and/or mannerisms, and frequently in terms of habitat. Youngsters are taught to fear boogie men and women, whose otherness may be defined by something as tangible as alcoholism or as intangible as an assumed ability to cast the evil eye. Some merely outsiders and others pariahs, these characters serve psychological as well as educational functions in their communities; they illustrate the dangers of talking with strangers (the possibility of disappearing into some peculiar abode), and their weirdness soothes the community as it measures its normalcy against their unusualness. That is certainly what the community does to Pecola Breedlove in *The Bluest Eye*; they can gauge how normal and beautiful they are by emphasizing Pecola's insanity and ugliness.

Omniscient narration gives readers an understanding of Shadrack's otherness, but the folks in the Bottom are never so privileged. They know that he went off to war normal and came back abnormal; the whys and wherefores of that transformation are mere abstractions and do not prevent them from defining Shadrack as one of the weirdos, however formed, who demands a special psychological and physical space in their worlds. A man who comes down the street ringing a cowbell and dangling a hanging rope every January third is not exactly an untainted representative of rationality, yet the community incorporates Shadrack's ceremony without diminishing itself or sanctioning him. They take note—from a distance when they can— of his cursing fits and drinking spells.

Still, like the local characters from oral tradition, he is able to make unspoken claims upon the community even as an outsider. The people in the

Bottom evince a degree of responsibility for Shadrack (as one of the wounded whose injury is more intense than their own) by buying the fish he catches and by enduring his curses and morbid parades. He provides diversion from their normalcy; though they do not wish to emulate him, his antics make them secure in their own identities. Seeing Shadrack expose his private parts could only make the ladies more appreciative of their husbands' clothing and make the husbands appreciate the covering that prevents them from being evaluated so publicly. Shadrack's cabin by the river could hold out to them a possibility for freedom, but it is negated by their knowledge of his mental cages. Tolerated but not loved, a part of the community but not truly in it, Shadrack exemplifies the type of character around whom legends and anecdotes grow, who is a source of entertainment as well as a source of dread, who seems through his life-style to be imminently dispensable, but who is the epitome of the community penchant for survival.[12]

It is appropriate that Shadrack is seen at the beginning and the ending of the novel, for the white man who made the Bottom a "nigger joke" and perpetuated white domination of black lives is representative of the system that has also overwhelmed Shadrack. His experiences in the army have been more costly than the slave's loss of land, and the effects have gone on longer. Not only has Shadrack been blasted mentally and suffered through more than forty years of that disorientation, but he must now watch with Nel as the remnants of the Bottom give way to a golf course and fancy houses.

In his strangeness, Shadrack is comparable to an overly sensitive poet/philosopher who has seen so much of the horror of life that he has been blasted beyond the reaches of mundane influences. He brings a knowledge to his people, but the ironic price of his experiences is that he has lost his ability to communicate in a language they understand. His bell and rope, initially more disturbing than enlightening, are more of a barrier to Shadrack's desire to impart truth than Tiresias's blindness or Diogenes's lamp. Rather than understanding that death can be put in perspective if it is given its recognizable place in human existence, the black folk of the Bottom are only reminded of its power to separate them from the living, of the mysteries it holds. To them, therefore, Shadrack is a loony who disturbs things that are best left alone; instead of reducing the fear of death, he evokes more.

Shadrack's mental blighting clearly sets him apart from the rest of the community. His insanity becomes one of the distinguishing physical characteristics that black folks have long used to recognize "otherness" in their midst. Such characteristics, like M'Dear's height and isolation from the community in *The Bluest Eye*, connect the possessor to powers beyond those of ordinary means. They hail such persons as conjurers, witches, or devil worshippers. Since the power identified with them can be used for evil as well as benign purposes, it ensures respect for them in the communities in which they dwell, respect that comes from fear or from belief. The inhabitants of the Bottom treat Sula's birthmark as such an indication of otherworldliness and use it to turn her into a witch. Who but a witch, the women probably rationalize, could use their husbands so thoroughly and discard them at whim? Who but a witch would progress to putting Eva in an old folks home?

The initial evidence against Sula is circumstantial, but it offers the beginning of the reinforcement of belief so central to the creation of outsiderness. From calling Sula a "roach" for putting Eva in the old folks home and a "bitch" for sleeping with Jude, the people in the Bottom come to recognize her true witchery when they discover she has slept with white men; that is the ultimate sign of deviation from their norm, and it puts Sula in league with all manner of strange beings. Knowing that strangeness does not mean weakness, they guard themselves accordingly: "So they laid broomsticks across their doors at night and sprinkled salt on porch steps" (113). After a couple of attempts to "collect the dust from her footsteps," perhaps with the intention of using it in a potion against her, they content themselves with the power of gossip. They "know" she has power when Teapot trips and falls on her steps. The extent of her power gets verification in what happens to another neighbor: "Mr. Finley sat on his porch sucking chicken bones, as he had done for thirteen years, looked up, saw Sula, choked on a bone and died on the spot" (114). They conclude that the birthmark over her eye "was Hannah's ashes marking her from the very beginning" (114).

The birthmark explains why Sula is not content with the life the other women in the Bottom lead, why she must travel all over the country in search of something that they cannot begin to imagine. Indeed, her ten-year absence from the Bottom serves to highlight a mysterious, legendary quality about her in the same way that many figures in traditional narratives have some unexplained or missing part of their lives. Sula's difference, like Shadrack's, must be labeled so that the community can go on about its business. Since her neighbors have no words to explain Sula's personality, and no previous encounters with anyone who could help them explain it, they label her difference as witchery and thereby justify shunning her. They can also soothe their ambivalent pride when she casts their husbands aside:

> Among the weighty evidence piling up was the fact that
> Sula did not look her age. She was near thirty and, unlike them,

had lost no teeth, suffered no bruises, developed no ring of fat at the waist or pocket at the back of her neck. It was rumored that she had had no childhood diseases, was never known to have chicken pox, croup or even a runny nose. She had played rough as a child—where were the scars? Except for a funny-shaped finger and that evil birthmark, she was free of any normal signs of vulnerability. Some of the men, who as boys had dated her, remembered that on picnics neither gnats nor mosquitoes would settle on her. Patsy, Hannah's one-time friend, agreed and said not only that, but she had witnessed the fact that when Sula drank beer she never belched. (115)[13]

Imagination gives the community diversity from its own stupored monotony; it comes together to make a monster out of difference in the same way that various groups in *Song of Solomon* respond to Pilate's lack of a navel. Sula's "don't give a damn" attitude makes her an easy target for the tales, for she lacks an egotistical concern for reputation. Not interested in fighting back, her very silence gives truth to the rumors as far as the women are concerned. And indeed, they do not really need justification for the tales they tell; rumor exists for its own satisfaction. When Teapot falls down Sula's steps and fractures his skull, it is much more exciting to attribute the incident to witchery than to call it an accident. There is as much pleasure in telling the tales, perhaps more, than in looking into the truth of Sula's life.

The community also judges Sula to be in league with the devil because Shadrack is civil to her. When Dessie sees him tip his hat to Sula, she is convinced that she is witnessing a greeting between two of Satan's disciples. And woe to her that she does so, for a "big sty" (117) is her reward for seeing what she should not have seen. Sula becomes the measure of evil for the community, their catch-all explanation for natural and unnatural occurrences, their chance to triumph, day after day, over the devil in their midst. Sula's place among them is as secure in its deviance as Shadrack's is in its insanity.[14]

While the Bottom may work hard to prove that Sula is a witch, it already has one in its midst. Ajax's mother is reputed to be "an evil conjure woman" (126) who, when Ajax is gone, sits "in her shack with six younger sons working roots." Her knowledge of good and evil is real, whereas the evidence of the knowledge assigned to Sula is "contrived." Perhaps because of her commitment to her sons, and theirs to her, this woman has found a place in the community; Sula is too antithetical to everything they believe in for them to accept her as readily. Ajax's mother would be beautiful, Morrison asserts, if she had any teeth or ever straightened her back, thereby emphasizing that her deviance is not the thing that sets her apart from her feminine self, which is a contrast to Sula. Stephanie A. Demetrakopoulos works through the implications of the masculine/feminine contrast of the two women in her discussion of the novel.[15]

If Shadrack represents the outer realm of the community's obligation and focus, then the deweys represent its center. Shadowy though they may be at times, they are nevertheless firmly entrenched in Eva's house, which provides a center for the Bottom. From a folkloristic perspective, the deweys extend the concept of twins (exemplified in the novel by Sula and Nel) into triplets. As such, they have identical relationships to those around them and serve in identical capacities. It does not matter that Eva asks for *a* dewey to perform a chore, for they are all orphans, dependent, easily intimidated, and as strange as their personalities and Eva's house make them; they are "a trinity with a plural name ... inseparable, loving nothing and no one but themselves" (38). Made comical by their antics and diminutive size, they remain children into their adult years. In their youth, they provided the comic relief to the mystery surrounding Eva, to the brooding Sula, and to the sexually active Hannah. They are also a part of the joking cycle in the novel, for they illustrate the almost comic perversity with which good intentions are sometimes pervaded. They are wild things in the Bottom, who, as a part of that tables-turned phenomenon, debunk the myth of maternal concern surrounding adoptions. Though Eva provides shelter and food for the deweys, she is about as much a mother to them as Teapot's Mamma is to him before his encounter with Sula.

The townspeople eventually notice that "the deweys would never grow. They had been forty-eight inches tall for years now" (84). Their size, combined with their acquisition of only the basic, functional command of language, gives their mental otherness a physical dimension. Yet they nevertheless figure more frequently as a concept than as separate entities in the novel; the lower-case references to them reinforce this idea. The question to ask, then, is "What is a dewey?" A dewey is a shadowy presence at 7 Carpenter's Road, hard to visualize but always concretely creating problems or running errands. A dewey is an individual who exists on the borderline between tolerable behavior and trying out for reform school. A dewey is contained lawlessness, just as a Shadrack is contained insanity. A dewey is rootless and uncommitted, existing from day to day with no knowledge of past or future. A dewey is an idea manifested in triplets whose very physical appearances defy that appellation. A dewey is the physical manifestation of Eva's power to control the environment around her.

Eva initiates the creation of the deweys as local characters, and Hannah and others perpetuate it when they force the teacher to admit all three youngsters—in spite of their differing ages—into the same grade. The denial of individual dewey reality gives way to one of Eva's pastimes: she creates the concept of the deweys for her own amusement. She names them and thereby determines their fate.[16] Community sanctioning of her joke makes it all the more appealing; it gives Eva a goddess-like characteristic. In that folk-like community of the Bottom, where legends and superstitions abound, the path by which the deweys come to be local characters allows us to glimpse a clear-cut origin that has few counterparts in oral tradition.

In a less dramatic way, Eva also contributes to the community perception of Tar Baby, the white mountain drifter who finds his way into a small back room at 7 Carpenter's Road. As uprooted as Shadrack and the deweys, Tar Baby is another figure about whom tales can develop—Is he really white? Why does he drink? Why does he live in the Bottom rather than in Medallion? What drives him to sing "In the Sweet By-and-By" so pathetically? Eva directs the course of information about Tar Baby's ethnicity and makes a joke of it: "Most people said he was half white, but Eva said he was all white. That she knew blood when she saw it, and he didn't have none. When he first came to Medallion, the people called him Pretty Johnnie, but Eva looked at his milky skin and cornsilk hair and out of a mixture of fun and meanness called him Tar Baby" (39–40). He provides Eva with another source of amusement. In her confinement to her sprawling house, she brings a world of diversions to fill the space when she does not wish to create her own. Tar Baby and the deweys are perhaps grateful for having the shelter of Eva's home; they desire about as much as she is willing to provide, thereby making her relationship to all of them as informal and as vaguely committed as their otherness and her temperament warrant. She can laugh at them or control them, because she is ultimately disinterested in them; as a part of the landscape she has created in that huge house, they have as much or as little claim to belonging as any of the other inhabitants. Like a perverted artist out of a Hawthorne tale, Eva gives them a place in her home as well as a place in the lore of the Bottom; together, they increase Morrison's population of "grotesques," as Darwin T. Turner labels her characters.[17]

However, to label them grotesques is perhaps to miss a fundamental component of the historical black communities that might have inspired the creation of the Bottom. Such communities have a large capacity for containing those unlike themselves, especially if the issue in question concerns sanity. Morrison writes of Shadrack: "Once the people understood the boundaries and nature of his madness, they could fit him, so to speak, into the scheme of things" (15). Shadrack and other characters might be conspicuously different from the norm, but there is a space for them within the larger community. If they do no more than provide a yardstick for measuring acceptable group behavior, they nevertheless serve a function. When the Bottom no longer has Sula to establish its limits of morality, there is a noticeable hole, a palpable emptiness in the community. There was a place for her there, even if that place was not in line with the majority of the community's norms.

What Eva does with the deweys and Tar Baby, together with how the community responds to Sula, enhances the notion that the Bottom is a consciously contrived black folk community in which the folk create and venerate their own traditions, much as the people do in Paule Marshall's mythical Bournehills and in Zora Neale Hurston's Eatonville.[18] Legends, superstitions (signs and beliefs), and rituals combine with the local characters to make *Sula* as akin to historic folk communities as any literary creation can be. In their observance of National Suicide Day, their most prominent ritual, the folks in the Bottom can be compared to contemporary communities observing rituals such as the Fourth of July or Groundhog Day, or to the Bournehillers' annual pageant to celebrate Cuffee Ned's rebellion. Cyclical, repetitive ceremonies provide these communities with a way of defining as well as explaining themselves.

The institutionalization of National Suicide Day is a measure of how thoroughly the community has absorbed Shadrack's strangeness as well as of how quietly that process of absorption takes place. The folks in the Bottom may not mark their wall calendars for the January third ritual, but they internalize the date and its events. Women mark labor and birth by that date as much as slaves in Alabama marked such occurrences by the year the stars fell. Even folks who choose to avoid doing things on National Suicide Day are nonetheless responding to its effect upon them. And the grandmother who maintains that "her hens always started a laying of double yolks right after Suicide Day" (16) contributes her share to the ritual by building a superstitious lore around it. Familiarity and repetition enable the inhabitants of the Bottom to contain National Suicide Day. Initially unable and later unwilling to deny it a place, they soon discover that what seemed horrible was more sounding brass and tinkling cymbal than destructive. Unfortunately, their effort to see National Suicide Day more as symbol than substance backfires on that day in 1941 when Shadrack leads his jubilant followers to a muddy death in the tunnel at the end of the New River Road.

Again Morrison executes a reversal by giving true meaning to an initially farfetched and hollow idea. The respect for death that made Shadrack so crazy after participating in the white man's big war is now paralleled by the "murder" of black people by the whites who commissioned and worked on the tunnel. Over a period of fourteen years, the whites have killed black hopes for working on the new road as well as on the tunnel. Some men have died and others have grown up and gone away while waiting for those hopes to be fulfilled. Their hopes have been as inconsiderable as those of the slave who desired good bottom land. It is perversely fitting, therefore, that National Suicide Day be given the tangible reality that silence and neglect have conferred on it for all those years, and it is equally perversely fitting that the song they sing, "Shall We Gather at the River," is one that has traditionally brought comfort to black people and the expectation that life after this world would be much better than that lived here. When the deweys, Tar Baby, and others die in the tunnel, their deaths denote the end of a particular kind of hope, the end of an era of belief that justice would be done through an unprompted, natural course. The tunnel catastrophe will provide tales for years to come about the "crazy" black folk of the Bottom who thought they could halt progress with their bodies. The story of their deaths will overshadow many of the tales that sustained these folk during their lifetime.

Just as it created local characters and instituted rituals, the Bottom also has its share of legends. Told for true, these stories take the shape of memorates, a first stage of legend formation in that the details of the narrative have not yet been fully fleshed out (and frequently the teller of the tale can claim to have been an eyewitness to the occurrence).[19] For example, people surmise various causes for the disappearance of Eva's leg, but a prominent, single-stranded, developed story has not been accepted over others. Still, the one detail believed to be true is generally agreed upon: Eva sacrificed her leg for the money that would ensure her family's survival. How that essential fact was brought about is where the accounts differ: "Somebody said Eva stuck it under a train and made them pay off. Another said she sold it to a hospital for $10,000—at which Mr. Reed opened his eyes and asked, 'Nigger gal legs goin' for $10,000 a *piece*?' as though he could understand $10,000 a *pair*—but for *one*?" (31). Sula absorbs the tale about Eva's leg, and, as an adult, uses it to try to equalize the distance between Eva and herself. When Eva claims that nobody can talk to her with disrespect, Sula maintains:

> "This body does. Just 'cause you was bad enough to cut off your own leg you think you got a right to kick everybody with the stump."
> "Who said I cut off my leg?"
> "Well, you stuck it under a train to collect insurance." (92–93)

Sula turns perhaps the most significant occurrence in Eva's life against her by suggesting that the circumstances surrounding the loss of the leg place Eva in a category similar to Shadrack. The irony is that Eva has contributed to the growth of the lore about her missing leg. When she mentions it, usually "in some mood of fancy, she began some fearful story about it—generally to entertain children. How the leg got up by itself one day and walked on off. How she hobbled after it but it ran too fast. Or how she had a corn on her toe and it just grew and grew and grew until her whole foot was a corn and then it traveled on up her leg and wouldn't stop growing until she put a red rag at the top but by that time it was already at her knee" (30–31). An active tradition bearer in much of the lore of the Bottom, Eva is no less stinting with tales about herself.

By contrast, Sula's derisive recounting of the tales about Eva's missing leg shows how she breaks with tradition and perhaps even alters the lore in an effort to undercut her biological relationship to Eva. By negatively reinforcing the stories, Sula shows a disrespect not only for Eva but for the tradition itself. This small exchange illustrates well her severing of ties with the community. The lore is not entertaining for her; she uses it to control Eva's behavior and finally to threaten her. She redefines the function of folklore by telling her stories as a leveling device to gain power over Eva and to diminish her self-concept in the process. She therefore simultaneously devalues the vibrancy and purpose of the oral tradition while strengthening her reputation as a *ba-ad* woman.

Morrison's community has its superstitions and folk beliefs in addition to its folk characters. Traditionally, the natural world has been the logical place for people in folk communities to look for signs and meanings to be revealed to them. The unnatural and peculiar things that happen before Hannah's burning are a sign to Eva that some significant occurrence is about to take place. She cannot find her comb, which is out of its "natural" place; there is an unusually strong wind that does not bring the release of rain; and Hannah dreams of a wedding in which the bride wears a red dress, the color of which Eva will later interpret to mean that it portended Hannah's burning death. Her knowledge that dreams go by opposites strengthens her interpretation of the death; the wedding, a happy occasion, really portends some impending misfortune. The plague of birds before Sula's return to the Bottom is looked upon as a portent of evil, for, like Eva, the folks have learned, from their closeness to nature, to read its signs and prepare themselves for whatever is coming.

Signs and beliefs such as the wind without rain, the bride in the red dress, the plague of birds, and Eva burning the hair she combs from her head (so that enemies cannot get it and use it to direct spells toward her—91) might be realistic enough to have their counterparts in *The Frank C. Brown Collection of North Carolina Folklore*, or some other collection, in that there is a demonstrated present occurrence linked to some future disastrous possibility.[20] However, the responses to Sula's birthmark form another kind of belief in the novel, one for which few historical parallels exist. Many characters believe that Sula is evil; when they view the birthmark, they project onto it features reminiscent of those assigned to boogie men. To Nel's impressionable children, Sula's birthmark is a "scary black thing" (97–98); Jude views it as a copperhead (103) and as a rattlesnake (104) when he sees Sula as a potentially dangerous element introduced into his home; and the people in the Bottom view it as "Hannah's ashes" (114).[21] Such reactions contribute to making Sula into a legend in the community. The mark becomes as distinguishing as any of those, such as blue or red eyes, limps, or warts, that Newbell Niles Puckett identified in his discussions of distinctive features of conjurers.

Through her creation of characters like Eva, Sula, Shadrack, and the deweys, and the legends and tales surrounding them, Morrison shows that folklore can be used for purposes of enhancing characterization, advancing plot, and putting forth themes. Such functions have been recognized by folklore scholars Alan Dundes and Hennig Cohen in their early studies of folklore and literature.[22] Yet Morrison goes further in attempting to recreate the very atmosphere in which folk cultures, with all their layers and characters, blossom and grow. Like Ernest Gaines in many of his works,[23] she makes her characters and her community the substance of a pervasive aura of folk tradition, a saturation frequently recognized more by suggestion than specifics, but that succeeds very well in showing Morrison's ties to black folk culture.

NOTES

Although Morrison copyrighted the novel in 1973, it was actually published on 7 January 1974. I am therefore using the 1974 date for consistency with other *publication* dates used throughout the manuscript.

1. Noted in Tate, ed., Black *Women Writers at Work*, 122, and Jane Bakerman, "The Seams Can't Show: An Interview with Toni Morrison," *Black American Literature Forum* 12 (Summer 1978): 59.

2. Morrison emphasizes that she chose the "nightshade" and "blackberry" for their connotative as well as their literal values. "Both plants have darkness in them: 'black' and 'night.' One is unusual (nightshade) and has two darkness words: 'night' and 'shade.' The other (blackberry) is common. A familiar plant and an exotic one. A harmless one and a

dangerous one. One produces a nourishing berry; one delivers toxic ones" ("Unspeakable Things Unspoken: The Afro-American Presence in American Literature," *Michigan Quarterly Review* 28 [Winter 1989]: 25). In her awareness of the plants, Morrison exhibits qualities of the folk healer. In structuring her novel around the positive and negative qualities of blackness drawn from natural imagery, she further enhances her ties to black folk traditions. She has also commented that she grew up in an environment where stories were told, where "black lore, black music, black language" were "prominent elements"; see Nellie Y. McKay, "An Interview with Toni Morrison," *Contemporary Literature* 24 (Winter 1983): 414–15.

3. For a discussion of passivity in fairy tales, see Kay Stone, "Things Walt Disney Never Told Us," in *Women and Folklore*, ed. Claire R. Farrer (Austin: Univ. of Texas Press, 1975), 42–50 and Marcia R. Lieberman, "'Some Day My Prince Will Come': Female Acculturation Through the Fairy Tale," *College English* 34 (1972): 383–95. For a slightly different view, see Kay F. Stone, "The Misuses of Enchantment: Controversies on the Significance of Fairy Tales," in Rosan A. Jordan and Susan J. Kalčik, eds., *Women's Folklore, Women's Culture*, (Philadelphia: Univ. of Pennsylvania Press, 1985), 125–45.

4. "Upon This Rock," one of the stories Dance has collected, illustrates the point well. Jesus tells a black man, a Jew, and an Italian to go out and collect stones during a day's walk. The black man, believing that he is being timed, rushes back with a pebble. The Italian brings a wheelbarrow full of stones, and the Jew shoves a mountain. When Jesus turns the stones into bread, "the Black man had a biscuit. The Italian had a wheelbarrow *filled* with loaves of bread. And the Jew had a *bakery*, of course." The next day, having been given the same directions, the black man goes out and brings back "a whole avalanche of mountains and boulders"; everyone must wait until four A.M. for him to push them to the gathering site. Upon his arrival, he discovers that the rules have changed from morning to evening. "And finally the Lord said, 'Upon *these* rocks I'll build my church.' And the Black man said, 'I be *damned* if you will. You gon' make *bread* today!'" (Daryl Cumber Dance, *Shuckin' and Jivin': Folklore from Contemporary Black Americans* [Bloomington: Indiana Univ. Press, 1978], 9–10).

5. Hurston, *Mules and Men*, and *The Sanctified Church* (Berkeley: Turtle Island, 1983).

6. See "Toni Morrison," in *Black Women Writers at Work*, ed. Tate, 130: "There was no other place in the world she could have lived without being harmed"; Sandi Russell, "It's OK to say OK," interview essay in *Critical Essays on Toni Morrison*, ed. McKay, 43–47: "Although the community didn't like Sula and what she did, they allowed her to 'be.' She couldn't have had these freedoms elsewhere" (44); and McKay, "An Interview with Toni Morrison," 413–29: Sula is "nevertheless protected there [in the Bottom] as she would not be elsewhere" (426).

7. Robert Graves, *English and Scottish Ballads* (London: Heinemann, 1963), 5–7.

8. See Axel Olrik, "Epic Laws of Folk Narrative," in *The Study of Folklore*, ed. Alan Dundes (Englewood Cliffs, N.J.: Prentice-Hall, 1965), 129–41.

9. Graves, *English and Scottish Ballads*, 89–91.

10. See Levine, *Black Culture and Black Consciousness*, 413–15.

11. As noted earlier, Barbara Christian makes a case for *The Bluest Eye* also being based on African-American musical structures. See *Black Women Novelists: The Development of a Tradition, 1892–1976*, 148–49.

12. Morrison has commented on her perception of black people's willingness to accept difference: "Black people have a way of allowing things to go on the way they're going.

We're not too terrified of death, not too terrified of being different, not too upset about divisions among things, people. Our interests have always been, it seems to me, on how un-alike things are rather than how alike things are." Tate, ed., *Black Women Writers at Work*, 123.

13. In the transformation to "ba-ad" woman, Sula's presumed peculiarities approximate those of some of the male heroes of African-American tradition. Consider one description of badman Stagolee: "Stagolee was so bad that the flies wouldn't even fly around his head in the summertime, and snow wouldn't fall on his house in the winter," Julius Lester, *Black Folktales* (New York: Baron, 1969), 113. Sula started on the road to "ba-adness" when she sliced off the tip of her finger to prevent the white boys from attacking her and Nel (54–55).

14. Philip M. Royster discusses how the Bottom uses Sula and Shadrack as scapegoats in "A Priest and a Witch against The Spiders and The Snakes: Scapegoating in Toni Morrison's *Sula*," *Umoja* 2 (Fall 1978): 149–68.

15. Holloway and Demetrakopoulos, *New Dimensions of Spirituality*, 58–59.

16. Barbara Christian has discussed the importance of naming in the novel, connecting it in Eva's case to the African concept of Nommo. See *Black Women Novelists*, as well as Jones and Vinson, *The World of Toni Morrison: Explorations in Literary Criticism*, 13–15, and Holloway and Demetrakopoulos, *New Dimensions of Spirituality*, 21–22, 41, 69, 75–76.

17. Darwin T. Turner, "Theme, Characterization, and Style in the Works of Toni Morrison," in *Black Women Writers (1950–1980): A Critical Evaluation*, ed. Evans, 361–69.

18. See Paule Marshall's *The Chosen Place, The Timeless People* (New York: Harcourt Brace & World, 1969) and Hurston's *Mules and Men*.

19. For more information on memorates and legend formation, see Sandra K. D. Stahl, "Personal Experience Stories," in *Handbook of American Folklore*, ed. Dorson, 268–76.

20. Wayland D. Hand, ed., *The Frank C. Brown Collection of North Carolina Folklore*, vols. 6 and 7 (Durham: Duke Univ. Press, 1961, 1964); see sections on "portents."

21. The narrator refers to Sula's birthmark as a "stemmed rose" (52, 144) and "like a stem and rose" (74). Shadrack, who does not share in the community disdain for Sula, sees the birthmark as a "tadpole" (157), a friendlier image than any of the other characters visualize. Karla Holloway views the varying images of Sula's birthmark as "physical manifestations" of the "African archetypes" of fire, water, and ground (*New Dimensions of Spirituality*, 68, 69).

22. See Dundes, "The Study of Folklore in Literature and Culture: Identification and Interpretation," 136–42, and Cohen, "American Literature and American Folklore," 238–47.

23. See, for example, Ernest Gaines's "A Long Day in November" in *Bloodline* (New York: Dial, 1968).

24. See Richard M. Dorson, *American Negro Folktales* (Greenwich, Conn.: Fawcett, 1967), 75–76, and Langston Hughes and Arna Bontemps, *The Book of Negro Folklore*, 6–8.

25. For a selection of Aunt Dicy tales, see J. Mason Brewer, *American Negro Folklore* (Chicago: Quadrangle Books, 1968), 69–74. These are somewhat diminished from pure trickster tales, but they nonetheless show a woman getting the better of her adversaries. And we need not necessarily look for feminine features of the trickster in discussing Sula, for Morrison, and several critics, have commented on how masculine Sula is in the courses of action she chooses; see the interview with Morrison in Jones and Vinson, *The World of Toni Morrison*.

26. See, for example, "Who Ate Up the Butter?" in Richard M. Dorson's *Negro Folktales in Michigan* (Cambridge: Harvard Univ. Press, 1956), 33–35, and "Playing Godfather," in Hughes and Bontemps's *The Book of Negro Folklore*, 6–8.

27. See Wolfgang Lederer, *The Fear of Women* (New York: Grune & Stratton, 1968) and Hurston, *Tell My Horse* (1938; rpt. Berkeley: Turtle Island, 1983), 143–51.

28. See Walter Blair, ed., *Selected Shorter Writings of Mark Twain* (Boston: Houghton Mifflin, 1962), 306–88.

29. This spirit of experimentation brings to mind the folktale in which Brer Rabbit introduces the alligator family to fire simply for the sake of observing their reaction. He lures them out of the water to a dry field of grass and sets it on fire ("Why Br' Gator's Hide Is So Horny," Hughes and Bontemps, eds., *The Book of Negro Folklore*, 23–30), thereby causing their silvery white hides to be burned to a crinkly brown (and explaining why they currently look the way they do). Compare this to Sula's penchant for making others uncomfortable solely for the sake of registering their discomfort: "In the midst of a pleasant conversation with someone she might say, 'Why do you chew with your mouth open?' not because the answer interested her but because she wanted to see the person's face change rapidly" (119).

PHILIP PAGE

Putting It All Together:
Attempted Unification in
Song of Solomon

In *The Bluest Eye* images of splitting dramatize a broken community, broken families, and especially broken identities. In *Sula* Morrison focuses on irreconcilable divisions between binarily opposed pairs. *Song of Solomon* initially posits a similarly split world, but this novel moves toward the attempted and ambiguous reconciliation of the divided parts. If *The Bluest Eye* lays out the problem of the creation and maintenance of viable identities for contemporary African Americans, and if *Sula* explores the frustrations of attempting to develop such identities through relationships with a significant other, Morrison's third novel expands that search to a quest for identity and meaning through knowledge of the ancestral and cultural past.[1] As in the first two books, the problem is one of fragmentation—families are "all split up" (291) to the extent that "it's a wonder anybody knows who anybody is" (328)—but here the attempted solution is not to find identity and meaning in a paired relationship, but to unify disparate elements and conflicting clues into a meaningful whole—in short, to "put it all together" (327).

Morrison sets up Milkman's miraculous quest for unity by chronicling the heterogeneity in his environment. His family is divided into two estranged branches, and, within his immediate family, his mother and father barely tolerate each other, and he rarely speaks to his sisters. Simultaneously, he is pulled in contrary directions by Macon, Ruth, Pilate, Hagar, and

From *Dangerous Freedom: Fusion and Fragmentation in Toni Morrison's Novels*. © 1995 by the University Press of Mississippi.

Guitar. In Part I of the novel, Milkman's response to these pressures modulates from confusion to withdrawal and then to resentment, and yet, particularly through his association with Pilate, there are signs of preparation for his identity-forming quest in Part II. In Part II, Milkman achieves a successful but interrupted integration, a process symbolic of racial schism in American history and of the shift from "Negro" to "black" in African-American culture.

In Morrison's first two novels, characters' immediate families tend not to provide stable bases for individual fulfillment but instead are splintered by unbridgeable gaps between parents and children. In *Song of Solomon* intra-family relations are even worse. The Bains family has been destroyed by the death of Guitar's father and the absence of his mother. The Dead family is indeed spiritually dead; Macon and Ruth's failed individual lives as well as their moribund relationship are reflected in the stagnated lives of their children and in the lack of healthy relationships among them. The household of Pilate, Reba, and Hagar, another of Morrison's female triads, has many positive qualities, but Pilate, who formed her own successful identity despite the violent break-up of her own family, is unable to transmit her strengths to her daughter or granddaughter (Scruggs, "Nature" 322). Both in her personal achievement and in her inability to pass on that achievement, Pilate's case further exemplifies Morrison's questioning of the power of parent/child relationships to foster individual wholeness. Moreover, the extended Dead family seems at first irrevocably split between the two households in their two opposing parts of town, much like the contrasts between the MacTeer and Breedlove households in *The Bluest Eye* and the Peace and Wright households in *Sula* (Barthold 180).

As in the first two novels, the past strongly shapes the disintegration of families and individuals, but for the Dead family the failure to know and incorporate the past is especially disabling. The family's separation from the past is revealed by its misnaming, which, like the "nigger joke" that named and created the Bottom (Christian, *Black Feminist* 51), is an absurd result of racism. Without their name (Solomon) and the wisdom it implies, the Deads are ignorant of their ancestry and hence of themselves, and they are alienated from their community, each other, and themselves. Lacking his spiritual inheritance, Macon substitutes the materialistic ethos of the dominant culture and therefore supposes that his rightful inheritance is the gold. Pilate tries to retain her spiritual connections to her past, in particular to her father, but, not knowing the full story of the past, she makes the erroneous assumption that the bones she keeps are not her father's but those of the white man she and Macon killed. Milkman's task of reintegration requires him to complete Pilate's quest by connecting past and present, thereby rediscovering the family name and converting the false inheritance to a true one.

The past also influences the characters in the form of ghosts, which serve as traces of the past. In this novel, as Freddie urges Milkman, "You better believe" in ghosts (109). For everyone there is the danger of becoming spiritually dead, of becoming, like Hagar, "a restless ghost, finding peace nowhere and in nothing" (127). Guitar's life is determined by the unexorcised ghosts of his parents: the callous response of his father's employer to his father's grisly death motivates Guitar's hatred of whites, and his mother's sycophantic imitation of Aunt Jemima precipitates his mistrust of women.

Each of Milkman's closest parental figures—Ruth, Pilate, and Macon— performs a version of ancestor worship. Ruth, cut off from any meaningful present or future, lives in the memory of her infatuation with her father. "In a way jealous of death" (64), she perpetuates the ghost of her father and the ghost of time past as symbolized by the watermark on her table.[2] Pilate retains the spiritual values of the past, and her close-to-nature lifestyle imitates her childhood life at Lincoln's Heaven. She treasures the signs of that former life—in her earring, her bag of bones, her rocks—but, alone, she cannot complete her quest for understanding of her self and her past. Macon, still suffering from the trauma of his father's murder, erroneously thinks he has successfully repudiated the past: "He had not said any of this for years. Had not even reminisced much about it recently" (51). He can no longer remember his father's real name (Jake) and thus has lost his past and himself. His servile assimilationism (worse than Helene's and Nel's), his accommodation to white standards, his soul-destroying materialism, and his lack of meaningful human contacts all result from his radical disassociation from his past. Having lost all the values of his upbringing in paradisiacal Lincoln's Heaven, he worships gold instead of his ancestors and has substituted material objects (keys, property, cars, money) for people. Having lost the land, he has become a landlord. His desiccated life is a dialectical reversal; he has become the opposite of what he longed to be. Despite his conscious repudiation of his ghosts, he ironically pursues his father's quest for material success and comfort in a white-dominated society.[3]

The persistent presence of Jake's ghost provides one meaningful link with the family past. Three times readers are told of his reappearances after he was blown up: by Macon (40), by Pilate (141), and in a curious third-person flashback allegedly told by Macon to Milkman (169). Presumably also, Jake's ghost is the "figure of a man standing by his friend" (187) that

Milkman sees when he and Guitar steal Pilate's bag of bones.[4] Jake's shallow burial, which led to the dumping of his bones in the cave, symbolizes that the past itself needs to be rediscovered and reintegrated into the present. Like Jake, the family past, as well as the African-American cultural and historical past, has been blown apart by the dominant white culture. Like the watermelon in *The Bluest Eye*, the break is a bad one, leading to the "disappointment" and "jagged[ness]" (*Bluest* 107) of an unwilled fragmentation. That disintegration, and its memory, like Jake and his bones, haunt the book like a ghost.

The past is figured in *Song of Solomon* not only in terms of the lost family name, the misdirected inheritances, and the reappearances of ghosts, but also in the novel's narrative form. Its dominant feature is the dozens of flashbacks in which almost a third of the text is narrated.[5] Almost all of these flashbacks are either told or remembered by the characters, not simply by the narrator, which suggests that the characters are endeavoring to regain contact with their pasts. In Part I, four of the characters who are trying to influence Milkman—Macon, Pilate, Guitar, and Ruth—remember episodes of their past and, more importantly, relate those episodes to Milkman. For example, Macon recounts his childhood at Lincoln's Heaven (51–54) and Ruth's questionable behavior upon her father's death (70–73), Pilate tells Milkman and Guitar her memories of Lincoln's Heaven (39–43), Guitar recalls his early days as a hunter (85), and Ruth tells her story of Milkman's birth (124–26). Milkman, hearing these past stories, is initially not interested. He rejects his family's past just as he rejects responsibility for his own present and future. But, despite his disinterest, the flashbacks provide him with a fragmented sense of his family's past that unconsciously leads to his desire to recover his lost heritage. The embedded stories about Macon and Pilate's childhood also prefigure Milkman's physical journey to Danville and Shalimar, as his quest becomes the effort to make sense of these fragments of time, place, and differing perspectives. He must learn to read correctly the palimpsest of his cultural, familial, and personal pasts.[6] More broadly, the incorporation and transformation of myths similarly imply the need for a broad "reading" of African-American experience in terms of European and African cultural heritages.

In Part II, the primary source of the flashbacks shifts from the other characters to Milkman as he "d[oes] his best to put it all together" (307). For example, he recalls his childhood (267), his whole life (282), Guitar's aphorisms (285), and his rudeness to his family and Hagar (304). He tries to interpret the past through the words of the Solomon song and through the place names on road signs. His quest to find the lost gold becomes his quest for his family's past and his own undiscovered identity.

It is fitting that he seeks the past in a journey to the South, for in Morrison's fiction the South always represents the past. For most of Morrison's characters—such as Pauline and Cholly Breedlove, Sethe and Paul D, or Joe and Violet Trace—the southern past is available only through memory, but Milkman is able to revisit the sites where his ancestors' past took place and thereby to identify himself with these ancestors.[7] As his knowledge of the past increases through the flashbacks and his own travels, his geographical journey expands, duplicating Pilate's geographical collection of rocks from the places she has visited. The stories Milkman collects are like Pilate's rocks: both are fragments of the characters' journeys, reminders of their own pasts and their cultural pasts. Just as the rocks provide the pleasure of connectedness for Pilate, the stories gradually give Milkman self-knowledge, empathy, a sense of place in the African-American culture, and a sense of belonging in the natural world.

Like the juxtaposition of temporal linearity and circularity in *Sula*, this novel simultaneously moves forward and backward in time. From the moment before Robert Smith's suicide on February 18, 1931 (Morrison's date of birth) to Milkman's leap 33 years later, it moves steadily forward, measuring its chronological movement with the stages in Milkman's life. At the same time, the novel spirals backward through the remembered and related flashbacks of the characters, through Milkman's spatial return to the sites of the past, through the evocation of characters from the past such as Circe and Susan Byrd, and through Milkman's unraveling of the secrets of his family's past. The "linear conception of time" is associated with Macon, whereas "Pilate's vision of time ... is cyclical and expansive" (V. Smith, "*Song*" 280–81). Part of Milkman's task is to fuse these two forms, the first traditionally associated with Euro-American culture and the second with African culture.[8] This double temporal movement creates a circular form, a plurality-in-unity, as the present and past mirror each other in the parallels between Smith's leap and Milkman's, between the singing of Solomon's song at the beginning and at the end, and between Milkman's birth and Pilate's death.[9]

Besides family divisions and the separation from the past, a third form of fragmentation in Milkman's home environment is the acute division between blacks and whites. As in *Sula*, nameless, usually powerful whites surround the black community and treat blacks with cruelty or indifference, for example the nurse who patronizes Guitar (7), the bankers who dominate Macon (20), the drunk Yankee who misnames the Deads (53), and the boss of Guitar's father who dismisses Guitar's mother with forty dollars and Guitar with divinity (61).[10] In *The Bluest Eye* and *Sula* the vise of discrimination remains in the background and relatively peaceful, but here whites murder Jake, Emmett Till, and the four little black girls, and blacks in the Seven Days plan and execute revenge.[11] This underlying principle of violent, racial division and its consequent displacements is symbolized by the image of the corpse of Guitar Bains's father, "sliced in half and boxed backward" (226).

Like the violent divisions in American society, here the black community is also radically divided. As opposed to the relative homogeneity of the black communities in *The Bluest Eye* and *Sula*, the Southside is divided between Macon and Ruth's neighborhood and Pilate's. It is divided politically between the assimilationists, like Macon, and the radical separatists, like the Seven Days.[12] This political division is reinforced by the references to historical events of the 1960s, in particular to the divisions within the civil rights movement between Malcolm X and Martin Luther King, Jr., and between Malcolm X and Elijah Muhammad.[13] The fragmentations within the novel's community thus figure the historic divisions within American culture and within African-American culture. The links between the characters' fragmentations and the fragmented society are suggested by Morrison's allusions to the murder of Emmett Till. This 1955 murder galvanized African Americans, and Milkman most deeply realizes his separation from his community when, ignorant of Till's death, he walks against the crowd (78) and is then chastised by Guitar for his racial apathy (86–89).[14]

The disparity between races is also suggested by the problematic question of "why." In *The Bluest Eye* the grown-up Claudia relinquishes the attempt to explain why things happened: "But since why is difficult to handle, one must take refuge in how" (9). Similarly, in this novel "why" is usually unknowable, which suggests that the causes of the racialized condition underlying the novel cannot be determined. Milkman endures the frustrations of not knowing why other characters behave as they do, for example, why Macon forbids him to visit Pilate's house (50), why Macon hits Ruth (87), or why Guitar wants to kill him (290). But Guitar expresses the general principle: "Listen baby, people do funny things. Specially us. The cards are stacked against us and just trying to stay in the game, stay alive and in the game, makes us do funny things. Things we can't help. Things that make us hurt one another. We don't even know why" (88). This principle applies to all of Morrison's novels: racial oppression leads to displacement and self-destructive behavior whose causes are inexplicable.

Like "why," "not" also articulates the racial disparities in Milkman's urban environment. The Southside community is relegated to denial—on "Not Doctor Street" (3), near "No Mercy Hospital" (4) to which blacks are denied admittance. The pervasive sense of denial of access, hope, rights, and privileges that dominates the black community is expressed in Railroad Tommy's bitter outburst to Milkman about all the things "he ain't going to have" (59).[15] The pernicious effects of this lack, of being the unprivileged members of a divided and hierarchical society, are apparent in the absences that Guitar lives with and that steer his life toward revenge: "Everything I ever loved in my life left me" (311). Hagar also suffers from the absence of things: "a chorus of mamas, grandmamas, aunts, cousins, sisters, neighbors, Sunday school teachers, best girl friends, and what all to give her the strength life demanded of her." The result is that she lives in a state of total absence: "Not wilderness where there was system, or the logic of lions, trees, toads, and birds, but wild wilderness where there was none" (138). Trapped in this nihilism, this dangerous freedom, and unwilling to embrace the wildness like Wild and Golden Grey in *Jazz*, Hagar's only recourse is to try to possess the one thing, Milkman, that she thinks she can possess, even though, as Guitar tells her, "You can't own a human being" (311). Then, upon losing Milkman, Hagar can think only of his absence, of "the mouth Milkman was not kissing, the feet that were not running toward him, the eye that no longer beheld him, the hands that were not touching him" (127).

Collectively, the African-American community can offset the negativity of denial. Not Doctor Street and No Mercy Hospital become "good" in the same sense that "baaad" can indicate its opposite in Black English. According to Roberta Rubenstein, the acceptance of the inverted names indicates the community's resistance to the dominant society (154). Kimberly Benston pushes this point to argue that through the names the Southsiders evade the "monologic violence" (87) of the white society and "protect memory as both continuity and concealment." In other words, the non-names, suggesting the community's subjugation and invisibility, become verbal icons for its internal unity in opposition to white authority. Through these non-texts, the residents signify upon their white oppressors and create meaningful communal identities in opposition to those oppressors.

In two other cases the absence of something becomes the vehicle for positive change.[16] The absence of gold in the cave outside Danville is crucial in shifting Milkman from the moribund materialistic values he acquired from Macon to the spiritual ones modeled by Pilate. Similarly, Pilate's lack of a navel, after causing her anguish and alienation, leads to her self-creation of a viable self (in contrast to Sula who, marked similarly by her birthmark, is less successful in her self-creation). Pilate "began at zero" by symbolically killing her old self by cutting off her hair and then "she tackled the problem of trying to decide how she wanted to live and what was valuable to her" (149). As a result of this self-deconstruction (Mobley, *Folk Roots* 113), she purges herself of fear, develops "compassion for troubled people" (150), "acquire[s] a deep concern for and about human relationships," becomes "a natural healer," stays in close touch with the spirit of her dead father, and becomes Milkman's protector and guide. As Milkman's spiritual guide, his *griot*, she models for Milkman the creation of self that is both within and without the community, she precedes him in her physical journey and her symbolic journey toward love and harmony, and she teaches him the values of a spiritual, Afrocentric, nature-centered, nonlinear perspective as opposed to Macon's material one.[17] Even though she cannot complete her quest until Milkman provides the missing clues, she provides a "template" (Benston 101) for her nephew by fusing disparate forces. As Milkman will pull everything together, Pilate has "deep connectedness" (Guth 581) with people, nature, community, and the past.[18] As Benston puts it, "she asserts ... the will-to-connection against a world insistent upon definition by division and differentiation" (99). She is Morrison's first character with a well-developed talent for fusion.

The fusion implicit in Pilate becomes explicit in Milkman. Although Sula and Nel are both fascinated by their opposite's house, they remain identified with their irreconcilably different houses and lifestyles; there is no middle ground, no character who straddles the two. In *Song of Solomon*, however, Pilate bridges the gap between the two houses when she abets Milkman's conception and birth, and then Milkman becomes a fully mediating character. He spends time at both houses, he develops significant relationships with characters in both houses, he appreciates the values of his father and his aunt, and he brings about the partial reconciliation of the two families.

At age four having "lost all interest in himself" (9), Milkman becomes vulnerable to the uses of others, becomes the subject of a struggle for his soul between five competing characters: Macon, Ruth, Guitar, Pilate, and Hagar.[19] He is bored with his father's assimilationist and material version of black capitalism, he is disgusted with his mother's necromantic fantasies, and he has no patience for Guitar's political obsession with racial injustice. Although Pilate's natural wisdom and openness intrigue him, they provide no direct route for his personal development, and his affair with Pilate's granddaughter becomes another boring "dead"-end. As Ruth reflects, "he became a plain on which ... she and her husband fought" (133). All five characters place claims on him to fulfill their own unfulfilled lives, and Milkman is vulnerable to their reification of him because he lacks the will to examine himself and his life.

The influencing characters offer contrasting ideas of love. Guitar tries to convince Milkman of the Seven Days' philosophy of unquestioning love for all African Americans, but that love leads each cult member into the strictures of revenge against whites and pushes Robert Smith over the edge of sanity and Henry Porter to the edge. Instead of love, Guitar becomes co-opted by his hate into the evil practices of the dominant social system he wishes to escape (V. Smith, *Self-Discovery* 152) and therefore, like Macon, Guitar exemplifies the dialectical reversal. In contrast, the love of Ruth and Hagar is personal rather than political, but their version of love is equally unacceptable to Milkman. Ruth indulges herself in worshipping her father and then converts that reifying love into "a passion" (131) for Milkman that denies his identity: "Her son had never been a person to her." Hagar, beset by her own problems, including Milkman's selfish treatment, allows her love for Milkman to congeal into the desire to possess him. Her love, like Beloved's love for Sethe, becomes an "anaconda love" (137) that would as soon kill Milkman as love him and that has devoured everything else within her: "she had no self left, no fears, no wants, no intelligence." Pilate's successful effect on Milkman's spiritual growth derives from her more empathic love. She loves individuals, in particular each member of her and Macon's families, and she unselfishly loves all people: "I wish I'd a knowed more people. I would of loved 'em all. If I'd a knowed more, I would a loved more" (340). Through that love, she achieves and conveys to Milkman the self-fulfillment that results from harmony with community and cosmos.

As Milkman gradually assimilates these varieties of love, he also synthesizes the other characters' attitudes toward the past. Guitar cannot escape the past, obsessed as he is by his father's death and his bitterness toward it. As a result the earth for him is still the "stinking hole" (227) of the outhouse into which he threw his peppermint stick, and his Seven Days' philosophy is his attempt to redress those perceived wrongs. Macon tries to redress the crimes committed against his father, not by killing whites but by outdoing them materially; consequently, he has lost his own spirit and the capacity for love. Ruth does not want to make up for the past but to preserve it, to retain her undying love for her father and to hold on to Milkman's devotion, exemplified by her prolonged nursing of him. She is therefore comforted by the watermark on her mahogany table because it reminds her of her life with her father: "she regarded it as a mooring, a checkpoint, some stable visual object that assured her that the world was still there" (11). First

Corinthians provides Milkman with a preferable model when she realizes that her past has not allowed her to become a whole adult and when she exercises her new-found courage by freeing herself from the crushing lies of Miss Graham's sentimentality and the mountains of red velvet. Pilate, again, is Milkman's most helpful guide, for she best combines respect for the past and constructive action in the present.

In addition to the themes of love and the past, Morrison uses multiple images of hunting to articulate the heterogeneous influences on Milkman. Guitar fondly remembers hunting as a boy and teaches Milkman never to hunt a doe, but Guitar's lesson is undercut when he becomes the hunter of people, first his white victims and then Milkman. Hagar resorts to tracking Milkman every thirty days, in her comic/tragic pursuit of something to hold herself together. Milkman becomes the hunter when he trails Ruth to the cemetery, but his purpose is valid, to learn Ruth's story as a counter to Macon's. Milkman's quest to Pennsylvania and Virginia is also a hunt, but a hunt in which the initial prey, the gold, becomes transformed into a search for himself and his ancestral origins. At the climax of that search is the literal hunt for the bobcat, in which Milkman becomes the hunted as well as the hunter (Mobley, *Folk* 124), has his epiphany of oneness with the cosmos, and acquires a new identity.

This pattern of differentiating various characters' orientations toward a value such as love or a mode of action such as hunting suggests the limitations of any single character's approach. Until Milkman begins to fuse the contrasting perspectives, each character tends to use love, the past, the hunt, or any other vehicle for his or her selfish purposes, which consistently fragments him or her from other characters and frequently harms everyone involved. Except for Pilate, the other characters remain trapped in their narrow, fixed, monologic approaches, which denies them the openness necessary for continuing growth.

The inadequacies of individual solutions are evident in individual characters' failures to interpret things around them. Macon widely misinterprets Pilate, thinking of her as a snake who bites the man who feeds it (54). Guitar wrongly concludes that Milkman's desire to go to Danville is designed to betray him and then erroneously assumes that the box Milkman helps load onto the train must contain the gold (259 and 299). Even Pilate, despite her sensitivity, misinterprets her father's ghost when he bids her to remember Sing, and she draws the wrong conclusion about the bones she finds in the cave.

For the first two thirds of the novel Milkman also fails to interpret correctly. Puzzled by his parents' stories, he tries to duck the confusing questions they raise. He ignores his sisters as entities to be interpreted: "He had never been able to really distinguish them (or their roles) from his mother" (68). He is left out of the signifying banter at the barbershop, a result of his isolation from his community and culture. His alienation implies his doubled fragmentation—cut off from the community and internally divided between loyalties to his competing mentors. Once on his quest, he still has difficulties with interpretations, for example wrongly concluding that Pilate took the gold from the cave near Danville (260) and not fully grasping Guitar's threatening message (266) and Guitar's new role as his enemy. For a while, he ignores the possibility that natural and manmade objects are signifiers: he suffers the "city man's boredom with nature's repetition" (228), and he is bored by the highway signs (228) and the "no name hamlet[s]" (262) he encounters.

No one version of love, of the past, of hunting, or of interpretation is adequate, but instead their plurality and their complex and ambiguous combinations are required. This novel is overtly fugal: it presents multiple lines, multiple reactions, and multiple versions of a topic or an entity, demonstrating that no single thread is adequate. It presents "a tough-minded and dynamic interplay of ideas which never come to rest in any simple resolution" but instead probe "the blues-like paradoxes and complexities of modern experience" (Butler 63). In a similar fashion, the novel relies not on just one mythic tradition but fuses elements of at least three: African, classical European, and Christian. As Jane Campbell notes, proper names in the novel "span centuries and hemispheres" (146), thus integrating multiple cultures and traditions. Even the location and identity of Milkman's hometown is a vague mixture (Butler 53–64; Scruggs, "Nature" 319; Imbrie 6), associated with Lake Superior, the Great Lakes in general, and yet with rivers. And the name of Milkman's ancestors' town in Virginia, a town not on any map (Heinze 140), slides among several names: Shalimar, Solomon, Shalleemone, and Charlemagne. By remaining vague and essentially multiple, both towns thus become ritualized places where myth can occur.[20]

Morrison embeds the need for pluralism by insisting on retelling the characters' stories, not only those of the major characters but also of such minor characters as Circe and Reverend Cooper and his friends. Although the novel is unified by a conventional third-person narrator, the characters retell or recall much of the novel's past. As in *The Bluest Eye*, many stories and many viewpoints are needed because no single one is sufficient.[21] The stories gradually create a plurality-within-unity, "a crazy quilt with a sense of pattern" (Fabre 111).

Milkman's role in this structure is to learn his own story, thereby finding his identity in his relation to his past and his community (V. Smith, *Self-Discovery* 136) and thereby becoming the unifying agent. As Rubenstein contends, he reconciles his two last names (154), and simultaneously he reconciles his two first names. Similarly, Linda Krumholz shows that Milkman's quest constitutes a reinterpretation of "milkman" and "dead," the former name suggesting his connections with nurturance, motherhood, and deliverance, and the latter his ties with his ancestors and his cultural heritage ("Dead" 557–58). He synthesizes the competing lives of his relatives and friends, and he unites the male and materialistic perspective of his father with the female and spiritual one of his aunt. "Milkman's story thus articulates a history of separations and re-connections" (Rubenstein 155) in which the progression moves from the fragmentations to the fusions.

At first, Milkman's reaction to his identity-less and reified situation is marked by confusion.[22] He not only loses interest in himself, but his imagination is "bereft" (9), and he is out of joint with himself and reality. He sits in the family car "riding backward" and feeling "uneasy" (31). As on those tortured family drives, he is "flying blind" rather than with purpose and insight. He is alienated from other children ("He hailed no one and no one hailed him" [32]), is dropped by his mother from the nursing chair, and is routinely scolded by his father. He develops a psychosomatic "short" leg, which results from his disorientation and in turn makes him feel even more out of plumb with the world. For Royster, Milkman is an "unconscious scapegoat," "a victim of his burdensome past, blind to his future, and unable to assert himself in his here and now" ("Milkman's" 431). His nickname, at first a mystery and then a source of shame, creates an odd sense of doubleness: is he Macon or Milkman? This disquieting doubleness is evident in his contemplation of the silver-backed brushes his mother gives him with the monogram *M.D.* and its pun not only on Macon/Milkman but on his initials and on "Doctor of Medicine," with its allusion to Dr. Foster. Milkman's misalignment with the world around him is perhaps best represented by the Poe-like scene in which he walks in the opposite direction from everyone (78), which leads him to wonder "if there was anyone in the world who liked him" (79).[23] Despite the difficulties of Milkman's backward and divided position, this early sense of double-consciousness gives him the perspective of the outsider/insider that eventually aligns him with other African Americans and that subsequently propels him on his quest.[24]

As Milkman learns about his immediate family history, this disorientation phase is followed by a period of withdrawal and denial. Unable and unwilling to assimilate the new information about his parents and his infancy, he becomes passively suicidal: he is bored with everything (90), feels that his life is "pointless, aimless" (107), and desires "above all ... to escape what he knew," (120) even if that means death at Hagar's hands.

At the same time, however, Milkman begins to resent the conflicting claims on him. Angered by what Macon tells him about Ruth, he "felt put upon; felt as though some burden had been given to him and that he didn't deserve it" (120). After he hears Ruth's side of the story, the feeling goes deeper: "he felt used. Somehow everybody was using him for something or as something. Working out some scheme of their own on him, making him the subject of their dreams of wealth, or love, or martyrdom" (165–66). In his view at this stage, his father, his mother, Guitar, and Hagar are lined up against him, making their "claims" against him.

Milkman's sense of being reified is accurate, but it is also ironic, because throughout Part I Milkman in turn reifies others. Spoiled by his parents and by his attractiveness to women, he blithely assumes the privileges of being cared for without accepting any responsibilities. As Lena accuses him, his misdirected urinations are indicative. Just as he pees on Lena (215), on the newly planted tree (214), and in kitchen sinks (213), he has figuratively "found all kinds of ways to pee on people" (215).[25] His depersonalization of others is evident in the "few and easily chosen" (90) Christmas gifts he buys for people and in his inability to even think of helping his mother in his dream about her and the threatening flowers (105–6). The person he most abuses is Hagar, in his cursory "dear John" letter (126), in his wish for her death (129–30), and in his verbal abuse (130).

Throughout Part I, while Milkman is being used by others and is using them, he nevertheless is being prepared for his quest in Part II. As in the preparation stage of the monomyth of the hero's quest as delineated by Joseph Campbell and Otto Rank, he becomes increasingly uncomfortable with his situation and his unformed identity. He learns from Pilate the mystery of being, symbolized by the egg, and he smells the odor of ginger with its hint of Africa. As he learns more, he is increasingly disquieted and feels more strongly the necessity of breaking away. He receives guidance, direct and indirect, from everyone around him: parents, sisters, community members (such as Freddie and the barbershop group), his spiritual guide (Pilate), and his friend/rival (Guitar). Toward the end of all this preparation, when Guitar yells at him to "live it! Live the motherfuckin life! Live it" (184), Milkman has a preliminary epiphany that anticipates the novel's ending: "All the tentativeness, doubt, and inauthenticity that plagued him slithered away without a trace, a sound" and "he felt a self inside himself emerge, a clean-lined definite self."

To document Milkman's growth, Morrison uses the issue of his fears.

At first, like the rest of the family, he is kept "awkward with fear" (10) by
Macon. Then he hears how Macon assuaged Pilate's fears after Jake's death,
and he learns a valuable lesson from Pilate: "What difference do it make if
the thing you scared of is real or not?" (40–41). When Hagar is trying futilely
to kill him, Milkman progresses from feeling the fear (113) to controlling it
(129), and his fear is replaced by the first stirrings of willpower: "But the fear
was gone. He lay there as still as the morning light, and sucked the world's
energy up into his own will." At this point, because of his own lack of
direction, he can only will negatively—for Hagar to die—but this indication
of will and the suggestion of a connection to cosmic energy prefigure his
later development. Next, Milkman expresses fear for Guitar, perhaps the first
time he feels anything akin to empathy: "Milkman rubbed the ankle of his
short leg. 'I'm scared for you, man' " (162). Then, as he thinks about Guitar's
self-imposed risks in joining the Seven Days, Milkman realizes that he
admires the lack of fear in the three most influential people in his life: "His
father, Pilate, Guitar. He gravitated toward each one, envious of their
fearlessness now" (178). This experience and his envy of fearlessness lay the
foundation for Milkman's transcendence of fear in Part II.

Milkman's quest in Part II enables him to fuse the competing
influences, heterogeneous forces, and complex pluralisms in his
environment, and from them to find meaning in terms of his identity, his
extended family, his community, and his culture. Not only is his development
"a movement from a linear to a cyclical perspective on existence" (V. Smith,
Self-Discovery 136), but it entails the integration of the two perspectives. Like
Pilate and unlike the other characters, Milkman transcends individualism
and finds himself in a grand harmony with all people and all things.[26]

Milkman's quest enables him to recapture his ancestral and cultural
past by embodying the essences of his family ghosts. He reaches the womb
of his family (the cave) by embracing the terrifying but guiding Circe, who
models Milkman's quest by fusing Western and African-American cultural
traditions, life and death, and present and past. He becomes Jake as he
rediscovers the lost paradise of Lincoln's Heaven in Shalimar. He then
becomes Solomon as he achieves the spiritual equivalent of flying, first in his
"dreamy sleep all about flying" (302) and then in his final leap (341).

Milkman also accomplishes this synthesis by partially reconciling the
claims of the characters who are battling for his soul. His trip to the South
begins as a response to his father's greed but becomes a repetition and
extension of Pilate's previous journeys in search of community and self. His
discovery of his origins, especially his solving of the mystery of Jake's bones,
not only corrects Pilate's assumptions and completes her quest but also

symbolically responds to his mother's preoccupation with the ghost of her father. Just as Milkman earlier bridges the gap between Pilate's and Macon's houses, so his quest unites the strengths of Pilate, Macon, and Ruth. His quest for his origins and therefore for his self answers Guitar's longing for love and racial identity as well as Hagar's need for attachment and recognition. In rejecting a present life that had proved intolerable and moribund, Milkman extends the preliminary questing gestures of not only these characters but also of Pecola, Cholly, Sula, Nel, and Ajax.

Milkman's success is most clearly conveyed through his acquiring the power to interpret correctly, to learn to read the layered meanings of texts. His initial inattention to highway signs is transformed into his fascination with them: "He read the road signs with interest now, wondering what lay beneath the names" (333). Guth identifies his "reclamation of the past" as a process of learning a new way of reading and interpreting (579), and Mobley argues that the text creates a "mosaic of narrative" in which "the reader's task is not unlike that of Milkman Dead, who must find the meaning in his complicated life story" (*Folk* 97). In a similar vein, Krumholz develops the intriguing parallels between Milkman's initiation and the "reader's ritual of initiation," which requires the reader, like Milkman, to develop new strategies and sensitivities of interpretation ("Dead" 567–69). As Milkman puts his puzzle together, the reader, like Morrison, must fuse the various pieces.

The primary "text" that Milkman must reinterpret is the actual song about Solomon. Solving the riddle of the song requires interpreting the names of his ancestors and leads to his understanding of his own name and his place in history and the community. The song comes to Milkman, and the reader, as fragments—a blues song, a children's ring game, words and names that suggest but do not clearly name Milkman's ancestors. Milkman's task is to fuse the fragments of the song as well as of the memories of Susan Byrd and others. As Barthold points out (183), the song's allusion to the biblical Song of Solomon conveys the sense of further merger, the marriage of holy bride and bridegroom.[27] The song becomes "the sacred text: a proclamation available to all, and the repository of secrets" (Fabre 113). Like Morrison's novels, the song is appropriately multiple, open-ended, and dialogic: it is "a site of preliterate re-weavings, scène, a fabric of languages alluding to a crazy-quilt of cultures, regions, religions, and affiliations" (Benston 104). In deciphering this text and his own genealogy, Milkman "reconstructs a dialectic of historical transcendence" (Willis 95), finding his own voice in the power of the sung word, literally uniting his maternal ancestor (Sing Byrd) with the song, thereby fusing native American and African-American cultures, and through this complex process synthesizing all the operative oppositions. As Mobley puts it, "As a performed ritual, the song signals a cathartic epiphany for Milkman" (*Folk* 127). Mobley also cites the song's effectiveness not only for Milkman but "as a kind of cultural glue" for the community and "as an illustration of Morrison's folk aesthetic and mythic impulse" for the reader. Since Morrison's maternal grandfather's name was John Solomon, the song is literally the song of Morrison. It is also the song about Solomon, the song that leads Pilate, Milkman, Macon, Ruth, First Corinthians, and Lena to Solomon and thus to their rightful name and place in history.

Milkman's adventure toward harmony reaches its climax when he is alone in the dark woods during the bobcat hunt.[28] Like Milkman's decoding of the song, his earlier boredom with and antagonism toward nature is reversed when he learns in this scene to hear and understand the unspoken language of the natural world: "He tried to listen with his fingertips, to hear what, if anything, the earth had to say, and it told him quickly that someone was standing behind him" (282). This power of interpretation not only saves Milkman's life but marks his integration with the underlying forces of life, establishes the solidity of his identity, and provides him with visionary wisdom. At this moment, he has put it all together, and thereafter he interprets everything with perfect accuracy: "he heard right up close the wild, wonderful sound of three baying dogs who he knew had treed a bobcat" (282) and "his sense of direction was accurate." Simultaneously, he becomes connected with the earth, no longer imagining a tilted, limping relationship: "he found himself exhilarated by simply walking the earth. Walking it like he belonged on it" (284). As a result, everything works for Milkman: he is accepted by the hunters; no longer weighted down with excessive jewelry, the peacock soars (286); and he finds loving companionship with Sweet. Having placed himself in harmony with community and cosmos, Milkman becomes the model human being—he shares the chores with Sweet, he solves the remaining puzzles of the riddle, he feels "connected" (296), he confronts Guitar in "the complete absence of fear" (298), and he revises his attitudes toward his family and Hagar, realizing his previous self-centeredness and lack of empathy. He is transformed, in short, into a hero ready for apotheosis.

Milkman's act of unifying so many disparate elements—himself, the competing claims upon him, self and community, North and South, urban and rural, and present and past—is all the more remarkable because his life and environment are fraught with counterexamples. Rather than achieving spiritual life, many characters suffer spiritual death-in-life: Ruth, Macon,

Lena, First Corinthians (for most of the novel), and all the men in Danville, who "as boys ... began to die and were dying still" (238). Many major characters die tragically, as well as innumerable minor ones (starting with Robert Smith) and many historical figures who are mentioned (John F. Kennedy, Martin Luther King, Jr., Malcolm X, Emmett Till, the four Sunday school girls).[29] In this world where "everybody wants a black man's life" (335), Milkman has cause to feel threatened and displaced: "Who were all these people roaming the world trying to kill him?" (273).

Milkman's ability to fuse everything is also remarkable because in his world people are continually trying to cut each other apart. Several deaths occur by cutting, as when Macon kills the white man in the cave with a knife, when Guitar's father is split in half by a saw, and when a nameless private in Georgia is killed "after his balls were cut off" (156). More murders by cutting are attempted or threatened: Pilate holds a knife to Reba's abuser, Hagar stalks Milkman with a butcher knife, Pilate threatens Macon in the cave with a knife, Milkman is cut with a knife in Solomon's store and in turn cuts Saul with a broken bottle, and Guitar tries to slit Milkman's throat with a wire. Metaphorically, cutting is attractive to Milkman: he is exhilarated to think of Guitar in "proximity to knife-cold terror" (178) and living "on the cutting edge." But it is also repellent: he feels that Guitar "had ripped open and was spilling blood and foolishness instead of conversation" (166). Much like the splitting in *The Bluest Eye*, the motif of cutting conveys the fragility of African-American lives and the difficulties of self-integration.

The cutting motif culminates in the bobcat-skinning scene (284–86), which extends Milkman's epiphany in the woods into his ritual rebirth. In contrast to Milkman's alienation from the black men in the barbershop, here he is initiated into the black male community. Collectively, they skin the cat, each man taking his turn with equal adeptness, as Milkman actively participates as "reader" and initiate. Since the skinning and evisceration of the bobcat eerily hint at "the physical horrors of lynching, castration, and mutilation suffered by black men (Krumholz, "Dead" 563), Milkman is thereby inducted into his racial identity and past. He is then offered the heart, symbolizing his acquisition of a new heart in communion with the natural world of the bobcat, and implying his rebirth as a new man and his penetration to the heart of himself, his ancestry, his community, and his universe. Significantly, in taking the heart he suspends thinking and acts on the intuition he has learned to trust in the woods: "Quickly, before any thought could paralyze him, Milkman plunged both hands into the rib cage" (285–86).

The cat-skinning scene is narrated by alternating the men's physical actions with Milkman's memories of Guitar's advice. This narrative ingenuity not only heightens the dramatic impact of the scene but also works as call and response, integrating Milkman and the men as well as Milkman and Guitar and pulling into ambiguous juxtaposition competing ideas about life and death and violence and love.[30] The "counterpointed text" (Lee, "*Song*" 70) of the passage and the unresolved oppositions it raises enact the comprehensive, fluid, both/and synthesis that Milkman has attained. His mind now operates dialogically: he is absorbed in the skinning while simultaneously recapitulating his relationship with Guitar. He has achieved double-consciousness and by implication multi-consciousness. Having entered the *différance*, he is wise enough to allow the double voices to remain open, not to insist on final answers to Guitar's and now his own pressing questions: *"Can't I love what I criticize?"* and *"What else? What else? What else?"* There are no further answers to such questions because there is nothing else but love, as Pilate's dying words and Milkman's fusion intimate.

One way of placing in perspective Milkman's quest, as well as Guitar's, is to turn to sociology. William E. Cross, Jr., proposes a model of "Negro-to-Black identity transformation" (158), defined as "nigrescence, the process of becoming Black" (157). Primarily from the late 1960s to the late 1970s, during the time that Morrison wrote *Song of Solomon*, many African Americans modified their "personal identity" and their "reference group orientation" from "Negro" to "Black" (Cross 39). Cross identifies five stages of this transformation: pre-encounter, encounter, immersion-emersion, internalization, and internalization-commitment (190–223). In the pre-encounter stage, Milkman's sense of his race is low and he shares Macon's antipathy for other blacks. Milkman's encounter, as for many blacks a series of episodes (Cross 200), is spread over his truth-revealing conversations with Macon, Ruth, and Guitar and his initiatory experiences in Danville and Shalimar. In Michigan he only experiences these encounters but does not personalize them, and the process leads him to "confusion, alarm, anomie, [and] depression" (Cross 201). In contrast, Guitar's encounter stage occurs all at once at the death of his father and is accompanied by his enduring anger toward whites.

The immersion stage, the emotional peak of the transformation, features the substitution of a new identity for the old one (Cross 202). Guitar reaches this stage well before Milkman when he becomes active in the Seven Days. In this "in-between" and emotionally exhilarated state (Cross 202), Guitar is energized by rage and racial pride. He adopts a morally dichotomized view of race and takes the path of militant confrontation (Cross 203–4). In his need to prove his own blackness, he turns inward toward black culture as he seeks the social support of the countercultural group, the Seven Days. Perhaps because of the traumatic origins of Guitar's encounter stage, he cannot progress beyond this "fascist" (Cross 205) position and remains fixed in pain, anger, exasperation, and racial hatred (Cross 208). Like Macon, whose father also died violently when he was young, and like most of the other characters in Morrison's first three novels, Guitar becomes static (Butler 68–69) and rigid (V. Smith, *Self-Discovery* 152), unable to continue the process of fusion and fragmentation.

Milkman's immersion takes the other direction identified by Cross, that of altruism, oneness with his people, and religious feeling (Cross 207). As the object of his quest changes from the materialistic to the spiritual, he undergoes repeated encounter experiences that finally lead him to the immersion stage. Specifically, he immerses himself in the quest for his ancestors, in finding his familial as well as his cultural roots, and in integrating himself with natural forces.

Unlike Guitar's fixation in the immersion stage, Milkman progresses into emersion and internalization. His return to Michigan marks his leveling off from the emotional peak of immersion and his regaining of emotional and intellectual control as he develops a more substantive and textured new self, all of which characterize emersion (Cross 207). Milkman also internalizes his new-found identity, as indicated by such markers as his "resolution of dissonance" (Cross 210); his pride, self-acceptance, and confidence; his inner peace; and his more complex relationships with others (Cross 211).

Despite the success of Milkman's nigrescence, his transformation remains truncated. Left suspended, his flight not completed, he is unable to use his new-found identity and integration to much effect. He does not proceed to Cross's fifth stage, internalization-commitment, in which one translates one's personal sense of blackness into a plan of action or a general sense of commitment (220). Moreover, his flight, like Solomon's before him, is tainted with ambiguity: are they flights from or to? Solomon left behind Ryna and twenty-one children, and Milkman leaves behind a dead Hagar and a dead Pilate. On the other hand, unlike Robert Smith, who tried to fly *away*, he flies *toward* Guitar (Davis 336), toward a mystical union with his double, who in turn seems to recognize the transcendence of the moment and to embrace his brother, his "main man" (341).

Milkman's transformation and successful hero's quest are miraculous. As he moves from his Michigan hometown to Pennsylvania and Virginia, the novel shifts from realism to myth and magic. Milkman's adventure, associated with mythic parallels, can happen only in myth. His quest works for him, as he works through his fears, creates a new identity, rediscovers his name, integrates with his community and his culture, and completes Pilate's earlier quest.

Milkman's chronicle has parallels with American culture. America has been nearly driven asunder by competing individual agendas, it endured its "knife fight" in the Civil War, and in the 1960s and 1970s it passed through another test of its unity. Despite its motto (*e pluribus unum*), it has always held plurality and unity in a precarious balance. Similarly, *Song of Solomon* details the perils of unquestioned unity (as in Macon's and Guitar's philosophies) and the necessary but arduous process of attaining a viable pluralism (as in Pilate's and Milkman's quests). Like Milkman, American culture has ghosts it tries to mourn and to recognize, riddles it tries to decipher, and a past it tries to rediscover, acknowledge, and appropriate. Like Milkman, it is preoccupied with examining itself to find itself and with learning to love so as to conquer fear. As this novel holds together a decentered subject, a unity inclusive of oppositions, fragments, and tensions, so America tries to recognize and reconcile its disparate voices. In such quests, there can be no final "answer," since final answers mean the closure of death; therefore Milkman lives *and* dies, flies *and* falls, embraces *and* kills Guitar. Similarly, as individuals and as a culture—like Claudia, Nel, and Milkman—Americans continue reading the texts in the necessarily endless process of self-discovery.

Milkman's suspension in mid-transformation underscores the power of his experience, suggesting that it cannot be or need not be brought back into the realm of ordinary life. Such transcendence provides the book much of its power, but it also leaves unexplored the issue of translating the miracle into reality. How can Milkman's mythical experience be approximated by ordinary mortals in ordinary conditions? In *Tar Baby* Morrison makes a second attempt to combine mythical experience with realistic conditions, and in *Beloved* and *Jazz* she examines the difficulties and the possibilities of replicating Milkman's idiosyncratic solution without the aid of mythical power.

NOTES

1. Much of the criticism on *Song of Solomon* has addressed how it explores the past by paralleling and modifying several mythic patterns. Most frequently cited is the hero's quest, or monomyth, as developed by Otto Rank and Joseph Campbell: see Michael Awkward ("'Unruly'" 491–94), Kimberly Benston, Gerry Brenner, Peter Bruck, Jane Campbell, Cynthia Davis, Genevieve Fabre, Leslie Harris (70–74), and Dorothy Lee ("*Song*"). Besides the parallels with classical Western mythology, critics have noticed the links with Christian traditions, obviously in the title, and in such characters' names as Pilate, Ruth, First Corinthians, and Lena (see especially Lee, "*Song*" 66–67). In addition,

analogues have been found in Gullah folklore (Blake), African-American folktales (Brenner), African cultural forms (Skerritt; O'Shaughnessy), and African epics (Krumholz, "Dead" 563–66).

2. I agree with Barbara Christian, for whom the watermark connects Ruth's past and present (*Black Feminist* 61), and with Charles Scruggs, for whom it symbolizes her buried life ("Nature" 325). For Lee, the watermark stands for Ruth's blemished life ("*Song*" 66), for Wilfred Samuels and Clenora Hudson-Weems it suggests her flawed existence (56), and for Susan Willis it represents Macon's rejection of Ruth (90).

3. Jane Campbell, arguing for the importance of ancestor worship in Milkman's quest to regain his lost African heritage, notes that Ruth and Pilate "maintain posthumous relationships with their fathers" (145). Similarly, Barbara Hill Rigney points out that characters in *Song of Solomon* resurrect their fathers and seek meaning in the legends of the past (*Voices* 65).

4. Without specifically identifying this figure as Jake, Terry Otten suggests that he reveals Milkman's contact with the spiritual power of the past (*Crime* 54).

5. Valerie Smith also notes the prevalence of flashbacks and discusses the importance of the characters' storytelling (*Self-Discovery* 135–50).

6. Deborah Guth focuses on Milkman's symbolic process of reading, a process that for her determines the novel's structure: "The plot of this novel of restoration is thus the transformative act of reading itself" (580).

7. Milkman thereby extends Nel's brief excursion to the South, in which she is entranced by her grandmother but is prevented from absorbing a lasting influence from her and the lost past she represents.

8. See Bonnie Barthold for a thorough discussion of these cultural distinctions.

9. Morrison has said that this novel, unlike her first two, is not circular: "*Song of Solomon* is different. I was trying to push this novel outward; its movement is neither circular nor spiral. The image in my mind for it is that of a train picking up speed" (Tate 124).

10. This payoff echoes the hollow promise of "$40 and a mule," which was made to African Americans after the Civil War.

11. As Melissa Walker points out, this novel takes place during the most violent years of the civil rights era, almost exactly those years that are omitted from *Sula* (140–41).

12. For discussions of the political implications of the novel, see Barthold (181–83), Ralph Story (149–58), Melissa Walker (129–46), and Willis (316).

13. Melissa Walker argues for the parallelism between Guitar and Malcolm X on the one hand and Milkman and King on the other, even going so far as to suggest that King's initials, MLK, are an abbreviation of "Milkman" (142–43).

14. Morrison's fascination with the Till case is also evident in her play, *Dreaming Emmett*.

15. Tommy's speech is reminiscent of Sula's list of the transformation of racial attitudes that will take place before she is loved: "when Lindbergh sleeps with Bessie Smith..." (*Sula* 145–46).

16. Rigney asserts that characters in this novel, such as Milkman and Pilate, are often defined by what they are not (*Voices* 24–25).

17. See Samuels and Hudson-Weems for a discussion of Pilate as self-creator (61–63) and trickster and *griot* (77), and see Valerie Smith for Pilate's contrasts with Macon and her circular sense of time ("*Song*" 279–81).

18. As Gay Wilentz claims, Pilate is the culture bearer, in communion with her father and therefore with her ancestral heritage (88). Marilyn Sanders Mobley similarly finds that Pilate is an effective guide because she mediates between the present and the past, this world and the next (*Folk* 114).

19. Several commentators—Otten (*Crime* 46), Philip Royster ("Milkman's" 419), and Rigney (*Voices* 33)—have described the novel as a *bildungsroman*. The tendency is to see Milkman between varying pairs of characters rather than as the object of a wider battle. Barthold (179), Susan Blake (78), and Valerie Smith (*"Song"* 280–81) place him between Pilate and Macon, whereas Ann Imbrie (482) says that he stands between Guitar's political stance and Pilate's humanist one, and Otten (*Crime* 50) positions him between the two dialectical poles of Guitar and Macon. Royster more broadly sees Milkman trying to resolve the opposing world views of Macon, Pilate, and Guitar ("Milkman's" 427). Another possible descriptor for the novel is *prufungsroman*, a novel of examination and trial.

20. Imbrie points out that Milkman's hometown is "primeval" (6), and Denise Heinze sees Shalimar as "a ritual ground" (140).

21. See Davis (336–37), Fabre (108), and Scruggs ("Nature" 316) for similar positions on this point.

22. In contrast to my view, Leslie Harris sees Milkman's childhood as a mythic time, followed by his alienation at around age thirty and then his quest (70).

23. This alienating image echoes James Baldwin's similar experience of moving opposite a crowd (*Notes* 95).

24. Benston even argues that Milkman's preoccupation with things behind him prepares him for appreciating Pilate's apprehension of what lies behind the apparent (100n).

25. Joyce Wegs associates Milkman's inappropriate urination with his "negative dominion" of others, that is, with "his self-concern, his indifference to others, and his childishness" (218). Milkman's errant urination also echoes Henry Porter's pissing down on people in his anger and alienation.

26. For similar formulations, see Awkward ("Unruly" 491) and Valerie Smith (*"Song"* 281–83).

27. Jane Campbell also comments on the implications of merging in the song (146).

28. Krumholz analyzes the significance of darkness as a figure for the liminal state in which Milkman "is initiated into his own blackness" as a new way of seeing and reading ("Dead" 560–62).

29. Fabre sees the prevalence of death as a metaphor for the Dead family and for the condition of African Americans (111).

30. I am indebted here to Guth (583) and Krumholz ("Dead" 562–63).

J. BROOKS BOUSON

"Speaking the Unspeakable":
Shame, Trauma, and Morrison's Fiction

Ann duCille, in her analysis of what she calls "the occult of true black womanhood," expresses concern about the "critical stampede" that has been attracted to black women. "Today there is so much interest in black women that I have begun to think of myself as a kind of sacred text. Not me personally, of course, but me as black woman, the other. Within the modern academy, racial and gender alterity has become a hot commodity that has claimed black women as its principal signifier" (83, 81). "[P]olitically correct, intellectually popular, and commercially precious," the black woman writer is constructed as the exotic, idealized Other, according to duCille (84). Toni Morrison, who published her first novel in 1970 and was awarded the Nobel Prize in Literature a scant twenty-three years later in 1993, has attracted the kind of critical stampede duCille describes. If Morrison was sometimes chastised by early reviewers for not transcending the "limiting classification 'black woman writer,'" among contemporary commentators "it has become almost unimaginable or unspeakable to mention the struggles that marked" Morrison's early career as a novelist (Peterson 462, 461). Now something of a sacred text herself, Morrison has "entered superstardom," becoming known as "*the* American and African American (woman) writer to reckon with" (Peterson 464). And just as Morrison's seven novels—*The Bluest Eye, Sula, Song of Solomon, Tar Baby, Beloved, Jazz,* and *Paradise*—have attracted

From *Quiet As It's Kept: Shame, Trauma, and Race in the Novels of Toni Morrison.* © 2000 by State University of New York.

intense critical scrutiny, so Morrison, herself, has been subjected to the scrutinizing gaze of her many interviewers.

"I see them select or make up details to add to the fixed idea of me they came in the door with—the thing or person they want me to be," Morrison has remarked of the people who have interviewed her over the years (Naylor 215). Portrayed variously by her interviewers, Morrison has been constructed as a romanticized exotic—if not mythic—black artist figure. She has been described as having a magnetic personality and a rich, compelling voice; as a moody and prickly person; and as a warm and amusing individual. One interviewer, who describes Morrison as a "larger than life" woman who has a "powerful way" of fixing people in her gaze and transfixing them with her voice, comments that Morrison "does not so much give an interview as perform one, in a silken voice that can purr like a saxophone or erupt like brass" (Fussell 280). "Morrison's voice recalls the rich sound of our best preachers," writes another. "She is, by turns, warm or wry as she reflects on the wonder of it all.... She is sister, teacher, aunt. She speaks with wisdom" (Washington 234). Another interviewer describes how in her conversation Morrison can rapidly "switch from raging about violence in the United States to joyfully skewering the hosts of the trash TV talk shows through which she confesses to channel-surfing late in the afternoon, assuming her work is done" (Schappell 86). Yet another interviewer remarks that Morrison is an enjoyable luncheon companion—"a woman of subversive jokes, gossip and surprising bits of self-revelation (the laureate unwinds to Court TV and soap operas)" (Dreifus 73).

If Morrison often plays to—or skillfully plays—her interviewers, she is, as her descriptions of her writing reveal, a driven woman, a woman who lives intensely within the private world of her writer's imagination and often finds her characters better company than the people who surround her. Writing to her is a "compulsion"; it is like "talking deep" within herself; it is an "extraordinary way of thinking and feeling" (Stepto 24, Tate 169, Watkins 45). An author who writes under a kind of necessity and who has insisted from the beginning of her writing career that art is political (*Black Creation* 3–4), Morrison has viewed part of her cultural and literary task as a writer to bear witness to the plight of black Americans. "[Q]uiet as it's kept much of our business, our existence here, has been grotesque. It really has," she has commented (Jones and Vinson 181). "My people are being devoured" (LeClair 121). One of her central concerns is "how to survive *whole* in a world where we are all of us, in some measure, *victims* of *something*" and "in no position to do a thing about it" (Bakerman 40). Indeed, she deliberately puts her characters "in situations of great duress and pain," and even in "grotesque" situations, in order to "know who they are." Through her "push towards the abyss," as Morrison remarks, she can discover why some people survive and some do not (Jones and Vinson 180–81). Writing provides Morrison with a "safe" place in which she can "think the unthinkable" (Bakerman 39) as she confronts the effects of shame and trauma on the lives of African Americans.

Despite Morrison's unrelenting and unflinching presentation of painful and shameful race matters in her novels, commentators have repeatedly focused on what some have called the magic realism of her novels, or they have placed her fiction in the context of a black feminist aesthetic or black oral tradition, or they have uncovered the black folk or communal values embodied in her work. Just as race matters, according to Morrison, remain unspeakable in American culture—and this despite the unending talk and academic theorizing about race—so race matters remain largely unspoken in the critical conversation that surrounds Morrison's works. Even those critics who have focused their attention on the social-psychological and historical-political concerns voiced in Morrison's fiction have tended to minimize—or even ignore—the sensitive, and at times painful, race matters that pervade and drive Morrison's novelistic narratives.

Insistently, Morrison focuses on inter- and intraracial violence in her fiction, even at the potential cost of alienating, or even unsettling or hurting, some of her readers. But because Morrison's novels are carefully designed and make self-conscious use of folklore and myths, critics have tended to avoid or downplay the violent, even perverse, subject matter of Morrison's novels. Dramatizing the physical and psychological abuse visited on African Americans in white America, Morrison shows that, as some trauma theorists have argued, trauma can result not only from a "single assault" or "discrete event," but also from a "constellation of life's experiences," a "prolonged exposure to danger," or a "continuing pattern of abuse" (Erikson 457). Morrison focuses not only on the collective memories of the trauma of slavery in works like *Beloved*, but also on the horrors of the postbellum years and of racist and urban violence in works like *Song of Solomon* and *Jazz*. She is also intent on portraying the trauma of defective or abusive parenting or relationships and also the black-on-black violence that exists within the African-American community. In Cholly's rape of his daughter, Pecola, in *The Bluest Eye*; in Eva Peace's setting fire to her son, Plum, in *Sula*; in Sethe's slitting her infant daughter's throat in *Beloved*; in Guitar's attempted murder of his friend, Milkman Dead, in *Song of Solomon*; in Joe Trace's hunting down and shooting his young lover, Dorcas, in *Jazz*; and in the Ruby men's massacre of the Convent women in *Paradise*, Morrison dramatizes what one commentator has aptly described as the "oppressor in the next room, or in the same bed, or no farther away than across the street" (D. Johnson 6). Morrison represents the speechless terror of trauma in recurring scenes of dissociated violence—vivid and highly visual scenes in which her characters experience violence from a detached perspective. And she also conveys the haunting and driven quality of traumatic and humiliated memory as she depicts the "rememories"—that is, spontaneous recurrences of the past—that plague her characters. Presenting jarring depictions of child and spousal abuse, incest and infanticide, self-mutilation and self-immolation, suicide and murder, Morrison's novels serve an important cultural function as they reflect and reflect on the incomprehensible violence that pervades the lives of many African Americans in our "catastrophic age," an age in which, it has been argued, trauma may "provide the very link between cultures" (Caruth 11).

Describing herself as living in "a present that wishes both to exploit and deny the pervasiveness of racism" and in a society in which African Americans have had to "bear the brunt of everybody else's contempt" ("Introduction" xiv, Angelo 256), Morrison also focuses attention on the ubiquity and complexity of shame in the African-American experience. Repeatedly, if not obsessively, Morrison stages scenes of shame in her fiction: scenes in which her characters, when they are looked at or treated with contempt by the shaming other, experience the inarticulateness and emotional paralysis of intense shame. Morrison dramatizes the painful sense of exposure that accompanies the single shame event and also the devastating effect of chronic shame on her characters' sense of individual and social identity, describing their self-loathing and self-contempt, their feelings that they are, in some essential way, inferior, flawed, and/or dirty. In *Beloved*, for example, Morrison depicts how Sethe is "dirtied" by slavery and schoolteacher's pseudoscientific racism; in *The Bluest Eye*, how Pecola's parentally transmitted shame is intensified by her inability to meet white standards of beauty in a culture that views black as "ugly"; in *Song of Solomon*, how Milkman Dead is weighed down by the "shit" of inherited family and racial shame; in *Jazz*, how Joe Trace is shamed by the "dirty" and "sloven" Wild, whom he believes to be his "secret mother"; in *Sula*, how Sula, who claims that she likes her "own dirt," hides her abiding sense of shame under a defiant display of shamelessness; and in *Paradise*, how the people of Ruby are shaped by their collective, and humiliating, memory of the Disallowing: the "contemptuous dismissal" of their dark-skinned forebears by light-skinned blacks. Mired in shame, Morrison's novels deal not only with the affects of shame, contempt, and disgust, but also with the feeling traps of shame-shame (being ashamed about shame in an endless, and paralyzing, spiral of feelings) and shame-rage (the inevitable and self-perpetuating sequence of emotions from shame to humiliated fury back to shame).

In novel after novel, as Morrison draws attention to the damaging impact of white racist practices and learned cultural shame on the collective African-American experience, she points to the shaping and shaming power of corrosive racist stereotypes and discursive repertoires in the construction of African-American identities as racially inferior and stigmatized. Investigating the class tensions and divisions within the African-American community, Morrison deals with the sensitive issues of internalized racism and the color-caste hierarchy as she repeatedly brings together dark-skinned, lower-class and light-skinned, middle-class characters, such as Pecola and Geraldine in *The Bluest Eye*, Son and Jadine in *Tar Baby*, and Pilate and Ruth in *Song of Solomon*, or as she in *Paradise* focuses on the color prejudice of the dark-skinned people of Ruby toward light-skinned blacks. If as a black writer dealing with race matters Morrison sometimes has found herself struggling with internalized racism as she works with and through a language that promotes, as she has described it, the "dismissive 'othering' of people" (*Playing in the Dark* x), she also deliberately, and with dialogic intent, invokes the shaming race- and class-inflected discourse of dirt and defilement, or the shaming language of the racial insult and slur, or shaming racist stereotypes, like that of the sexually promiscuous black woman and the lawless and potentially violent black underclass male. Just as hegemonic discourse has constructed blackness as a sign of a fundamental and stigmatizing difference, so Morrison, in a classic countershaming strategy, repeatedly constructs whiteness as a sign of pathological difference in her novels. While Morrison is also intent on representing black pride in her novels—such as Milkman's discovery of his "golden" racial heritage in the folk tale of the flying African in *Song of Solomon*, or Violet and Joe Trace's sense of expansive black pride and self-ownership as they train-dance their way to black Harlem in *Jazz*, or the pride of the people of Ruby in their utopian all-black town in *Paradise*— she also shows how the humiliated memories and experiences that result from living in a racist society reverberate in the lives of her characters.

While in Morrison's novels we find evidence of the desire to bear witness to the shame and trauma that exist in the lives of African Americans, in Morrison's insistent aestheticizing of shame and violence, we also find evidence of the reactive desire to cover up or repair the racial wounds she has exposed. Countering the depictions of the white oppressor and the black oppressor in the next room, Morrison's novels also enact a reparative urge in their dramatizations of the potentially healing power of the sense of safety and connection offered by the African-American community and in their antishaming and restitutive fantasies of what Morrison calls the African-American ancestors: that is, "timeless" elder figures who are "benevolent, instructive, and protective" (Morrison, "Rootedness" 343). Morrison, then, seems bent on effecting a cultural cure both through the artistic rendering and narrative reconstruction of the shame and trauma story and also through the fictional invocation of the protective power of the black folk community and the timeless ancestor figures. But the precariousness of that cure is revealed not only by her repeated depictions of the intergenerational transmission of victimization and shame but also by her constant restagings of familial and cultural scenes of shame and trauma in each successive novel as she confronts in her fiction the historical legacy of slavery and the persisting conflicts and challenges that continue to haunt African Americans in the race-divided American society where race still matters.

The Impact of Trauma and Shame on the Individual

As Morrison shows that race matters not only in the collective cultural experience of African Americans and in the construction of group identity but also in the experience of the individual, she represents, with almost clinical precision, what has, in recent years, become of interest to psychiatry and psychoanalysis: the impact of shame and trauma on the individual psyche and the family structure. Unlike traditional psychoanalytic inquiries which have tended to ignore the importance of social forces on the construction of group and personal identity,[1] recent investigations of the impact of trauma and shame on the individual as well as sociological inquiries into the ubiquity of shame and pride in daily social interactions can help bring into bold relief the effect of racist practices on African-American identity. A race-cognizant application of shame and trauma theory—which has mainly studied the painful effects of shame and trauma on individuals and families within the dominant white culture—shows that African Americans have been forced to deal not only with individual and/or family shame and trauma but also with cultural shame and racial trauma as they are designated as the racially inferior and stigmatized Other and thus become the targets of white discrimination and violence. An indispensable addition to the analysis of sensitive race matters, psychoanalytic and psychiatric accounts of the impact of shame and trauma on the individual provide an invaluable and necessary starting point for an analysis of Morrison's representations of shame and trauma in her fiction.

Trauma and the Individual

"The ordinary response to atrocities," writes psychiatrist Judith Herman, "is to banish them from consciousness. Certain violations of the social compact are too terrible to utter aloud: this is the meaning of the word *unspeakable*" (*Trauma* 1). Although awareness of horrible events intermittently penetrates public consciousness, it is seldom for very long. Not only do "[d]enial, repression, and dissociation operate on a social as well as an individual level," but the study of trauma itself "has a curious history—one of episodic amnesia" (*Trauma* 2, 7).[2]

Freud—by establishing within psychoanalysis the theory that sexual trauma is a product of fantasy—effectively denied the historical reality of traumatic occurrences, and psychoanalysts who followed the classical Freudian model "sought the determinants of the unconscious meaning" of trauma "in pathogenic fantasies rather than in shattering facts" (Ulman 62). But the shortcomings of the classical psychoanalytic model of trauma have become apparent to recent psychiatric and psychoanalytic investigators like Judith Herman, Bessel van der Kolk, Dori Laub, and Elizabeth Waites who find the source of the dissociated memories that haunt the trauma survivor not in repressed feelings and fantasies but in actual events.

Involving "threats to life or bodily integrity, or a close personal encounter with violence and death," traumatic events confront individuals "with the extremities of helplessness and terror" (Herman, *Trauma* 33). In such threatening situations, the sympathetic nervous system is aroused, causing the endangered person to feel a rush of adrenaline and enter a state of alertness. Traumatic responses occur when both resistance and escape are impossible, overwhelming the individual's self-defense system. Because traumatic events produce "profound and lasting changes in physiological arousal, emotion, cognition, and memory," the traumatized individual "may experience intense emotion but without clear memory of the event, or may remember everything in detail but without emotion" (Herman, *Trauma* 34).

When actual experiences are so overwhelming that they "cannot be integrated into existing mental frameworks," they are "dissociated, later to return intrusively as fragmented sensory or motoric experiences" (van der Kolk and van der Hart 447). Dissociation, rather than repression, is common to the trauma experience. Indeed, "Many trauma survivors report that they automatically are removed from the scene; they look at it from a distance or disappear altogether, leaving other parts of their personality to suffer and store the overwhelming experience" (van der Kolk and van der Hart 437). Paradoxically, situations of extreme and inescapable danger may evoke a state of "detached calm" in which events are still registered in awareness but seem "disconnected from their ordinary meanings." These altered states of consciousness can be viewed as "one of nature's small mercies, a protection against unbearable pain." Not unlike hypnotic trance states, these detached states of consciousness "share the same features of surrender of voluntary action, suspension of initiative and critical judgment, subjective detachment or calm, enhanced perception of imagery, altered sensation, including numbness and analgesia, and distortion of reality, including depersonalization, derealization, and change in the sense of time" (Herman, *Trauma* 42–43).

In the aftermath of traumatic occurrences, explains Herman, individuals find themselves "caught between the extremes of amnesia or of reliving the trauma, between floods of intense, overwhelming feeling and arid states of no feeling at all" (*Trauma* 47). As the intrusive symptoms of reliving the trauma lessen, numbing or constrictive symptoms—feelings of alienation, disconnection, inner deadness—come to predominate (*Trauma* 48–49). Because traumatic experiences become encoded in an abnormal type of memory that spontaneously erupts into consciousness in the form of flashbacks and nightmares, and because even apparently insignificant reminders can provoke these memories, what would otherwise seem a safe environment can end up feeling dangerous to survivors (*Trauma* 37).

While the "social context into which human babies are born relies on the family as a primary buffer against trauma," writes Elizabeth Waites, the "often correct assumption that families protect the best interests of children is so expedient that it often becomes a barrier against recognizing the traumatic potential of families themselves" (69). In abusive families—in which parent-child interactions may mingle protective with brutal behavior or in which punishment may predictably follow indulgence, or in which the sole predictable thing about the abuse is that it is inevitable—traumas that are dangerous, if not life-threatening, are repeatedly inflicted and rarely acknowledged as mistakes (68–69). The disruptive symptoms of post-traumatic stress in children can have a significant impact not only on developing competencies but also on character development, and thus, the attempt to recover from childhood trauma can be made more difficult by the complex ways in which responses to trauma become woven into the structure of the personality (64–65). Because victimization is often vigorously denied by both the perpetrator and the victim, and because victim-blaming is a common individual and even socially institutionalized response, the childhood victim can develop a scapegoat identity or incorporate self-punitive behavior into his or her self-concept (68). Even adult victims who are psychologically healthy prior to an assault commonly suffer disturbances not only in self-regulation but also in self-esteem and self-representation as a result of trauma (104–05).

Survivors of childhood and adult trauma—who feel not only "unsafe in their bodies" but also that their emotions and thinking are "out of control"— are "condemned to a diminished life, tormented by memory and bounded by helplessness and fear" (Herman, *Trauma* 160, 49). Confronting individuals with "the futility of putting up resistance, the impossibility of being able to affect the outcome of events," trauma shatters "assumptions about predictability and mastery" and thus "inflicts a 'narcissistic wound to the fabric of the self'" (van der Kolk, "Foreword" ix). Because a "secure sense of connection with caring people is the foundation of personality development," traumatic events, in calling fundamental human relationships into question, can "shatter the construction of the self that is formed and sustained in relation to others" (Herman, *Trauma* 52, 51). Moreover, trauma can affect autobiographical memory: that is, "the integration of particular events into a coherent, temporally organized, and self-referential pattern." The distortion of autobiographical memory caused by trauma can have subtle or profound effects not only on "self-presentation and self-representation" but also on the "integration of self-experience" into the coherent pattern that is phenomenologically experienced as a "stable personal identity" (Waites 29, 31). Trauma affects not only the individual but also, as studies of those victimized by the Holocaust have shown, victim-survivor populations, and the effects of trauma can be transmitted intergenerationally (see, e.g., Danieli).

Shame and the Individual

Like the study of trauma, the study of shame has, until recent times, been largely neglected. Indeed, it is suggestive that shame, which induces secrecy and a hiding response, is an "only recently rediscovered feeling state" (S. Miller xi). Since 1971, "there has been a rapid increase in the literature on the psychology of shame, thus redressing a long-standing neglect of the subject," writes shame theorist Helen Block Lewis. "Once clinicians' attention is called to shame, it becomes apparent that, although it is easily ignored, shame is ubiquitous" ("Preface" xi).[3]

This neglect of shame, in part, can be attributed to "a prevailing sexist attitude in science, which pays less attention to nurturance than to aggression" and thus "depreciates the shame that inheres in 'loss of love'" (Helen Lewis, "Preface" xi). Because of the Freudian view that attachment is regressive and that women are shame-prone as a result of their need to conceal their "genital deficiency," there is an implicit hierarchy in classical psychoanalytic discourse, which views shame as preoedipal and guilt as oedipal (Helen Lewis, "Role of Shame" 31). To Freudians, guilt was the "more *worthy* affective experience" compared to shame, which was viewed as "the developmentally more primitive affect" (Andrew Morrison, *Shame* 5). Shame, then, until recently, has had a "stigma" attached to it so that "there has been a shame about studying shame in the psychoanalytic and psychotherapeutic fields" (Goldberg x). But with the movement away from the classical Freudian oedipal conflict-guilt model of personality and the intensifying focus on the narcissistically wounded and shame-ridden self— beginning in the 1970s and with increased interest in the 1980s and 1990s— shame has become the subject of psychoanalytic scrutiny, most notably in the work of affect and shame theorists like Silvan Tomkins, Helen Block Lewis, Donald Nathanson, Andrew Morrison, Gershen Kaufman, and Léon Wurmser.

Contrary to Freud, as recent psychoanalytic investigators have shown, "there is no concrete evidence that shame precedes guilt in development"; moreover, shame "exists equally strongly in men and women" (Helen Lewis, "Role of Shame" 31, Andrew Morrison, *Shame* 13). An inherited, physiological response, shame is an innate affect, hardwired in the brain, and there also appears to be a biological, genetic disposition to experience *extreme* forms of shame, which may begin with "a *constitutional* predisposition to overstimulation" (Goldberg 41). Pointing to the biological sources of this painful emotion, shame investigators argue that one can observe a proto or primitive form of shame behavior in infant-parent interactions—manifested in such infant behaviors as shyness, gaze aversion, hiding the face, and stranger anxiety (see, e.g., Nathanson, "Timetable"). One likely reason for the "inarticulateness" of shame is that the "brain is arranged so that key aspects of emotional life ... can operate largely independent of thought" and thus "emotional input is experienced before cognition" (Goldberg 41). Moreover, the "special affinity" of shame for autonomic reactions, such as blushing, sweating, and increased heart rate, "suggests that it is an emergency response to threatened affectional ties" (Helen Lewis, "Introduction" 16–17).

An intensely painful experience, shame "follows a moment of *exposure*," an uncovering that "reveals aspects of the self of a peculiarly sensitive, intimate, and vulnerable nature" (Nathanson, "Timetable" 4). Shame sufferers feel in some profound way inferior to others—they perceive themselves as deeply flawed and defective or as bad individuals or as failures—and this internalized shame script grows out of early shaming interactions with parents or significant others. Shamed individuals may experience "a brief moment of painful feeling"—a jolt or jab of pain—followed by a compulsive and often repetitive "replaying" of the shaming scene, often in scenarios in which shamed individuals imagine themselves responding to the shaming incident in a more satisfactory way; or they may experience "painful confusion and unwanted physical manifestations," such as blushing and rapid heartbeat, and feel "at a loss for words and also at a loss for thoughts" (Scheff, "Shame-Rage Spiral" 110–11). Shame, then, is a disorganizing experience, and it can leave individuals feeling "overwhelmed" and "small, helpless, and childish." In describing their feelings, shamed individuals often voice common shame fantasies: that they could "crawl through a hole' or 'sink through the floor' or 'die' with shame" (Helen Lewis, "Introduction" 19). Shame is not only a "quickly spreading and flooding affect," but it also can induce feelings of "shame about shame" (Wurmser, *Mask* 55).

At once an interpersonal and intrapsychic experience, shame derives from the shame sufferer's "vicarious experience of the other's scorn," and, indeed, central to the shame experience is the "self-in-the-eyes-of-the-other" (Helen Lewis, "Introduction" 15). At the core of shame, writes Léon Wurmser, is the "conviction of one's *unlovability*" because of an inherent sense that the self is "weak, dirty, and defective" (*Mask* 92, 93). In the classic shame scenario, in which the "eye is the organ of shame par excellence," the individual feels exposed and humiliated—*looked at* with contempt for being inferior, flawed, or dirty—and thus wants to hide or disappear (Wurmser, "Shame" 67). Fear of visual exposure, as Wurmser explains, leads to the wish to disappear as the person one has shown oneself to be, or to be viewed as different than one is (*Mask* 232). Shame-imbued people may suffer shame vulnerability—that is, "a sensitivity to, and readiness for, shame"—and shame anxiety, which is "evoked by the imminent danger of unexpected exposure, humiliation, and rejection" (Andrew Morrison, *Shame* 14, Wurmser, *Mask* 49).

Experiencing a heightened sense of self-consciousness, shame sufferers may feel inhibited, inferior, incompetent, dirty, defective, scorned and ridiculed by others. Shame, and its related feeling states—chagrin, embarrassment, mortification, lowered self-esteem, disgrace, and humiliation—can lead to withdrawal or avoidant behaviors, which reflect the desire of shamed individuals to conceal or hide themselves in an attempt to protect against feelings of exposure. Other classic defenses against shame function to help shamed individuals recover from painful feelings of exposure and helplessness. For example, "feeling weak may be 'repaired' by arrogance, self-glorification, aggressiveness," and the "powerful, surging" feeling of anger may work to temporarily overcome the "helpless feelings of being disregarded and insignificant" that often accompany shame (Goldberg 69). Many expressions of rage can be understood as attempts "to rid the self of shame," while contempt represents "an attempt to 'relocate' the shame experience from within the self into another person" (Andrew Morrison, *Shame* 14). Other defenses against shame include the defiance of shamelessness—that is, the deliberate flaunting of one's shame—and turning the tables in the attack-other script, in which the shamed individual actively shames and humiliates others (see Wurmser, *Mask* 257–64, Nathanson, *Shame and Pride* 360–73).

Describing the "natural, inevitable sequence from shame into humiliated fury and retaliation and thence into guilt for 'unjust' or 'irrational' rage," Helen Block Lewis has called shame a "feeling trap" ("Introduction" 2). Drawing on Lewis's work, Thomas Scheff and Suzanne Retzinger point to the potentially lethal consequences of the shame-shame or shame-rage feeling traps. A feeling trap, as they explain, "involves a series of loops of shame (being ashamed of being ashamed), which causes further shame, which can continue indefinitely," or it involves a self-perpetuating chain of emotions in which unacknowledged shame leads to anger which, in turn, results in further shame (104–05). Moreover, when an individual has emotional reactions to his or her own emotions and to those of another person, both individuals can become mired in a feeling trap—"a *triple spiral* of shame and rage *between* and *within* interactants," which, in turn, can lead to the emotional impasse of an interminable conflict (126). "Shame-rage spirals may be brief, lasting a matter of minutes, or they can last for hours, days, or a lifetime, as bitter hatred or resentment" (127). Moreover, shame-anger chains, according to Scheff and Retzinger, can endure "longer than a lifetime, since hatred can be transmitted from generation to generation in the form of racial, religious, and national prejudice" (105).

Cultural Shame and the Deference-Emotion System

"Shame is a multidimensional, multilayered experience," observes Gershen Kaufman. "While first of all an *individual* phenomenon experienced in some form and to some degree by every person, shame is equally a *family* phenomenon and a *cultural* phenomenon. It is reproduced within families, and each culture has its own distinct sources as well as targets of shame" (*Shame* 191). While American society "*is* a shame-based culture ... shame is *hidden*. There is shame about shame and so it remains under strict taboo" (*Shame* 32).

Shame, which is often called the "master emotion" (see, e.g., Scheff, *Bloody Revenge* 53–54), has profound consequences for individuals in their daily interactions with others. Indeed, "Shame and pride seem to be an almost continuous part of human existence not only in crises but also in the slightest of social contacts," according to Thomas Scheff. Cross-cultural investigations of politeness behavior suggest "the universality of shame" in revealing how cultures "provide elaborate means for protecting *face*, that is, protecting against embarrassment and humiliation" (*Bloody Revenge* 51). In daily social interactions, states of shame and pride "almost always depend on the level of deference accorded a person: pride arises from deferential treatment by others ("respect"), and shame from lack of deference ("disrespect"). Gestures that imply respect or disrespect, together with the emotional response they generate, make up the *deference / emotion system*, which exerts a powerful influence on human behavior" (Scheff, Retzinger, Ryan 184–85). Stuart Schneiderman's observation that the "closest approximation" in American history to having "'no face' is being black in America" points to the significance of issues surrounding pride and shame and the deference-emotion system in the social formation of African-American identity (124). In a similar way, shame theorist Andrew Morrison, in his discussion of what he calls "learned cultural shame" over feelings of being different, remarks, "The African American people, often judged by white American society as inferior, have endured the stigma of being different since their history on this continent began. The sense of difference and inferiority imposed by the dominant culture leads to internalization of that judgment by the affected group" (*Culture of Shame* 35).

Race Matters: Shame, Trauma, and the African-American Experience

Just as individuals who suffer from shame may struggle with the conflicting need to "confess" and "retain" the shameful secret and just as trauma survivors seem driven by "the twin imperatives of truth-telling and secrecy" (Goldberg 169, Herman, *Trauma* 1), so there has been a corresponding cultural impulse to publicly reveal and conceal the humiliations and traumas endured by oppressed groups like African Americans. Even as the process of recovering the silenced black voices in American history and culture goes forward and even as racism and the social construction of African-American identities have become the subject of intense scholarly scrutiny, so there is a corresponding countermovement in the American culture to deny or minimize the continuing significance of race and the historical legacy of racism and racist oppression on the cultural memory and collective experience of contemporary black Americans.

Describing the historical traumas suffered by African Americans, black psychiatrist James Comer argues that the trauma of slavery was compounded by the fact that children born into slavery were "socialized and developed in ways that defined them as inferior" (154). "Snatch a free man from his own culture, enslave, exclude, degrade and abuse him; and his sense of worth, value and adequacy will be destroyed, reduced or under constant and severe challenge," writes Comer (165).[4] After slavery was abolished, the dominant white culture continued its tactics of physically terrorizing and psychically shaming black Americans. African Americans "found themselves controlled by a government and an economy run by openly racist whites.... [U]ntil 1915, more than 90 per cent of the black population lived in the most restrictive and oppressive section of the country, and over 50 per cent of all blacks lived as serfs." And until the 1940s, "[f]raud, theft, economic reprisal and open violence against blacks existed." Between 1882 and 1935, more than 3,000 blacks were lynched and between 1882 and 1955, over 4,700 blacks died in mob action. While the "motives for violence were mixed," the underlying purpose was to maintain white privilege (165–66). In Comer's account, African Americans carry with them collective memories not only of white antagonism and abuse but also of the sound of "contemptuous white laughter" in the sight of the tragedy of black life (170).

In a similar way, Cornel West describes the impact of racist violence and racial contempt on the collective historical experience of African Americans. "One of the best ways to instill fear in people is to terrorize them," comments West. "Yet this fear is best sustained by convincing them that their bodies are ugly, their intellect is inherently underdeveloped, their culture is less civilized, and their future warrants less concern than that of other peoples. Two hundred and forty-four years of slavery and nearly a century of institutionalized terrorism in the form of segregation, lynchings, and second-class citizenship in America were aimed at precisely this devaluation of black people." Although ultimately this "white supremacist venture was ... a relative failure," the white endeavor to dehumanize blacks "has left its toll in the psychic scars and personal wounds now inscribed in the souls of black folk" (122–23). Also remarking on the pain of racial wounding, bell hooks discusses the association in the black imagination of whiteness with terror. "All black people in the United States, irrespective of their class status or politics," she writes, "live with the possibility that they will be terrorized by whiteness" (*Killing Rage* 46).

The comments of hooks and West point to the psychic scars and personal wounds suffered by African Americans in the race-divided American society. Historically treated with disrespect—indeed, viewed by the dominant white culture as shamed objects of contempt—African Americans bear the wounds of the intergenerationally transmitted racial shame described in Comer's account of how blacks carry with them the sound of "contemptuous white laughter" and also in W.E.B. Du Bois's well-known turn-of-the-century description of the "double-consciousness" of African Americans, "this sense of always looking at one's self through the eyes of others, of measuring one's soul by the tape of a world that looks on in amused contempt and pity" (9). Du Bois's account of the double-consciousness of African Americans derived from viewing the self through the eyes of contemptuous others recalls Helen Block Lewis's description of the accentuated sense of self-consciousness experienced by the shamed individual. Explaining that the shame experience is "directly about the self, which is the focus of a negative evaluation," Lewis writes, "Because the self is the focus of awareness in shame, 'identity' imagery is usually evoked. At the same time that this identity imagery is registering as one's own experience, there is also vivid imagery of the self in the other's eyes. This creates a 'doubleness of experience,' which is characteristic of shame" ("Shame" 107).

The black Antillean psychiatrist Frantz Fanon provides a vivid account of the shame sufferer's doubleness of experience in his remarks on the black feeling of inferiority that "comes into being through the other" and in his description of the experience of being seen as an object of contempt—as a "Dirty nigger!"—in the eyes of whites (110, 109). Viewed through the shaming gaze of whites, "Negroes are savages, brutes, illiterates" (117). Fanon describes his feeling of being "dissected under white eyes, the only real eyes," and of having his body "given back" to him "sprawled out, distorted" (116, 113). The fact that he wants to hide from the gaze of whites—"I slip into corners, I remain silent, I strive for anonymity, for invisibility"—reveals his reactive desire to defend against feelings of shameful exposure. "Shame. Shame and self-contempt. Nausea. When people like me, they tell me it is in spite of my color. When they dislike me, they point out that it is not because of my color. Either way, I am locked into the infernal circle," writes Fanon as he, in recounting the racist myths that undergird the cultural construction of blackness, reports not only on the experience of being treated as the racially inferior and stigmatized Other but also on the process of the "internalization—or, better, the epidermalization"—of a sense of inferiority (116,11).

Describing the black shame that arises out of internalized racism—that is, the absorption by African Americans of "negative feelings and attitudes about blackness held by white people"—bell hooks similarly observes that many blacks see themselves as inferior, as "lacking" in comparison to whites and that they overvalue whiteness and "negate the value of blackness" (*Killing Rage* 186, 148, 158). The accounts of Fanon and hooks reveal not only that the "deliberate shaming" of an individual can be used as a "severe punishment" (Helen Lewis, "Introduction" 1–2), but also that shame sufferers, in internalizing the disgust and contempt of the shaming other, can develop a deep sense of self-hatred and self-contempt. Wurmser's description of how basic shame—the inherent sense that the self is weak, defective, and dirty—leads to a deep sense of "pain, hurt, woundedness" (*Mask* 93) provides a compelling description of racial shame: the profound hurt felt by those treated as the racial Other, as shamed objects of contempt. While shamed individuals, as Silvan Tomkins observes, are governed by the "wish not to hear the rasping, tongue-lashing voice of the internalized shamer and condemner," they also may identify with "that not so small voice" (265).

In a white male American culture that is "shame phobic"—for it places value on "achievement, competition, power, and dominance" (Goldberg 78)—African Americans not only have been viewed as objects of contempt, they also have served as containers for white shame.[5] Because white Americans have historically projected their own shame onto blacks, African Americans have been forced to carry a cripplingly heavy burden of shame: their own shame and the projected shame of white America. Gershen Kaufman, in his analysis of the complex interplay of identity, culture, and ideology in intergroup hostilities, such as the historical hostility between whites and blacks in American society, explains how the ideology of group hatred and prejudice is fueled by affects such as shame, disgust, contempt, and rage. Not only is violence targeted at particular groups "shaped by distinct ideologies of superiority and hate," writes Kaufman, but each group enacts its scripted role in the "actions and reactions" played out between various groups. In a culture that devalues those who are different, people belonging to minority groups are viewed with contempt. Indeed, "it is the affect of contempt which partitions the inferior from the superior in any culture or nation. As such, contempt is the principal dynamic fueling prejudice and discrimination" (*Shame* 240–41).

That scholars investigating race have described the study of racism as a "dirty business" or have remarked that it is "virtually impossible to write or say anything on the topic of race that is not in some way objectionable or embarrassing" (Gordon ix, LaCapra 2) points to the profound shame attached to the vexed issues surrounding antiblack racial prejudice and the racial caste system. Commenting on how the "much-heralded stability and continuity of American democracy was predicated upon black oppression and degradation," Cornel West observes that "[w]ithout the presence of black people in America, European-Americans would not be 'white'—they would be only Irish, Italians, Poles, Welsh, and others engaged in class, ethnic, and gender struggles over resources and identity. What made America distinctly American for them was not simply the presence of unprecedented opportunities, but the struggle for seizing these opportunities in a new land in which black slavery and racial caste served as the floor upon which white class, ethnic, and gender struggles could be diffused and diverted. In other words, white poverty could be ignored and whites' paranoia of each other could be overlooked primarily owing to the distinctive American feature: the basic racial divide of black and white peoples" (156–57). Toni Morrison makes a related observation on the experience of immigrants in her analysis of what she calls "race talk," a discursive repertoire that places emphasis on so-called essential racial differences, and that, in constructing African Americans as the deviant and racially inferior Other, is used to provide an ideological rationale for the continuing economic and social oppression of blacks. "[R]ace talk," as Morrison describes it, is an "explicit insertion into everyday life of racial signs and symbols that have no meaning other than pressing African Americans to the lowest level of the racial hierarchy. Popular culture, shaped by film, theater, advertising, the press, television, and literature, is heavily engaged in race talk. It participates freely in this most enduring and efficient rite of passage into American culture: negative appraisals of the native-born black population. Only when the lesson of racial estrangement is learned is assimilation complete. Whatever the lived experience of immigrants with African Americans—pleasant, beneficial, or bruising—the rhetorical experience renders blacks as noncitizens, already discredited outlaws" ("On the Backs of Blacks" 97–98). Describing how race functions as "a metaphor ... necessary to the construction of Americanness," Morrison writes, "Deep within the word 'American' is its association with race.... American means white, and Africanist people struggle to make the term applicable to themselves with ethnicity and hyphen after hyphen after hyphen" (*Playing in the Dark* 47).[6]

Until the black revolution of the 1960s, "To be called 'black' in America meant to live in a state of shame ...," remarks shame theorist Donald Nathanson, who views the 1960s expression of the "cultural need to 'shove it to whitey'" as a "shame-reversing" attack-other script (*Shame and Pride* 465). Although the Civil Rights Movement also provided a healthy reversal of black shame by "transforming shame into pride and a sense of relative well-being for many blacks in this country (e.g., 'Black is Beautiful' as a new rallying cry)" (Andrew Morrison, *Shame* 187), racial prejudice and discrimination continue to be significant facts of black American life. "[I]t is time to 'get real' about race and the persistence of racism in America," writes Derrick Bell (5).[7] In the United States where racism is "an integral, permanent, and indestructible component" of American society, African Americans "remain" what they "were in the beginning: a dark and foreign presence, always the designated 'other'" (ix, 10). The "racism that made slavery feasible," in Bell's view, "is far from dead in the last decade of twentieth-century America; and the civil rights gains, so hard won, are being steadily eroded" (ix, 3). For bell hooks, "Confronting the great resurgence of white supremacist organizations and seeing the rhetoric and beliefs of these groups surface as part of accepted discourse in every aspect of daily life in the United States startles, frightens, and is enough to throw one back into silence." hooks describes how "painful" it is to "think long and hard about race and racism in the United States" or to read the information found in Andrew Hacker's 1992 book, *Two Nations*, which reports that many white Americans believe that Africans and African Americans languish "'at a lower evolutionary level than members of other races.'" To hooks, "The anti-black backlash is so fierce it astounds" (*Killing Rage* 3, *Two Nations* 27).

Like bell hooks and Derrick Bell, Morrison has commented on the continuing significance of race in American society. To Morrison, "declarations that racism is irrelevant, over or confined to the past are premature fantasies" ("Official Story" xx). America remains "Star-spangled. Race-strangled" ("On the Backs" 100).[8] Yet while antiblack racism continues to plague African Americans, postmodern theorists have put "race" under erasure.[9] Remarking on the erasure of race in contemporary theory, Morrison observes that "race" remains "a virtually unspeakable thing, as can be seen in the apologies, notes of 'special use' and circumscribed definitions that accompany it—not least of which is my own deference in surrounding it with quotation marks. Suddenly ... 'race' does not exist." African Americans insisted, for three hundred years, that "'race' was no usefully distinguishing factor in human relationships" only to have "every academic discipline, including theology, history, and natural science" assert that "'race was *the* determining factor in human development." Then, when black Americans "discovered they had shaped or become a culturally formed race, and that it had specific and revered difference, suddenly they were told there is no such thing as 'race,' biological or cultural, that matters and that genuinely intellectual exchange cannot accommodate it." Morrison counters the theoretical erasure of race by insisting that "there *is* culture and both gender and 'race' inform and are informed by it. Afro-American culture exists..." ("Unspeakable Things" 3). Blackness, to Morrison, is a socially constructed category and a social fact in our racialized and race-conscious society. Responding to the description of race as "'both an empty category and one of the most destructive and powerful forms of social categorization,'" Morrison describes "race" as a "powerfully destructive emptiness" ("Introduction" ix).[10]

Anthony Walton, describing his experience as an African American in the 1990s, writes, "I have, for most of my adult life, wondered what, exactly, is the stain we black Americans carry, what is it about our mere presence, our mere existence that can inflame such passion, embroil the nation in such histrionics for so long a time?" (255). In a society in which racial shame remains a social fact and a shaping force in the construction of black identities and in which, in Morrison's words, "blackness is itself a stain, and therefore unstainable" ("Introduction" xviii), it is telling that Morrison, herself, was subjected to a form of public shaming when she received the Nobel prize in literature. Not only did journalists from the United States, Britain, and Europe capitalize on Morrison's race and gender in their stories, as they made use of the opportunity "to 'spice up' their headlines with a variety of eye-catching combinations" of the words "'winner,' 'black,' 'Nobel prize,' 'woman,'" but also "[w]ith amazing cross-cultural consistency, reviewers adopted an apologetic and defensive tone that seemed intended to 'account for' the literary significance of Morrison's fiction by dispelling doubts about its worth, rather than by celebrating its uniqueness" (Fabi 253–54). And Morrison was also dismissed and belittled by some aspiring laureates, who referred to her as an "affirmative action" laureate. "White America demonized black America in the days of Jim Crow. Still true today, though cosmetic changes have disguised some of the uglier aspects of the arrangement," remarks Adam Begley. "Need proof? Think of the way some people try to shrink a rival with the phrase *affirmative action*" (54; see also Reilly).

Trauma, Shame, and Storytelling in Morrison's Novels

Intent on representing painful race matters in her novels, Morrison repeatedly, if not obsessively, stages scenes of inter- and intraracial violence and shaming in her novels. She also uses her fiction to aestheticize—and thus to gain narrative mastery over and artistically repair—the racial shame and trauma she describes. In her commentary on the opening of her first novel,

The Bluest Eye, Morrison provides insight into her narrative method. She explains that the opening sentence spoken by her child narrator—*"Quiet as it's kept, there were no marigolds in the fall of 1941"*—attracted her because the phrase "Quiet as it's kept" is "conspiratorial" and implies that there is a "secret between us and a secret that is being kept from us." Although the next sentence divulges the shameful secret—*"We thought ... it was because Pecola was having her father's baby that the marigolds did not grow"*—it also, by foregrounding the flowers, "backgrounds illicit, traumatic, incomprehensible sex coming to its dreaded fruition." The novel's opening, thus, "provides the stroke that announces something more than a secret shared, but a silence broken, a void filled, an unspeakable thing spoken at last" ("Afterword" 212–14).

Morrison seems driven to speak the unspeakable in her fiction. But in foregrounding the flowers and backgrounding the illicit and traumatic, she also defensively aestheticizes the shame and trauma she represents in her novels, and she reminds her readers that violence in fiction is "always verbally mediated" and thus it appears "as something *styled*" (Kowalewski 4). In her constant exposure of shameful and traumatic secrets, Morrison, at times, deliberately evokes the oral quality of gossip through her meandering narrative style and her use of narrative fragments in the progressive and repeated, but constantly interrupted, telling of her characters' stories. But even while Morrison *consciously* affects an improvisational or oral style in her fiction, she also is an author who is caught up in the desire to reveal and conceal, to tell and not tell, which typifies our culture's approach to shame and trauma. Thus readers of Morrison's fiction may come away with the sense of narrative withholding or hesitancy as they follow and piece together a novelistic narrative that circles redundantly around the illicit, traumatic, incomprehensible secret or secrets it represents. If through her use of aesthetic design and fragmented narrative structure Morrison partly defends against the shameful secrets and physical horrors she depicts in her fiction, her description of her imagined reader as a co-conspirator and confidant also reveals that she is intent on involving her readers emotionally in her work.

"Writing and reading," remarks Morrison, "mean being aware of the writer's notions of risk and safety, the serene achievement of, or sweaty fight for, meaning and response-ability" (*Playing in the Dark* xi). An author who makes readers aware of the "response-ability" of her fiction and who demands reader involvement with her texts, Morrison compares the African-American artist to the black preacher who "requires his congregation to speak, to join him in the sermon, to behave in a certain way, to stand up and to weep and to cry and to accede or to change and to modify—to expand on the sermon that is being delivered" (Morrison, "Rootedness" 341). Likening herself to the black preacher and also to the jazz musician, Morrison must, as she describes it, "provide places and spaces so that the reader can participate" (Russell 44). Morrison wants from her readers "a very strong visceral and emotional response as well as a very clear intellectual response" (McKay 147). While Morrison attempts to put her readers "into the position of being naked and quite vulnerable" and to rid them of all "literary" and "social experiences" so she can "engage" them in the novel, she also wants her readers to trust her, for she is "never going to do anything so bad" that her readers "can't handle it" (Ruas 109, Moyers 274). "My writing expects, demands participatory reading," Morrison remarks. "The reader supplies the emotions.... He or she can feel something visceral, see something striking. Then we [you, the reader, and I, the author] come together to make this book, to feel this experience." Morrison risks hurting her readers, but she also holds them "in a comfortable place," as she puts it, so they won't be "shattered" (Tate 164).

Demanding participatory reading and having both a cognitive and emotional impact on readers, Morrison's novels exert interactional pressures on readers, who may be held in a comfortable place—through what one commentator calls Morrison's "rational telling of extreme events" (Byerman, "Beyond Realism" 55)—and yet also feel compelled and unsettled, if not emotionally distressed, by what they read.[11] In dramatizing shame, Morrison openly appeals to her readers' active curiosity by positioning them as eavesdroppers and voyeurs—as observers of family or communal secrets— and as receivers of shameful gossip. In her strategic public disclosure of shameful secrets, Morrison also risks shaming her readers, for just as exposed individuals feel shame, so the observers can experience shame if they have "seen too much" or "intruded too deeply into the hidden" (Nathanson, *Many Faces* 65). And if the literary container provides a potentially safe space from which to experience reconstructed stories of shame-laden traumas, Morrison's novels are also powerful forms of emotional communication, works, as we shall see in our investigations of critic-reader reactions to Morrison's fiction, that are capable of invoking in readers a range of intensely uncomfortable feelings and that can also induce readers to respond in affective and collusive ways as they participate in the text's drama. Critic-readers, for example, sometimes report feeling not only afraid or ashamed but also guilty, disgusted, anxious, angry, or even numbed as they read Morrison's novels. In their critical responses to Morrison's works, many commentators also become unwitting participants in the classic shame drama of blame assessment as they attempt to discover who or what is to blame for the plight of Morrison's characters, or they are induced to enact shame- and trauma-specific roles—including those of the advocate or rescuer or the contemptuous shamer or hostile judge—as they respond to Morrison's troubled, and troubling, characters.

If the forceful emotional tug and pull of Morrison's novels, with their repeated enactments of shame-shame and shame-rage feeling traps, can unsettle or even vicariously shame and traumatize readers, who become enmeshed in narratives that focus on human brutality and the dis-ease of contemporary culture, readers, as we shall see, often are induced to assume a more comforting role dramatized in Morrison's novels: that of the understanding witnesses or the supportive community of listeners who help begin the process of healing shame and trauma by responding empathically to the painful stories of Morrison's shame- and trauma-haunted characters.

"Even as intellectuals and politicians posit the declining significance of race, 'racial difference' remains America's preeminent national narrative," writes Ann duCille. Thus, while race may be "an empty category, a slippery concept, a social construction, a trope," it still matters (1). We need to theorize race "not as meaning*less* but as meaning*ful*"—as a site of difference "filled with constructed meanings that are in need of constant decoding and interrogation" (58). Morrison, in her own critical writings—most notably in *Playing in the Dark*—is intent on making visible the racist mythologies that "render blacks publicly serviceable instruments of private dread and longing" ("Introduction" xviii). But she also is aware that "for both black and white American writers, in a wholly racialized society, there is no escape from racially inflected language" (*Playing in the Dark* 12–13). As Morrison remarks, "I am a black writer struggling with and through a language that can powerfully evoke and enforce hidden signs of racial superiority, cultural hegemony, and dismissive 'othering' of people and language which are by no means marginal or already and completely known and knowable in my work" (*Playing in the Dark* x–xi). Although Morrison herself sometimes finds it difficult to maneuver around racially inflected language and discursive repertoires, she also is intent on depicting the rich complexities and complicating differences—such as differences in gender, class, education, and culture—that shape African-American identities.

If, quiet as it's kept, much of African-American existence has been grotesque, Morrison is intent on speaking the unspeakable in her novels as she exposes to public view the painful collective and private shame and trauma suffered by black Americans in our race-conscious and wholly racialized American society. Although those who have investigated shame and trauma often report on the tendency of people to turn away from the shameful and traumatic, Morrison has an uncanny power not only to fascinate but also to draw readers into the fictional worlds she creates. Quiet as it's kept, Morrison's fiction is shame- and trauma-driven, as we shall see in the following pages. Yet despite the painful and shameful subject matter of her novels, Morrison, by creating verbally rich and complexly designed fiction, has earned the pride of place among contemporary American novelists as she explores the woundedness of African-American life in an idealized art-form that conveys, but also aesthetically contains and controls, intense feelings of anger, shame, and pain.

NOTES

1. In *Psychoanalysis and Black Novels*, Claudia Tate explains why psychoanalytic theory has been largely shunned by black intellectuals. "Instead of regarding individuals and their stories as products of a dialectic of material circumstances *and* their internalization of them, psychoanalysis, as it generally operates, centers the individual's primary nurturing environment, not the external circumstances that precondition that environment." The psychoanalytic model "relegates the bleak material circumstances of real lives to the background," and thus scholars who study African-American literature "shun" psychoanalysis since it effectively "effaces racism and recasts its effects as a personality disorder caused by familial rather than social pathology" (16). Because of the continuation of racial oppression and "the demand for black literature to identify and militate against it," remarks Tate, "black literature evolves so as to prove that racism exists in the real world and is not a figment of the black imagination" (17).

In the course of this study, I show that the application of shame and trauma theory to the works of Morrison does not efface but instead illuminates the impact of pernicious racist practices on the black American cultural experience. Describing how shame "attends the process of subjection," Joseph Adamson and Hilary Clark write, "Whenever a person is disem-powered on the basis of gender, sexual orientation, race, physical disability, whenever a person is devalued and internalizes the negative judgment of an other, shame flourishes" (3, 2–3).

2. In her discussion of the "forgotten history" of trauma, Judith Herman shows how "[p]eriods of active investigation have alternated with periods of oblivion" (*Trauma* 7). Although Freud, in his investigations of hysteria, grasped the truth of the actual sexual trauma suffered by his female patients, he "retreated ... into the most rigid denial." Rather than acknowledging "the exploitive nature of women's real experiences," Freud "insisted that women imagined and longed for the abusive sexual encounters of which they complained" (19). But when soldiers fighting in the First World War "began to break down in shocking numbers" and behave like hysterical women—"They screamed and wept uncontrollably. They froze and could not move. They became mute and unresponsive. They lost their memory and their capacity to feel"—the "reality of psychological trauma was forced upon public consciousness once again" (20).

Yet interest in trauma waned after the end of the First World War only to be revived again during the Second World War and later the Vietnam War. But it was not until 1980 that the American Psychiatric Association finally gave "formal recognition within the diagnostic canon" to a new category of mental disorder—the post-traumatic stress disorder (28). Only after 1980 did it finally become clear that the post-traumatic stress syndrome is seen in women survivors of rape, domestic battery, and incest (32). It has also been argued that women suffer from the "traumatic stresses" of "everyday" violence against and oppression of women (see Brown).

3. An insightful discussion of the similar neglect of the study of shame in literary scholarship is found in Joseph Adamson and Hilary Clark's introduction to *Scenes of Shame*—a collection of essays by literary critics and psychoanalysts who investigate the shame dynamics of works by authors such as Hawthorne, George Eliot, Faulkner, Anne Sexton, Nietzsche, and Kierkegaard. Adamson and Clark also provide an excellent overview of shame theory in their introduction. See also Joseph Adamson's application of shame theory to the analysis of Melville's works in *Melville, Shame, and the Evil Eye*.

4. African-American historian Nell Painter describes the psychic damage caused by slavery in her essay, "Soul Murder and Slavery: Toward a Fully Loaded Cost Accounting." Painter explains that there has been a "reluctance to deal with black people's psychology" following the 1960s debate on Stanley Elkins's book, *Slavery: A Problem in American Institutional and Intellectual Life* (1959). Elkins, who compared the trauma of Nazi concentration camps to that of slavery, claimed that African-American slaves, like concentration camp inmates, *"internalized"* the attitudes of their masters and that slavery produced "psychologically crippled adults who were docile, irresponsible, loyal, lazy, humble, and deceitful, in short, who were Sambos" (130–31).

Elkins was criticized for ignoring not only the importance of slave families and communities but also the fact of slave resistance and revolt. Yet Painter is troubled by the fact that "since the thunder and lightning of the Elkins controversy—even after the appearance of extensive revisionist writing—scholars and lay people have avoided, and sometimes positively resisted, the whole calculation of slavery's psychological costs. The Sambo problem was solved through the pretense that black people do not have psyches." Arguing that it is "imperative" to reject those claims that deny the "psychological personhood" of slaves (131), Painter discusses the psychological damage resulting from both child abuse and the sexual abuse of women in slavery. But she also argues that both slave families and religious belief offered crucial means of support that helped slaves "resist being damaged permanently." Moreover, Painter claims that the white slave owners "inflicted the psychic damage of slavery upon themselves, their white families, and, ultimately, on their whole society" (139).

5. Like other "demonized" enemies described by Rafael Moses in his discussion of projection and the political process, black Americans have served as the "embodiment" of the "unconscious wishes" and "split-off affects" of the white culture (see 140–41). Moreover, as a scapegoated group in white America, African Americans have been players in the blaming drama that is part of the shame scenario. When shame is projected, "it can be a source of shame in the person receiving the projection," who is now blamed for the negative attributes of the projector. The scapegoating ritual acts out this process, for the designated scapegoat, who is unable to resist the projected shame, carries "all of the blame" and thus those who are freed from blame "become the shamers rather than the shamed" (Nancy Morrison 56).

Black psychiatrist James Comer describes how in the "white mind" the African American became a "receptacle" for the projection of white guilt and anxiety about "'bad' impulses," that is, sexual and aggressive feelings (131). "The conduct of the whites who participated in murdering and lynching blacks suggests that these grisly events served as a catharsis by purging the evil the whites feared in themselves and 'projected' onto the blacks. Black victims were castrated, tortured, burned and mutilated by white men, women and children in drunken, orgy-like atmospheres" (134).

Joel Kovel's analysis of white racism, with its polarizing binarisms of black/white and polluted/pure, also describes the projective—and shaming—mechanisms that have led to the scapegoating of black Americans. The "nuclear experience" of "aversive" white racism, writes Kovel, "is a sense of disgust about the body of the black person based upon a very primitive fantasy: that it contains an essence—dirt—that smells and may rub off onto the body of the racist" (84). Kovel roots racist aversion in a "bodily fantasy about dirt, which rests in turn upon the equation of dirt with excrement: the inside of the body turned out and threatening to return within. And within this nuclear fantasy, black people have come to be represented as the personification of dirt ..." (89–90). Treating the black as Other, the white racist assigns hated or impure aspects of the self onto the black. "It is precisely this process of purification that creates the need to see another as the exemplar of impurity and to treat him as if he were exactly that" (91). Thus, "The fantasy of dirt and purification is the central theme of white racism from a subjective standpoint," according to Kovel. "It is a quintessential fantasy of Otherness—for the black body from which the white ego flees is his own body, lost in the Cartesian split of the cogito, and projected into the dark Otherness of the black" (xlv).

For an interesting analysis of the role played by the "discourse of dirt and defilement" in the Clarence Thomas Supreme Court confirmation hearings see Kendall Thomas, "Strange Fruit," 376–85.

6. Adrian Piper explains the difficulty inherent in this struggle with terminology. Remarking on the various terms used to designate African Americans—such as "blacks," "Negroes," "colored people," "Afro-Americans," "people of color," and "African Americans"—Piper comments that it "doesn't really matter" which classifying term is used "to designate those who have inferior and disadvantaged status, because whatever term is used will eventually turn into a term of derision and disparagement by virtue of its reference to those who are derided and disparaged, and so will need to be discarded for an unsullied one" (30).

7. Bell is arguing against the optimistic belief that racism was "a terrible and inexplicable anomaly stuck in the middle of our liberal democratic ethos," or the hopeful claim about the "declining significance of race" in American life—the view that "class has become more important than race in determining black life-chances in the modern industrial period" (Hochschild 3, W.J. Wilson 150). Because much of the work studying racial prejudice "assumes that racism derives largely from ignorance and false consciousness," observes Christopher Lane, the belief is that knowledge will enhance "cultural understanding" and diminish "inter- and intragroup hostility" (4, 5). In Lane's view, such assumptions ignore underlying issues that can be illuminated by psychoanalysis and that shed invaluable light on the psychic forces that drive racial resentments and hatreds.

8. In a speech that Morrison gave at Howard University on March 3, 1995 (which has not been published but has been quoted in several news reports), she remarks that "the genius of racism is that any political structure can host that virus. Any developed country can become a suitable home for fascism" (Morgan 35). Presenting a chilling "little

scenario," Morrison draws a comparison between the rise of fascism in Nazi Germany and the current plight of African Americans. "Before there was a Final Solution, there was a first one. And after the first, there was a second, and after the second, there was a third. Who knows how many more? Because the descent into a final solution is not a jump. It's one step and then another and then another." The initial step is to "construct an inferior enemy and use that enemy as both focus and diversion." This step is followed by "overt and coded name-calling, verbal abuse." After gathering "from among the enemy collaborators who agree with and sanitize the process of dispossession," the next step is to "pathologize the enemy" by, for example, recycling "'scientific racism' and the myth of racial superiority." The resultant criminalization of the "enemy" serves to "rationalize the building of holding arenas ... especially for the males and absolutely [for] the children. Last, maintain at all costs silence" ("Holocaust in D.C.").

9. As postmodern theories of racial formation have observed, writes Epifano San Juan, race is "'an unstable and "decentered" complex of social meanings constantly being transformed by political struggle.' ... Race can no longer be considered a fixed, ontological essence or a unitary, transcendental category predicated on the epistemological reasoning supplied by anthropology, biology, and other physical sciences. Rather it is a framework for articulating identity and difference, a process that governs the political and ideological constitution of subjects/agents in history" (7). The term "race" denotes a "social construct, a historical conceptualization of how the U.S. social formation was structured in dominance by the construction of every inhabitant as a racialized subject" (6). While "[p]ostmodern critiques of racism have decisively shifted attention away from empirical methodologies to scrutiny of the foundational assumptions of Western rationality," racism "as an ideological and political phenomenon has to be grounded first 'in the material conditions of existence,' the network of modes of production and interacting ideological and political levels" (12, 13).

Responding to the antiessentialist strain of contemporary race theory, Henry Louis Gates remarks on the "treacherous non sequitur that moves us from 'socially constructed' to essentially unreal. We typically go from 'constructed' to 'unstable,' which is one non sequitur, or to 'changeable by will' (which is a bigger problem still, given that 'will' is yet another construction)" (324). On the level of theory, Gates finds the attempt to "dismantle the scheme of differences" important: "it is important to remember that 'race' is *only* a sociopolitical category, nothing more: but it is also important to question the force of that 'only.' In its performative aspect, the proclamation of nonexistence of the Negro usually sounds like the old darky joke about the nigger in the chicken coop, denying his existence on the poultry's behalf. Spivak poses the question: can the subaltern speak? Possibly she can— but a chicken, never. We are, of course, accustomed to other tensions and disjunctions between theory and praxis. What a leading deconstructive theorist describes as 'the sense of loss of historical agency that accompanies the fragmentation of the self characteristic of social abstraction' has bred its own resistance, manifest in the claims of—indeed, in the authority of—experience. Thus Barbara Christian forcefully defends the specificity of the black woman's cultural work as a preserve both discursive and experimental ..." (325).

See also Joyce Ann Joyce's "'Who the Cap Fit'" and Diana Fuss's "'Race' Under Erasure? Poststructuralist Afro-American Literary Theory" in *Essentially Speaking* 73–96. If Morrison refers to herself as an "African-American" writer despite the claims of some that such a label is essentializing, it is also the case that a "strategic essentialism becomes an almost indispensable tool" for a writer like Morrison who wants "to speak to and about a people whose individual lives may be markedly different, but who nonetheless suffer from a common form of racial hegemony" (McBride 774).

10. "Very few African Americans of a certain generation," writes Morrison, can "forget" the description of blacks found in the Encyclopaedia Britannica's infamous eleventh edition: "'[T]he mental condition of the negro is very similar to that of a child, normally good-natured and cheerful, but subject to sudden fits of emotion ... capable of performing acts of singular atrocity ... but often exhibiting in the capacity of servant a dog-like fidelity.'" Because illogic and contradiction are understood as basic characteristics of blacks, "when race is at play the leap from one judgment (faithful dog) to its complete opposite (treacherous snake) is a trained reflex" ("Official Story" xi). In her analysis of the "block and blocked thinking of racial stereotype," Morrison similarly remarks on the opposing fictions and interchangeable racial tropes used to depict African Americans. "Without individuation, without nonracial perception, black people, as a group, are used to signify the polar opposites of love and repulsion. On the one hand, they signify benevolence, harmless and servile guardianship, and endless love. On the other hand, they have come to represent insanity, illicit sexuality, and chaos." Since these are "interchangeable fictions from a utilitarian menu," they can be "mixed and matched to suit any racial palette. Furthermore, they do not need logical transition from one set of associations to another" ("Introduction" xv).

Morrison illustrates the exchange of racial tropes that occurs in racist thinking in her discussion of the shaming public spectacle of the Senate's investigation of Anita Hill's charges against Clarence Thomas, which provided "unprecedented opportunity to hover over and to cluck at, to meditate and ponder the limits and excesses of black bodies" ("Introduction" xvii). Anita Hill's testimony that Thomas sexually harassed her, rather than initiating a search for the truth on the part of the Senate investigators, "simply produced an exchange of racial tropes." As Thomas seemed in danger of "moving from 'natural servant' to 'savage demon,'... the force of the balance of the confirmation process was to reorder these signifying fictions. Is he lying or is she? Is he the benevolent one and she the insane one? Or is he the date raper, sexual assaulter, and illegal sexual signal, and she the docile, loyal servant?" ("Introduction" xvi). The accusation of sexual misconduct would have probably disqualified a white candidate, whose suitability would have been tainted by such accusations. "[B]ut with a black candidate, already stained by the figurations of blackness as sexual aggressiveness or rapaciousness or impotence, the stain need only be proved reasonably doubted, which is to say, if he is black, how can you tell if that really is a stain? Which is also to say, blackness is itself a stain, and therefore unstainable." If, to keep the Supreme Court "stain-free," Thomas had to be "bleached, race-free," Anita Hill's allegations of sexual misconduct "re-raced" Thomas: that is, "re-stained him, dirtied him," and thus the "'dirt' that clung to him following those allegations, 'dirt' he spoke of repeatedly, must be shown to have originated elsewhere. In this case the search for the racial stain turned on Anita Hill. Her character. Her motives. Not his" ("Introduction" xviii–xix).

11. If Morrison sees her role as a writer to bear witness, the reader's role in reconstructing Morrison's narratives is not unlike that of listeners of real-life shame and trauma stories who must uncover the shameful secret and reconstruct the fragmented narrative of the trauma sufferer. Because Morrison is aware that she risks hurting—that is, vicariously shaming and traumatizing—her readers, she, not unlike the therapist-listener, must create a safe-holding environment (see Goldberg 169 and Wilson and Lindy 6, 27,

38) for her readers, enabling them to both experience and process the shame- and trauma-driven stories of her characters. While Morrison protects her readers, she also wants her readers to feel something visceral and, indeed, readers of Morrison's fiction may experience intense emotional responses through the interaffective process that psychoanalysts refer to as the "contagion of affect."

Because both shame and trauma are contagious, therapists who deal with real-life shame or trauma sufferers often report experiencing discomforting, if not painful, affects in their role as witness-listeners. They may feel vicarious shame at another's vulnerability. Listening to the story of the shame sufferer may provoke their own sense of "failure" or "self-deficiency," or they may experience a sense of "helplessness," or they may want to "turn away" from another's shame (Andrew Morrison, *Shame* 6, Nathanson, *Shame and Pride* 319, Lewis, *Shame and Guilt* 15–17). In a similar way, those who listen to the trauma story may "experience degrees of hyperarousal" proportionate to the hyperarousal manifested by the traumatized individual; or they may experience "vicarious traumatization" in which imagery associated with the trauma story intrudes into their waking fantasies or dreams; or their "sense of personal vulnerability" may be heightened and they may share the victim's "experience of helplessness" (Wilson and Lindy 17, Herman, *Trauma* 140, 141). Identifying not only with the victim's helplessness but also with his or her rage, listeners may "experience the extremes of anger, from inarticulate fury through the intermediate ranges of frustration and irritability to abstract, righteous indignation" (Herman, *Trauma* 143). And listeners may also suffer "witness" or "bystander guilt" or may identify with the victim "through the experience of profound grief" (Herman, *Trauma* 145, 144). Adding to the complexity of the witness role, the listeners may also enter into shame- and trauma-specific role enactments. Shifting and dynamic, these roles range from positive roles—those of the fellow survivor, the helpful supporter, the rescuer or comforter, the advocate—to negative ones in which listeners are positioned as collaborators or hostile judges or contemptuous shamers or even as perpetrators (see, e.g., Wilson and Lindy 62–82).

MARIA DıBATTISTA

Contentions in the House of Chloe: *Morrison's* Tar Baby

Is "Once upon a time" the oldest narrative entry into the world? So conjectures Toni Morrison in support of her belief, vigorously defended in her Nobel Laureate Address, that narrative is "one of the principal ways in which we absorb knowledge" (7). Whatever else can be inferred from such a statement, it is clearly *not* the remark of a born realist. Whoever resorts, as Morrison does in her Nobel address, to fairy tale or fable to convey her attitude toward her craft belongs to the tribe of storytellers whose imagination may feel cramped by the form of the classic realist novel, with its absolute ban on the fabulous, mythological or miraculous. Morrison's own narratives are more hospitable to the presence of other-worldly creatures, to ghosts and nature spirits, for example. Despite the fact that her books are routinely reviewed and classified as novels, one wonders, in light of the Nobel address, as august an occasion for self-definition as is likely to present itself, if Morrison even thinks of herself as primarily a novelist.

This question may strike the millions of readers who devour her books as hopelessly academic (which, of course, it is and is meant to be). Still, the popular press does not greet each new work as the newest claimant to that elusive title, the Great American Novel, but as yet another example of Morrison's credentials as the great American storyteller. As is often the case, the popular label gets at something fundamental about the nature of her art

From *The Aesthetics of Toni Morrison: Speaking the Unspeakable*, edited by Marc C. Conner. © 2000 by University Press of Mississippi.

and about the difference, often overlooked or dismissed as inconsequential, between the storyteller and the novelist. One of Walter Benjamin's most luminous essays, "The Storyteller," insists on the difference, distinguishing the storyteller, rooted in the community and customs of the oral tradition, from the novelist, the solitary creator who communicates to readers as isolated as himself (86). Even in these general, admittedly sketchy terms we can still begin to appreciate how Morrison is a storyteller before she is a novelist, a rapt teller of tales before she is a detached observer of historically entangled lives.

Much, as this essay hopes to show, hinges on this distinction for Morrison's practice as a Black American writer of fiction. The distinction is an aesthetic one, and one that has fallen out of fashion, but upon it Morrison works out the paradoxes of her talent. Foremost among them is that the historical "conscience" of her narratives is most eloquent in the registers of fantasy than in her recordings of fact. It is the fabulist, the teller of tall tales, and not the novelist in her that communicates the most painful, damning knowledge of her race and of her history. Morrison's power to appall, to call the world to account for the evil it has not yet vanquished, the good it has not yet realized, is most vividly realized through the intimacies of the morally efficient tale rather than in the sprawling, factual narratives of the loose and baggy novel. Her imaginative indictments of the real have frequently been identified as a species of "lo real maravilloso," or as it is commonly, if inaccurately, called, magical realism. This is, if nothing else, a misnomer for the way Morrison presents the real, as we commonly understand the real to entail the way things are before imagination has transformed or belied or replaced them. In Morrison's view, the primary fact about the real is its palpable unreality. There is consequently nothing marvelous about the real, only the human ability to endure and, in exceptional cases, transmute it. Her characters, whatever the sexual or class or racial differences separating them, would, if asked, probably all subscribe to the emotional protest of Valerian Street, the imperious white male of *Tar Baby*, at the painful gap between what the world is and what life should be: "'I have lived in it and I will die out of it,'" Valerian declares of his "real" existence in social space and historical time, "'but it is not the world. This is not life. This is some other thing'" (234). The conviction drives Morrison's characters to seek life elsewhere, outside the precincts of the classical, scrupulously realist novel. The novel may *dramatize* such feelings, and often does, but it may never resolve or assuage them by pretending that the world is other than what it is— materially real and historically inescapable. Morrison's fiction resists making this final admission. Her art consists in always finding—or making—that "some other thing," a life and a world elsewhere, in Richard Poirier's resonant phrase. As an imaginative writer, she will not *fully* concede to the world its undislodgeable reality. She continues to dream of a belated blossoming of the real into a humanly acceptable world, even if, as in the conclusion of *The Bluest Eye*, her characters must live with the historical intuition that for them any hopes for a future flowering come "much, much, much too late" (160).

She is not alone among contemporary novelists in seeking deliverance in both fanciful and genuinely mythopoeic forms. "The anti-myths of gravity and of belonging bear the same name: flight," claims the narrator of Salman Rushdie's *Shame*, who, with a fabulist's bravura, would defy the physical laws and human bonds that tie us to the earth (86). Such defiant anti-myths emotionally exalt Morrison's protagonists as well. Her most-cherished characters are creatures of air. Flight is the dream-narrative they carry within them, inwardly buoyed, like Milkman in *Song of Solomon*, by the "sense of lightness and power" (298) the dream of flying gives them. Novelistic persons, by contrast, are weighted by gravity, grounded in the things of the earth. The burden of history is heavy upon them. Morrison's characters feel this weight, indeed often are crushed beneath it, yet they never renounce their dream of taking to the air. Their predicament preserves the antithetical meanings of flight as one of the primal words in Morrison's vocabulary: flight as a mode of transcendence most commonly associated with the imagination, especially when it takes the exalted form of prophecy; and flight as an escapist fantasy, a desperate departure from the oppressive jurisdiction of the real.

It was Harold Bloom who first took public exception to assessing Morrison's art primarily in terms of the cultural politics that ground her in time and place. He found a deeper appeal—and truth—in her representations of "the pure madness of integrities of being that cannot sustain or bear dreadful social structures." Bloom advised us to look to the "negative magic of the romancer" to account for Morrison's strengths as "a potential strong novelist." For Bloom, such strengths are not born in ideological creeds, but originate in ancestor texts: "Literary texts emerge from other literary texts and they do not choose their forerunners" ("Introduction," *Toni Morrison*, 3–4). Perhaps not. Yet in one exceptional instance Morrison not only chose a forerunner, but demanded that we read her fiction beside and against it. The title of Morrison's fourth novel, *Tar Baby*, aligns her fiction with a folkloric, primarily oral tradition, the tradition, that is, of gregarious and credulous storytellers rather than solitary and factual novelists. *Tar Baby* is in many ways Morrison's most generically mixed work and the one that, in her own interpretation, is the most obsessed with the question of masks: "The Tar Baby tale seemed to me to be about masks. Not masks as covering what is to be hidden, but how masks come to life, take life over, exercise the tensions between itself and what it covers" ("Unspeakable Things" 30). In her brief elucidation of this idea, Morrison refers primarily to the masks assumed by her characters. But it is Morrison's authorial mask of storyteller and mythographer that concerns me here and which makes me question whether Bloom, however astute in redirecting critical attention to the aesthetic character of Morrison's fiction, is altogether precise in awarding her the palm of "strong novelist." Arguably, her imaginative potencies might lie elsewhere, a proposition that cannot be confirmed until we confront the mask through which she works out her own complicated, often troubled relation to her literary heritage and unless we are willing to accept the possibility that the mask she adopts may conceal, as masks are wont to do, a divided nature.

This may strike some readers of Morrison as a misguided, even patronizing approach to a writer-critic who shows no hesitancy, much less ambivalence in identifying herself with "the dark and abiding presence" of black Africanism in American literature, a presence she insists is indisputably "there for the literary imagination as both a visible and an invisible mediating force" (*Playing* 46). Given this attestation, perhaps there is nothing at all remarkable in her having named one of her narratives after one of the most enduring, if also one of the most discomfiting figures in Afro-American folklore. But why select the tar baby, as mute, intractable, mesmerizing and maddening a black presence as any conjured up by white writing, to serve as the visible emblem and mediating force for her own literary imagination? Even after concluding the book, it is impossible to determine whether the title is meant to be read as eponymous or symbolic, whether it designates a character—or characters—within the book or a stereotype to be faced down and repudiated. Or is the tar baby a symbol of less determinate and even more troubling meaning, and if so, does Morrison intend to make the symbol more or less disquieting?

Transparency of meaning, much less transparency of being, is, of course, what the tar baby is designed to frustrate. The tar baby ostensibly presents an image of blackness that is infantile, impassive and inert; it embodies all the negative attributes stereotypically assigned to a certain kind of Black character—outwardly unresponsive, inactive, even sullen. Such a stereotype conforms, curiously and interestingly enough, to the way Morrison will later characterize whiteness in her influential account of how the Afro-American presence proved decisive in the shaping of American literature. In *Playing in the Dark*, Morrison, after reviewing the evidence provided by such classic American works as *Moby Dick* and *Huckleberry Finn*, concludes that "if we follow through on the self-reflexive nature of these encounters with Africanism, it falls clear: images of blackness can be evil *and* protective, rebellious *and* forgiving, fearful *and* desirable—all of the self-contradictory features of the self. Whiteness, alone, is mute, meaningless, unfathomable, pointless, frozen, veiled, curtained, dreaded, senseless, implacable" (59). All these contradictory and unfathomable, but finally artistically challenging, even irresistible attributes are manifest in what Joel Chandler Harris called "The Wonderful Story of the Tar Baby." In the tale, whatever its variations, whether, that is, it is Farmer John or Brer Fox who contrives the tar baby, the nature of the encounter is unchanged. Brer Rabbit approaches the tar baby, extends a greeting, and on receiving no response becomes increasingly exasperated. He at first slaps, then punches, then wrestles with the tar baby, each movement ensnaring him ever more securely for the predator/enemy in the wings. The non-responsiveness of the tar baby makes it initially as much an object of curiosity as of pique. Why is the greeting not returned? Is silence to be understood as a personal affront or a sign of idiocy? Or is the tale meant to illustrate a more practical lesson about the superiority of guilt to instinctive or blind aggression, especially under provocation? Or does it convey a more quietist moral—one that assumes commanding ideological force in the doctrine of non-violence—that the violence born of frustration is not only self-defeating, but indeed, self-imperilling?

Such are the questions it seems natural to put to the tale, but merely to pose them is to fall into the very trap in which Brer Rabbit, normally so clever himself, was so easily, if uncharacteristically, ensnared. The tar baby is, after all, a ruse. It is endowed with a human shape to give the impression of life where none actually exists. It presents to the onlooker who happens upon it all the arresting and unnerving features of the uncanny, at once familiar and estranged. In its apparently obstinate silence, it offends against our most civilized sense of who we are and what is due to us according to the protocols of ordinary human exchange. Its silence, which we might regard as a folkloric equivalent of Bartleby's "I prefer not to," takes us outside the bounds of sociability into some dark terrain beyond the reach of normalizing speech acts. As such, it may conveniently serve as an emblem for the written work itself, which stubbornly maintains its silence before any questions we might put to it. The title, then, not only announces a subject but issues a warning. We might read this caution as follows: reach out to this enigmatic presence that solicits you with its illusion of life; struggle to grasp this mute, inglorious image of blackness put in your path; grapple with it, chasten or reshape it, but don't expect to hold or subdue or destroy it. Or else: anything that makes blackness visible, as "un-pass-byable" as the tar baby itself, has a power, however negative or dangerous, that should not be ignored or repudiated.

Such may be the monitions that lurk in Morrison's title and dictate her literary strategies. *Tar Baby*, published in 1981, appeared after a turbulent decade when Afro-Americans were not only creating new and increasingly powerful self-images, but also contesting any depiction that did not conform to their sense of how the world appeared and felt to them. What mattered was to foreground race, not expunge or sanitize its presence in social and political representations. A decade after the publication of *Tar Baby*, Morrison was to import the racialization of American popular and political culture into the sedate preserves of the American literary canon. In *Playing in the Dark*, her influential dissection of the language of race and color in American literature, Morrison proposes that "the act of enforcing racelessness in literary discourses is itself a racial act. Pouring rhetorical acid on the fingers of a black hand may indeed destroy the prints, but not the hand. Besides, what happens in that violent, self-serving act of erasure to the hands, the fingers, the fingerprints of those who do the pouring? Do they remain acid-free? The literature itself suggests otherwise" (46). This is indeed a reasonable suggestion to draw from the literature, as long as the object of rhetorical tampering is an unnatural whiteness, a bleached-out human and social reality.

But what are the literary consequences if we reverse the terms of this proposition, as Morrison seems to have done in playing with a tar baby? What if, instead of pouring rhetorical acid on her fingers, the writer suspends them in a racial emulsion? Presumably, the signature imprint of race would then, like a photographic plate or a strip of film, yield up its hidden and hitherto invisible image. Yet there is always the attendant danger of a residue sticking to the developing hand, a residue that may constitute as telling a sign of violent and self-interested encounter as any act of erasure. The image of the manipulative hand that can destroy as well as create reappears in Morrison's Nobel Lecture, where it serves as a figure for the writer's relation to language. To illustrate her conception of the writer's vocation, Morrison retells a story, one found, she claims, in several cultures, about a wise old woman, a "rural prophet" whose fame extends beyond her community to the city, where her legend "is the source of amusement." Young skeptics, bent on exposing her as a fraud, approach her with a question they believe that, given her blindness, she will not be able to answer: "'Old woman, I hold in my hand a bird. Tell me whether it is living or dead.'" She does not answer at first, bringing her interlocutors to the brink of laughter, but at last delivers her Solomonic judgment: "'I don't know whether the bird you are holding is dead or alive, but what I do know is that it is in your hands'" (10–11).

The meaning Morrison herself chooses to read into this fable is that the bird represents language and the clairvoyant old woman the "practiced writer" embedded in a venerable, but endangered tradition. I have no quarrel with this reading, which allows Morrison to remind us of the many ways language can die: "out of carelessness, disuse, indifference, and absence of esteem, or killed by fiat" (14). Yet what detains me is the distinction hovering at the edges of her fable between what we might call the writer's custodial hand, which cherishes and protects the cultural lore entrusted to its keeping, and the manipulative hand that, concerned only with asserting its own power, suffocates the living language within its deadly grasp. Interpreted in light of this recurrent imagery of manipulation, the tar baby suddenly reveals itself as a race-specific emblem for the black artist's ambiguous relation to black matter—black culture, black history and black story, especially the unspeakable and unspoken story that will not be told until *Beloved*, a story that possibly could not be told until Morrison herself had survived her own encounter with the tar baby put in her path.

In assessing the validity of reading *Tar Baby* as a cautionary tale about the risks inherent in black writing, subjective and objective genitive, we might consider Morrison's own interpretation of the tale. "It was," she remembers thinking, "a rather complicated story with a funny happy ending about the triumph of cunning over law, of wit over authority, of weakness over power." This reading, while granting the story's complicated morality, immediately disposes of any troublesome after-thoughts about the "funny happy ending" by supplying the appropriate moral: the story celebrates the triumph of cunning over law, wit over authority, weakness over power. This is a plausible, if somewhat tidy account of how the denouement works on our moral sensibility, yet it fails signally to satisfy the one person most invested in it—Morrison herself. As she later confides, the story continued to worry her, a worry linked to the uncanniness of the aesthetic object: "Why did the extraordinary solution the farmer came up with to trap the rabbit involve tar? Why was the rabbit's sole area of vulnerability having good manners? Why did the tar baby's silent complicity seem to me at once natural and obscene? Of the two views of the Brier Patch, the farmer's and the rabbit's, which was right? Why did it all seem so contemporary and, more to the point, so foreboding?" (quoted in O'Meally, "Tar Baby" 36). In eliciting the contemporary resonance of the tale, Morrison knew she would be resuscitating its foreboding elements as well. These forebodings appear to be connected to her sense of the way the story questions the moral good of good manners, rendering it vulnerable to an impolite silence that is at once natural and obscene. Yet why should an act of discourtesy inspire such hysterical reaction on the part of the rabbit and such writerly distress, amounting to a dark foreboding, in Morrison? There hardly seems to be much matter for unnerving concern, unless we take into account Morrison's own relation to the story.

Morrison figures this relation in a gesture that falls far beneath Brer's Rabbit's impatient, chastising cuff. "I did not retell that story," Morrison confided. "And needless to say, I did not improve it. I fondled it, scratched and pressed it with my fingertips as one does the head and spine of a favorite cat—to get at the secret of its structure without disturbing its mystery" (quoted in O'Meally, "Tar Baby," 36). Here the writerly hand is not depicted pouring acid on its materials, but gently pressuring its valued object to surrender its secret. Importantly, the secret of the tale must be coaxed rather than dragged forth to ensure that its core mystery is left intact. The enigma of the tale must be deciphered, but not demystified, a rather neat, but, for Morrison, an essential distinction. With such hermeneutic dexterity, Milkman decodes the children's playground song in which is encrypted the story of his ancestry, without disturbing its power to enchant. Such reverence for occult realities dictates Morrison's approach to the mythological and folkloric material. Her narratives appeal to the numinous registers of fable for enlightenment, for a salivific meaning not to be found in the demythologized world of everyday life, the world, that is, represented most scrupulously by the novel. Rather than strike at an elusive, even offending mystery (as Ahab contemplated striking the sun if it dared insult him) into forced counter-response, Morrison strokes and caresses it. What she does not do is address it from a safe distance. Contact, with all the risk of entanglement, even soilage that might entail, is the only envisioned course. But why take these risks or hazard such contaminations?

The opening sentence of *Tar Baby*—"He believed he was safe"— suggests one possible motive. Morrison may simply feel that safety in any case is impossible and, as we shall see, ignoble to boot. In her own commentary on the beginning of this work, she relates how she carefully set the verb "believed" within an anapestic rhythm to produce the desired, but deceptive effect of existential as well as metric stability. "If I had wanted the reader to trust this person's point of view," she writes, "I would have written 'was safe.' Or, 'Finally, he was safe.' The unease about this view of safety is important because safety itself is the desire of each person in the novel. Locating it, creating, it losing" ("Unspeakable Things" 30). To this inventory of those made uneasy by the prospect of locating, creating or losing safety we must add Morrison herself.

This, too, the opening pages of the narrative make clear in a near-paroxysm of narrative unease. The book commences with a nameless figure plunging into the sea believing that he can master its currents, gain the shore, and with it, his freedom. But it is no ordinary sea to which he commits himself. Everywhere there are symbolic signs that a romancer, not a naturalist, is imagining a world for him to navigate. Even the signatories of the made human world are imbued with a romantic luster: the ship from which he dives bears the regal name Konigsgaarten, the king of the seas, and the port town that awaits its docking is Queen of France. It is the first image of potential, perhaps predestinated mating in a book whose last, hallucinatory image of coupling is the marriage flight of a queen soldier ant and her chosen consort, "the man who fucked like a star" (292). Novelistic descriptions of human love-making, even of the most passionate order, cannot hope to compete with such stellar instances of sexual transport. Contributing to the exciting sense of romantic ordeal is the swimmer's encounter with the "water-lady" whose insistent hand "was forcing him away from the shore": "[she] cupped him in the palm of her hand, and nudged him out to sea" (5). Morrison again figures authorial power—here her own power as a "negative romancer"—in the image of the intruding and intervening hand. In this instance, however, the fateful hand is acting upon and within a primordial environment in which race is not yet an issue. Blackness is the color of the sea or of the night sky, a temporary if spectacular coloration, not an indelible racial marker. The water-lady and her sheltering, but insistent hand is the narrative delegate for Morrison's own romance proclivities. In and through her, she enjoys trying her own writerly hand at recounting one of those thrilling sea-adventures that, since the days of Odysseus, challenge the storyteller, schooled in tradition, to exercise his ingenuity. Yet generically as well as episodically speaking, the swimmer's safety is never seriously threatened by the hand of a water-lady or the female romancer she might personify as author. The only real peril he encounters takes the form of an impersonal natural force. Caught in its grip, the swimmer is "down, down and found himself not at the bottom of the sea, as he expected, but whirling in a vortex. He thought nothing except, I am going counterclockwise. No sooner had he completed the thought than the sea flattened and he was riding its top" (4).

Riding can take on the dimensions of mythological feat in Morrison's fiction—one remembers the eerie last line of *Song of Solomon* celebrating the shamanistic knowledge that inspires Milkman's suicidal leap: "If you surrendered to the air, you could *ride* it" (337). Surviving the downward thrust of the whirlpool thus delivers the fugitive not only from a treacherous

natural phenomenon but from a literary hazard—the vortex of realism, we
might call it. Milkman refuses to be engulfed by it, demonstrating an
imaginative as well as physical courage that Morrison, his creator, apparently
affirms. This aspect of her narrative desire to defy the tenets, indeed the
physical laws which realism is bound to honor, is epitomized in the figure of
the water-lady, who presumably desires to prevent the swimmer from
reaching shore. Once grounded in the verisimilar world, he might find safety,
but *her* existence would be imperilled, deprecated as the insubstantial stuff of
fable. The water-lady wants to detain him "at sea," captive to the world of
romance. The vortex which competes for his life is an antagonist force that
cannot be so fancifully personified. Its eddies are formed by commingling
currents of physical facts; at their center is a vacuum in which fantasy and
dream may find room to circulate, but no safe, permanent quarter. This the
nameless fugitive subliminally apprehends. What saves him from such an
engulfing physical realism is not a supernatural agent, but a reflex of his own
observing consciousness. Completing the thought—or, to be accurate,
impersonally remarking his own movement—seems to work as a counter-
charm to the spiraling downward motion. This moment of self-
objectification *rhetorically* delivers him to the surface, where he will
eventually make his way to a shore which at first he cannot see, which is just
as well, advises the narrator, fond of both legend and irony, "because he was
gazing at the shore of an island that, three hundred years ago, had stuck
slaves blind the moment they saw it" (8).

The race descended from these slaves still roams the island, which
bears the name, Isle of Chevaliers, after their own uncanny power of riding
"through the rain forest avoiding all sorts of trees and things" (152–53). Such
is the "fisherman's tale" that is later recounted to the fugitive about the
legendary race of blind horsemen who will call out to him in the last pages
of the book. His informant also tells him that "Personally I think the
blindness comes from second-degree syphilis" (153). But in Morrison's
fiction, science is generally ineffectual in challenging the knowledge—and
solace—offered by fable. "Realistic" explanations of the world do not deter
her imaginative (hence most beloved) characters from taking flight into the
dream territories that shimmer, like a mirage, beyond the horizons of the
Real. The book will end with the fugitive running "Lickety split. Lickety-
split. Lickety-lickety-lickety-split" to join those blind chevaliers who "race
those horses like angels all over the hills" (306). In rhythmic homage to Brer
Rabbit's high-tailing it out of danger, Morrison elects to return her fiction to
the idiom as well as the realm of folktale. A book that begins with an
empowering, if morally questionable belief in safety thus concludes with a

final scramble into myth and the legendary community one might find there. Morrison has commented on this symmetry in a manner that interests us. The close of the book, she points out, entails the "wide and marvelous space between the contradiction of those two images: from a dream of safety to the sound of running feet. The whole mediated world in between" ("Unspeakable Things" 31).

The "whole mediated world in between" I take to refer to the province of the novel and it is clear by the ending of this, as of many of her works, that Morrison is not ready to settle down there. The novel for her is a space for imaginative transit, never a final destination. The prosaic world does not inspire her deepest loyalty, although it necessarily commands her respect and quite often her most hilarious as well as most heart-breaking satire. As a novel about the prosaic world, *Tar Baby* can only be said to begin at the point numerically and typographically marked with a 1, consigning the previous narrative to prologue or antechamber to the main structure of the narrative. The opening sentence of this new chapter confirms the necessity for imaginative re-orientation: "The end of the world, as it turned out, was nothing more than a collection of magnificent winter houses on Isle des Chevaliers" (9). Nothing is more efficient in Morrison's rhetorical arsenal for demolishing the empire of fancy than the corrective force of that knowing, almost patronizing phrase—"as it turned out." It summarily chastises any extravagant imaginings with the incontrovertible evidence of facts—like names and places that have a specific provenance in time. But it also must be said that there is a fine disdain for the wealth of material facts the novel may offer in the way the narrator dismisses a collection of magnificent winter homes as a mere "nothing" compared to the wonderlands fancy can conjure.

The characters who inhabit these novelistic environs are neither the archetypal adventurers of romance, nor the dispossessed sons or mistreated daughters of fable and fairy tale. They are the settled members of a household presided over by Valerian Street, heir to a candy fortune who has retired to the Isle de Chevaliers. They live in a "'handsomely articulated and blessedly unrhetorical house'" (11) whose name, L'Arbre de la Croix, suggests that Valerian's refuge will soon, if it has not already, become his Golgotha. In this house are congregated the principal players of Morrison's interracial drama: Valerian the patriarch, his wife Margaret, the former beauty queen (or Principal Beauty as she is sarcastically called), their black servants Sydney and Ondine, "Philadelphia Negroes" of correct deportment, and their niece Jade, whose education Valerian has sponsored. There is also a resident "ghost" in the family ensemble, the Street's son Michael. Around him Morrison accumulates all the novelistic lore of social activism that links

Tar Baby to a certain historical era—to the days of Dick Gregory for President, of agitation for Indian rights and the return to a barter rather than free market economy.

It is into this household that the fugitive intrudes, bearing with him all the explosive power of romance. Morrison arranges for him a somewhat comical, if suspenseful entry. Margaret, determined to resolve a dispute with her husband, goes to her room to look for a poem, but instead discovers a black man hiding in her closet. Sydney, with the aid of .32 caliber pistol, escorts him to the dining room where the family is assembled, while Ondine volunteers to call the Harbor police. Everyone reacts with proper alarm, except Valerian, who cordially greets his "guest" and asks him if he cares to have a drink. Valerian's welcoming gesture catapults us into a novel of Faulknerian outrage. The women are outraged at the offense to their womanhood (which has been affrighted); Sydney and Ondine, who have never been invited to share the table with Valerian and Margaret, are outraged at the discourtesy to themselves. Later Valerian will compound the offense to domestic propriety by christening the fugitive-intruder Son, a name that signifies his symbolic rather than biological place in Valerian's affections.

Only belatedly do we come to know that the black man has a name, William Green, and that he comes equipped with a decidedly "novelistic" history—childhood memories, a broken marriage, a nomadic life as an "undocumented man" in "an international legion of day laborers and musclemen, gamblers, sidewalk merchants, migrants, unlicensed crewmen on ships with volatile cargo, part-time mercenaries, full-time gigolos, or curbside musicians" (166). Had Morrison made *this* derelict life the center of her novel, Green might well have found himself the protagonist of a naturalist novel in the Dreiserian mode. But she made a Caribbean Isle, not the grimy backstreets of port towns or the crowded alleyways of third-world bazaars the setting of her story. It is in a landscape hospitable to myth that she confers this novelistic identity upon him, as if to see if it will survive there or revert to some other, more primordial state of being. We can gauge his progress—or regress, as the case may be—simply by noting the names that define him at any given time in the narrative, whose human relations are coded, as it were, by the presence or absence of color. Morrison enjoys scrambling colors in her racial palette, especially in this novel where red, white, green, yellow, and of course black stand as primary signatures of character as well as indices of social status. Naming her lovers Green and Jade, for example, hints at a complementariness that sexually draws them to each other despite the vast difference in class, education, and experience separating them.

The courtship of Jade and Son will proceed in counterpoint to the emotional disintegration of the House of Valerian. Two narrative tracks are thus laid, as it were, side by side, sometimes crossing and bisecting each other, but bound for separate narrative destinations. Let us consider first the "novelistic" trajectory. By the book's novelistic but not literal end, the moral compromises and self-flattering, exculpatory fictions that have kept the Valerian household emotionally solvent are liquidated in a veritable orgy of truth-telling. This family plot is thus put in the service of the reality principle. It seeks out social and personal truth in its most unpalatable, but also most undeniable form. To do this it must vanquish the human disposition to replace unbearable reality with fantasy-anodynes, a disposition symbolized by Valerian's name, whose family name, Street, comments ironically on any personal fancies he might entertain to disguise the truth of his life. Street is a rather common thoroughfare—as compared, say, to the more aristocratic boulevard or avenue. Valerian bespeaks of aristocratic, even imperial pretensions, and indeed Valerian prides himself in being named after a Roman Emperor. But the name Valerian also possesses a more ambiguous, even sinister significance. Valerian is a plant form with spiky flowers from whose roots is derived a sedative and anti-spasmodic. Sedation appears to be one of its "true and ancient properties," to invoke the standard Morrison adopts in dedicating the novel to her female progenitors and relations.

This dedication is worth pausing over, since within it is secreted the moral by which the fiction and its characters will be called to account: "Mrs. Caroline Smith, Mrs. Millie McTyeire, Mrs. Ardelia Willis, Mrs. Ramah Wofford, and Mrs. Lois Brooks—and each of their sisters, all of whom knew their true and ancient properties." Unlike *Song of Solomon*, which bears the singular and intimate dedication, Daddy, *Tar Baby* pays homage to an entire line of female forbears. How uncompromisingly historical is that catalogue of names, particularly striking given Morrison's belief in the demiurgic power of names. These names are culled from the unremarkable ledgers of daily life. You might find such names in a phone book, where I suspect, some of them might still be found. What distinguishes these women is not the symbolic import of their names, but the knowledge they possess and preserve in the form of "ancient properties." This collective inheritance is at once evoked and jeopardized by the epigraph that succeeds and complements the dedication, take from First Corinthians 1:11: "For it hath been declared unto me of you, my brethren by them which are of the house of Chloe, that there are contentions among you." Paul's admonition carries with it an entreaty to end division, and a way of attaining that end: "Now I beseech you, brethren, by the name of our Lord Jesus Christ, that ye all speak the same thing; and that there be no divisions among you; but that ye be perfectly joined together in the same mind and in the same judgment." Paul, voicing a millenarian ideal of spiritual accord, summons us to a heavenly community in which we all will be of the same mind, share the same judgment and so speak the same things. But the novel is a dialogic form that gives expression to different minds and utters diverse judgements on the things of this world. The novel's generic obligation to render unto Caesar everything that is Caesar's, to render, that is, the material and historical world with impartiality, may explain why Morrison, for whom First Corinthians is a formative "precursor" text, regards the novelistic inheritance as spiritually inadequate to her needs. No matter how bleak the story she has to tell, the history she must relate, she never loses faith in this Pauline vision of a spirit and a community perfected through love.

But if the dedication and epigraph announces the spiritual disposition of the narrative that follows, it also declares a personal lineage. The author who now bears the name of Toni Morrison was born Chloe Anthony Wofford, a name she changed to Toni during her years at Howard, and to Morrison in 1958 upon her marriage. Reading *back* into the dedication through the epigraph, we see Morrison reclaiming her ancestral house, publicly honoring the female clan from which she descends and whose enduring, formal existence we might recognize under the name of the House of Chloe. This is the only instance I know of in Morrison's writings where her given name is read as a prophetic signature in the Joycean mode, reconnecting her, as Stephen Dedalus's name links him to the artificers of old, to her true and ancient properties. Among these we must reckon the true and ancient properties of storytelling.

Tar Baby, like many of Morrison's fictions, is filled with storytellers who act as her surrogates. They devise or invent stories in order to make sense of the world; for them narrative truly functions, as Morrison puts it in her Nobel Address, as a form of knowledge. But the sense they make may not always *make* sense. Narrative may be a way of knowing, but making up stories can as easily occlude as disclose the truth about things. "You making up a life that nobody is living," Sydney reprimands Ondine when she begins to tell her version of why Michael will never return, as his mother expects, for Christmas (36). Or sometimes the sheer inventiveness of the storyteller can exhaust the resources of a language, and hence obliterate any way of determining what is fact, what invention, what an outright falsehood. Thus Thérèse, a blind, shamanistic old woman not unlike the one Morrison celebrates in her Laureate address, fabricates a story about Son and Jade rooted in the belief that Son is a horseman descended from the hills, a story whose every detail departs further and further from the truth: "The more she invented the more she rocked and the more she rocked the more her English crumbled till finally it became dust in her mouth stopping the flow of her imagination and she spat it out altogether and let the story shimmer through the clear cascade of the French of Dominique" (108). Untranslated and perhaps untranslatable, Thérèse's story can convince and instruct no-one. Its shimmering form fails to grasp or arrest an image of truth: whatever wisdom she possesses is drowned in the cascade of her invention, which dazzles but does not enlighten.

Morrison's own instincts about how best to tell a story and coax forth the secret of its structure represent a modification and refinement of the survival instinct manifest in the fugitive's talent for fashioning a story to suit his audience: "The sex, weight and demeanor of whomever he encountered would inform and determine his tale" (5). Morrison pays tribute here to storytelling as an invaluable human resource for the defenseless or disadvantaged—tales can function as survival narratives, securing our safety by enlisting the listener on our behalf. The personal proximity the storyteller enjoys, the proximity that skill can turn into valuable intimacy, is unavailable to the novelist. Moreover, the tale the novelist has to tell is embedded in a reality that may not be so easily altered to suit the audience and occasions of its telling. For there is another instinct at work in the novelist even more powerful than the instinct to survive, an instinct whose vicissitudes deeply concern Morrison. She alludes to it in a particularly stark moment in the narrative when Valerian Street finally is told the reason why, in his childhood, his son Michael had hidden under the sink: "The instinct of kings was always to slay the messenger, and they were right. A real messenger, a worthy one, is corrupted by the message he brings. And if he is noble he should accept that corruption" (243).

This remark falls under the convention of authorial commentary, but in this instance the observation seems to refer less to the events within the narrative than to the author's attitude toward her material and her mission as a truth-teller. This may be why this thought is expressed as a maxim, a proverbial truth not so much about the historical fate of royal messengers as the likely fate awaiting that truth-teller, the novelist. It is as a novelist, not as a storyteller, that Morrison recounts the corrupting message that Valerian does not want to hear—how his young wife, despite her protestations that "I am not one of those women in the *National Enquirer*," abused their young son ("you stuck pins in his behind. You burned him with cigarettes") (209). That the *National Enquirer* might be seen as a rival, or at least a consumer, of the *kinds* of horror that Morrison recounts suggests how extensive the perceived threat of "corruption" can be. The family history of child abuse in the Valerian household and the sensational story of how Son accidentally murdered his wife, caught in a liaison with a teenage boy, are fodder for tabloid mentalities. Morrison writes in the tradition of Faulknerian outrage, understanding, as Faulkner did, how uncomfortably and often comically close are the tales and the rhetoric of the sensationalist press and their chosen style of novelistic reportage. It is a style adapted to the conditions of life in the Gothic and grotesque landscapes of dream and dementia, the style of history's losers and victims. For Morrison, as I have argued, this understanding of possible contagion is figured in the image of the authorial hand immersing itself in such "dark" material that it may itself become stained, hopelessly entangled in the evil it reports. Being a messenger, then, means being corrupted by the message that no-one wants to hear.

Morrison displays her fearlessness, some might say her disregard for credibility, in dramatizing her divided artistic allegiances in a scene which involves both an allegorical and real encounter with tar. Jade, the most "novelistic," cosmopolitan character in the novel, at home in Paris and New York and having no relation to Nature except as a pleasure ground, wanders off the road where her car has stalled and suddenly finds herself in a bog, up to her knees in tar. Jade, who will later be called a "tar baby" by Son, is here experiencing the panic of a female Brer Rabbit. What assails her is not the materiality of tar, but the reality of blackness that her own light-colored skin has allowed her to avoid. We first come to know Jade "psychologically" through a recurrent dream. In the dream she relives an uncanny moment in a Paris supermarket when a splendid black woman with skin the color of tar, carrying three eggs, catches Jade in her gaze and then directs a stream of spit at her feet. The egg-bearing "woman's woman—that mother/sister/she" (46)—transports Jade to some primordial realm of femaleness located "at the edge of the world."

Son, too, thought he had glimpsed some dreamscape at the "end of the world" where he might make a home. But unlike him, Jade is not a creature responsive to the lure of supermundane beings and their apocalyptic ultimates. She is a "character" in a novel who finds the very idea of such a woman and such a world repugnant, if mesmerizing. She is continually haunted by spectral women fingering eggs and baring their milk-giving breasts, but none will be as insistent as the forest-women who regard her, at first desirously, then reproachfully, as she struggles to liberate herself from tar:

The young tree sighed and swayed. The women looked down from the rafters of the trees and stopped murmuring. They were delighted when they first saw her, thinking a runaway child had been restored to them. But upon looking closer they saw differently. This girl was fighting to get away from them. The women hanging from the trees were quiet now, but arrogant—mindful as they were of their value, their exceptional femaleness; knowing as they did that the first world of the world had been built with their sacred properties; that they alone could hold together the stones of the pyramids and the rushes of Moses's crib; knowing their steady consistency, their pace of glaciers, their permanent embrace, they wondered at the girl's desperate struggle down below to be free, to be other than they were. (183)

Jade, schooled to live in the metropolitan world, takes flight *from* this elemental, antediluvian first world of the world, this world of exceptional femaleness, all breasts and eggs. There is something grotesquely comic in Morrison's flagrant sexual symbolism here, which makes us sympathize with Jade's disgust with the local culture of female necromancy (a culture that shares the dark humor that often infuses folktale, like naming a swamp *Sein de Vieilles*). What detains us in this gynocratic phantasmagoria is the talismanic phrase "sacred properties," which emotionally reconnects us to the women cited in the book's dedication. We cannot dismiss the implication that Morrison herself is the legatee destined to receive and in her turn transmit custodianship of those ancient properties, the well-spring of the first stories told of the world, from the saga of pyramids built by slaves to the divine story of Moses found in the bulrushes.

For Morrison these properties signify and ensure the endurance of tradition—consistency, change that is non-convulsive, but deeply considered and steadily pursued. Of these, the most important as well as most difficult for Morrison to remember is the *glacial pace* by which human life and human culture should be advanced. Temperamentally, she is kin to Thérèse and prefers a cascade of invention to the glacial and stately tread mandated by tradition. She is more likely to break into a narrative run, lickety-split, lickety-split, than retard the momentum of the stories that are spilling out of her brain. Two kinds of exceptional femaleness are brought together in this passage, and in their encounter we might detect the figure of Morrison the storyteller, imaginatively at home in the elemental world of myth, confronting Morrison the truth-teller, who must, like Jade, make her living, even if it corrupts her, in the mediated world.

In *Tar Baby* the contention between these two narrative selves is never completely resolved. Perhaps this is the why the narrative concludes not with a celebration of female properties, but with the cheering on of a "certain kind of man," in the hope, perhaps, that he will find a way out of the impasse in which Morrison has landed him. This is how Morrison understands him:

> He was dwelling on his solitude, rocking the wind, adrift. A man without human rites: unbaptized, uncircumcised, minus puberty rites or the formal rites of manhood. Unmarried and undivorced. He attended no funeral, married in no church, raised no child. Propertyless, homeless, sought for but not after. There were no grades given in his school, so how could he know when he had passed? He used to want to go down in blue water, down, down, then to rise and burst from the waves to see before him a single hard surface, a heavy thing, but intricate. He would enclose it, conquer it, for he knew his power then. And it was perhaps because the world knew it too that it did not consider him able. The conflict between knowing his power and the world's opinion of it secluded him, made him unilateral. But he had chosen solitude and the company of other solitary people—opted for it when everybody else had long ago surrendered, because he never wanted to live in the world their way. There was something wrong with the rites. He had wanted another way. Some other way of being in the world.... (165–66)

Such a man may rightly expect to be welcomed among the blind chevaliers who live beyond the reach of any human laws, customs or rites. It is, I suppose, one way of being in the world and one way of defying, like Milkman, the unbearable gravity of being.

But it is not the way of being in the world of the novel, which encompasses multilateral, not singular humanity. Morrison is drawn to such unilateral beings, those isolatoes that populate American romances, who carry within them the seeds of some primordial maleness, the generative power celebrated in *Song of Solomon*. But the exhilaration in recovering a lost patrimony that exalts that fiction at its end becomes muted in her succeeding work. *Tar Baby*, indeed, occupies a problematic place in Morrison's career, interposing between the patriarchal exaltation of *Song of Solomon* and the maternal pathos of *Beloved*. At its conclusion, its lovers are in flight, Jade taking to the air, Son to the hills. We gather, then, that contentions still persist in the House of Chloe. Yet with this knowledge comes a compensatory vision, a vision granted us at a certain point in the narrative, a point of rest and contemplation in which Morrison instructs as follows:

> At some point in life the world's beauty becomes enough. You don't need to photograph, paint or even remember it. It is enough. No record of it needs to be kept and you don't need someone to share it with or tell it to. When that happens—that letting go—you let go because you can. The world will always be there—while you sleep it will be there—when you wake it will be there as well. So you can sleep and there is reason to wake. A dead hydrangea is as *intricate* and lovely as one in bloom. Bleak sky is as seductive as sunshine, miniature orange trees without blossom or fruit are not defective; they are that. (242, emphasis added)

This is the only purely aesthetic sentiment expressed in *Tar Baby*, and certainly the most serene expression of Morrison's lyricism. It surfaces unexpectedly, like a sudden infusion of grace, in the midst of a series of moral reckonings: Margaret, the monster-mother begging Ondine for forgiveness and friendship; Valerian indicting himself for the "crime of innocence" that makes him "inhuman and therefore unworthy" (241, 243). The oddity of this moment cannot be minimized. The things of this world are perceived for what they are rather than for what they might signify and what they are, it turns out, is beautiful. Beautiful and *intricate* ... one last time, at least in this essay, we encounter a trope of entanglement and perplexity. The world will always be there to enchant and ensnare us—this is the humbling truth subtending Morrison's storytelling art—and its strange consolation.

Strange, because such a vision seems hardly supportable, given the history of the world, and indeed for Morrison, most often it is not. Morrison, of course, has shown herself in her writing to be uncommonly sensitive to the sheer gorgeousness of the language of pain and contention, as reported in the House of Chloe. But she is equally haunted by the Pauline judgment that the world is subject to perpetual indictment for the very qualities—loveliness and intricacy—that appeal to the artist in her. Another storyteller-novelist tormented by similar self-divisions, Salman Rushdie, poses the same quandary in *The Moor's Last Sigh*. "How to forgive the world for its beauty," a Mephistopholean-inquisitor demands to know at the close of the Moor's long journey into art, "which merely disguises its ugliness; for its gentleness, which merely cloaks its cruelty; for its illusion of continuing, seamlessly, as the night follows the day, so to speak—whereas in reality life is a series of brutal ruptures, falling upon our defenseless heads like the blows of a woodsman's axe?" (391). How indeed? Rhetorically as substantially, the argument remains unsettled. But the arraignment of the world as a place of insidious beauty and treacherous illusion could not have been so forcefully, so vividly made without Rushdie's final simile of the woodsman's axe. It is to fable and fairy tale that we must look to understand, indeed to bear, the mortal blows that life rains upon us.

So we conclude, then, as we begun, by meditating on the kind of knowledge to be found in fable, where the woodsman's axe still falls with deadly authority. We know that there will be contentions among us—the House of Chloe issues bulletins to that effect. We suspect to the point of certainty that the romancer in Morrison, always poised for flight, and the novelist in her, mired in the corruptions of truth, will continue to struggle for mastery over the Real. Yet for readers of Morrison, incapable, as Morrison's imaginary creatures are, of taking flight lickety-split into folktale and myth, there is comfort in knowing that the world is not cursed, only intricate. Certainly Morrison appears to find solace in reaching that point in her art when she can let go, relax her grip and admit, without bitterness, that the world will always be there. In such moments of respite and reprieve, when the world is apprehended as merely but *fully* there, its beauty sufficient to our needs, the romancer and the novelist in Morrison, seem, however impermanently, reconciled. The denunciatory force of Morrison's social representations are not so much opposed, but consumed in such moments of harmony. These are the times of concord in the House of Chloe, when all, if only for a brief while, are of the same mind and judgment.

MICHAEL WOOD

Sensations of Loss

"The language of a novel is the system of its 'languages.'"
—M.M. Bakhtin, *The Dialogic Imagination*

One of the most striking features of Toni Morrison's fiction is the brilliance of its apparently casual, often bleak insights; what it knows without seeming to know at all. "The neighbors seemed pleased when the babies smothered.... They did all the right things, of course: brought food, telephoned their sorrow, got up a collection; but the shine of excitement in their eyes was clear" (*Paradise* 21). The reporter who interviews the mother of the smothered babies is sympathetic, her eyes are "soft"; "but the shine was like that of the neighbors" (22).

Sometimes, especially in the earlier novels, these insights are discreetly highlighted as authorial knowledge, and in *Jazz* they are given to an identifiable female narrator, who is always shrewd and entertaining but sometimes wrong. Most often, though, the insights are closely aligned with particular characters. In these cases there is no authorial knowledge, we might say, or there are several knowledges. The author knows only what her characters know, and they know different, contradictory things. The narrative voice is steady, ample, eloquent, recognizably Morrison's own; but what it says comes from marked places within the fiction, articulating what is seen along quite different lines of sight. This effect is allowed its furthest,

From *The Aesthetics of Toni Morrison: Speaking the Unspeakable*, edited by Marc C. Conner. © 2000 by University Press of Mississippi.

most difficult development in *Paradise*, and an understanding of how it works there will teach us a good deal about the density of the novel's argument about race, the complexity of its meditation on history, and the deep ambiguities generated by the dead and living bodies of its multiple conclusions. My suggestion is that in *Paradise* Morrison not only re-enacts, by example, the questions raised by the emergence of competing knowledges, but also refigures knowledge itself in the light of what fiction can and cannot do; construes knowledge as a dialogue between canceled and continuing possibilities.

Who knows about the neighbors' and the reporter's excitement about the smothered babies, for example? Who sees the shine in their eyes, to whose perception do they "seem" pleased? An omniscient narrator would not need to report appearances in this way, and the mother of the dead children is too bewildered and distraught to reach for these interpretations. Too inarticulate to formulate them at any time, perhaps, but the feelings can only be hers, she is guiding us here. She is doing the seeing, even if she is not conscious of it; Morrison has lent her the shape and lucidity of the sentences. This is not an unusual or original technique—it is much used in Flaubert, Faulkner, Woolf, Henry James, and García Márquez—but I think its reach and its delicacy have been underestimated. We seem to be much more comfortable with intense and plausible impersonations of character or a declared ironic distance from them. We are also more comfortable with various versions of *style indirect libre*, where the author/narrator ironically, unobtrusively borrows the tone and language of a character. Morrison uses this method too, but it is at its most interesting when it starts to slide back toward the other one.

"God at their side, the men take aim" (18). These men are murdering women the way earlier generations burned witches, and for similar reasons, so the narrator cannot be telling us they really had God at their side. If the men are likely to have said to themselves that God is at their side—and some of them are—then this is a moment of *style indirect libre*. If the men are likely to have felt a mixture of excitement and fear and outraged virtue, but to have lacked an image with which to represent and cancel these feelings—as most of them probably did—we are back with a narrator who finds language for feelings which are not hers, but which are there in the fiction, waiting to be named. There are nine men involved, so it is appropriate for a range of meanings to lurk in the single simple phrase.

Commentators tend to agree about the attributes of Morrison's style, even when they disagree about whether they like it or not. When Jill Mathus writes of a "rich and startling lyricism" (156), and Henry Louis Gates and

Anthony Appiah evoke "a densely lyrical narrative texture that is instantly recognizable" (xi), they are being complimentary about what James Wood sees as a problem of purple prose (236–45). Phrases taken in isolation may incline us to Wood's view, but the issue of taste is immediately complicated by other issues, and I want to look at the question from the reverse side: not how Morrison speaks for her characters but how they speak through her and if they speak through her. What happens when the lyricism, like the knowledge, is theirs rather than hers? And when it is not?

> Mile after mile rolled by urged and eased by the gorgeous ache in Bennie's voice. (35)

> Somewhere in the house the child continued to cry, filling Sweetie with rapture—she had never heard that sound from her own. Never heard that clear yearning call, sustained, rhythmic. It was like an anthem, a lullaby, or the bracing chords of the decalogue. (129–30)

> The wind soughed as though trying to dislodge sequins from the black crepe sky. Lilac bushes swished the side of the house. (190)

> She entered the vice like a censored poet whose suspect lexicon was too supple, too shocking to punish. (261)

> September marched through smearing everything with oil paint: acres of caradamom yellow, burnt orange, miles of sienna, blue ravines both cerulean and midnight, along with heartbreakingly violet skies. (232)

These five quotations picture the worlds and feelings and activities of five different women. The first is Mavis, the mother of the smothered children, who has run away from the rest of her family and is on the road, driving west. Bennie is a hitchhiker who sings all the time: "Songs of true love, false love, redemption; songs of unreasonable joy.... Mavis sang along once in a while, but mostly she listened..." (34). The "gorgeous ache" is not what Bennie's voice possesses, or not necessarily. It is what Mavis hears in it, what Mavis misses when Bennie is gone. More precisely, it is what Mavis would call it if she had such words. It is a name for what she cannot name, the sound of an experience turning into a regret, an absence. Of course there may be an ache behind the ache in Bennie's voice, the force of Bennie's own real pain, but the adjective "gorgeous" pulls us emphatically away from that.

The second woman is Sweetie, mother of four extremely sick children, who seem never to have had a moment's health. Her own mind is stretched to the breaking point by weariness and worry, and she has walked away from her house into the wind and snow. She sees the girl who tries to help her as a personification of Sin, and the women who take her in as hawks and demons. The child she hears crying is either a product of her own imagination—released from sickness into temporary madness she hears the sound of health—or one of Mavis's dead children, who have been haunting the house since Mavis arrived. Either way the yearning is Sweetie's, rather than that of the child, and the images offered to us—anthem, lullaby, decalogue—all come from her emotional world, if not from her vocabulary.

The third woman is Patricia, schoolteacher and amateur historian. Troubled by all she knows and suspects, she opens her window and looks out across the yard towards her mother's grave. The soughing wind and the sequins are her metaphors—slightly old-fashioned, a literary consolation which cannot quite console, as if Patricia had quoted a poem which does not cheer her up as much as she thought it would.

The fourth woman is Seneca, the girl who seeks to help Sweetie, and who finds her own consolation and distraction in cutting herself repeatedly, obsessively. Here the simile—even the word "vice"—cannot be hers, and seems so far removed from anything she can be feeling that we have to suspect the intervention of the novelist herself, or one of her literary surrogates. The writer sees the girl's thrill at the self-scarring, but must translate it, for herself and for us, into something less secret, more negotiable. "Too shocking" looks like a cover for something which is beyond or beneath shock.

The fifth quotation evokes the landscape of a brief and beautiful love affair. The oil paint and its colors are a metaphor for the riotous change in the life of Connie, who has fallen in love with a man for the first time at the age of thirty-nine. Nothing in the language or the perception belongs to her—nothing except the tumult and the brightness, that is. Paint here plays something of the role of literature in the previous example: it talks to us about the character, but not from within the character's mind.

What do these instances show us? Above all that we should not praise or blame Morrisons lyricism without a closer look. In these five examples alone, we get at least three different stylistic moves. The writer borrows a character's perception and mood, her angle of vision, and offers her own language in return—as we saw in our earlier example about the excitement of the neighbors and the reporter. She slips into a character's imagery and lets it speak for itself. And she looks at and names a character's condition, translating not from the character's point of view into the writer's language, but from the writer's point of view into the writer's preferred figure of speech. All three moves are equally valid, of course, although I think the first two work better for Morrison, and certainly, as I now hope to demonstrate, take us deeper into her work.

The instances I have cited are particular and personal, intricately situated and not pretending to objectivity. But none of them is contentious, although a couple of them reflect bitter observations. Even the contentious claims in *Paradise* may seem smoother or more polite than they are, because it is tempting for readers to identify with certain arguments and characters in the novel rather than others, even against others. That is, when a character articulates what we think, or think we think, or would like to think, this version seems to override all others, to belong to a removed realm of truth, and probably to be the author's own view. Now there may be such a realm, but it is not available to any of the characters in *Paradise*, and it is not available to Morrison or to us for much of our lives—not available at all in relation to disputes about race and history and memory. However, it is important to see that the temptation itself is part of Morrison's art. She is not inviting us to an elementary relativism (everything depends upon your point of view); she is asking us to think our principles and prejudices through to the point of whatever resists them.

I find myself wanting to believe, for example, that Patricia the schoolteacher is simply right about the racism of the town where she lives, its scorn for blacks of lighter color than that of its deep-black founding fathers. On their way to establishing their first town in 1890, the fathers were denied entry into a black city in Oklahoma, and this refusal, mimed every year in the town's nativity play, as a whole set of Josephs and Marys is turned away from the inn by people like themselves, is at the heart of the town's ongoing mythology: "Their horror of whites was convulsive but abstract. They saved the clarity of their hatred for the men who had insulted them in ways too confounding for language.... Everything anybody wanted to know about the citizens of Haven or Ruby lay in the ramifications of that one rebuff out of many" (189). There is much in the novel to support Patricia's view, and we need to hear what she is saying. But she is wrong in thinking she knows everything we could want to know. Indeed, if we knew only what Patricia knows about Haven or Ruby, we would know almost nothing. We need to remember too that Patricia is not a neutral observer, she is the daughter of a man who married a lighter-skinned woman, and two sentences later, she is looking out of her window at her mother's grave, and seeing the metaphorical sequins we have already encountered. Patricia's view is not invalidated by its context, of course; but it is contextualized.

I am also tempted to believe that Richard Misner, the Baptist minister and a relative newcomer to the town, is simply right about the way the older people in the town are locked into their past: "Over and over and with the least provocation, they pulled from their stock of stories tales about the old folks, their grands and great-grands, their fathers and mothers.... Testimonies to endurance, wit, skill and strength. Tales of luck and outrage. But why were there no stories to tell of themselves? About their own lives they shut up. Had nothing to say, pass on" (161). The echo of *Beloved* in the phrase "pass on" alerts us to the importance of the issue, but then again this point of view, couched in something much closer to *style indirect libre*, rich as it is in its partial truth, is distinctly limited and fully situated. Richard is "enraged" by these people (160). He is worried about his own contribution to the town's troubles, because he has been encouraging younger people to speak up. He belongs to a generation marked by the assassinations of Martin Luther King, Jr., and Malcolm X, and he feels the romance of Africa in a way that most of his parishioners do not. "'Africa is our home,'" he says (210), and home is a dream of belonging beyond all conflict and conquest, a version of paradise before the fall: "'I don't mean heaven. I mean a real earthly home.... Not some place you went to and invaded and slaughtered people to get. Not some place you claimed, snatched because you got the guns ... but your own home, where if you go back ... past the whole of Western history, past the beginnings of organized knowledge, past pyramids and poison bows, on back to when rain was new, before plants forgot they could sing and birds thought they were fish, back when God said Good! Good!—there, right there where you know your own people were born and lived and died'" (213). This is beautiful, but it does not feel like reliable history or politics. Patricia, who is listening to Richard as he gets launched, says, "'You preaching, Reverend.'" He says he is not, he is talking. "'I'm talking to you, Pat'" (213). He is talking and preaching. We do not have to distrust him to know we need to see the world from other angles as well.

A more contorted, more troubling instance: by the end of the novel the upright Steward Morgan has become a cold-blooded killer, and we are right to see him as such. But he is also, at another point, twice said to have "innocent eyes" (156). Who sees his eyes this way? The narrator seems to be reporting generalized community views at this stage, is not close to any particular character except Steward himself, who is not likely to be thinking of how his eyes look. Is this innocence an illusion, mere appearance? Or is it that a certain kind of stubborn, handsome innocence could drive a man to murder, that Steward is guilty because he is innocent? The tangle of paradox reminds us of other powerful and difficult formulations in Morrison's work: "'If I hadn't killed her, she would have died'" (*Beloved* 200).

These divergent perspectives do not result in the suggestion that all possible interpretations are equal. We need to feel pretty strongly that some of these partial views are sufficient in order to understand why they are not. We are implicated in these affairs, cannot afford to sit back and watch the spectacle as if it was not happening to us. That fiction is something that happens to us, if not (fortunately) as finally as history happens to us, is one of Morrison's most demanding and enabling convictions.

This conviction is everywhere visible in her writing, but it finds especially interesting technical reflections in *Paradise*—in the ease and frequency of flashbacks, for instance, which make old times seem contemporary, and the present seem full of layers: "She crossed Central Avenue toward them.... She walked fast.... He carried the equipment box through the dining room" (53). These sentences occur in quick succession, but nothing except our own piecing together of the story allows us to identify the first two as part of a memory and the third as current narration. So too in the proffering of the figurative version of an event before the literal one: "Then a mighty hand dug deep into a giant sack and threw fistfuls of petals into the air. Or so it seemed. Butterflies" (90). And in the subtle slippage from waking world to dream and back: "Having misread the warning, she was about to hostess one of the biggest messes Ruby had ever seen. Both of her dead sons were leaning against the Kelvinator, cracking the shells of Spanish peanuts. 'What's that in the sink?' Easter asked her. She looked and saw feathers—brightly colored but small like chicken feathers—lying in a heap in her sink.... She woke up wondering what kind of bird was colored that way" (154–55). The dead sons are there before there is any indication that this is a dream. The dreamer's first interpretation of the warning is that the feathers refer to the buzzards which have been flying over the town; her second that the strange feathers in the sink indicate that things and people are not in their place. What she cannot possibly know is that her husband's extra-marital affair released in his mistress "the wing of a feathered thing, undead" (226). Even though she has learned of the affair by the time of her dream, she can know only through telepathy, or the echoing magic of fiction, that she and the other women meet up in their imagery.

In all of these cases the freedom of fiction not only permits the imagining of alternatives to the given world, it infiltrates the world itself, reshapes it. It is true the world to be reshaped is fictional, but then the historical world too has often been altered by powerful fictions—of racial superiority among other notable things. The open intervention of fiction within Morrison's fiction is not floating self-reference but a model for the mind's capacity to change what it sees—its real but not limitless capacity.

Does the title of the novel speak of paradise, or of paradises, the plural hidden in the singular, the way multiple perceptions are hidden in the continuity of Morrison's voice? Would there be a way of folding the plural back into the singular? Is paradise, a closed garden in most mythologies, a place of negative purity, as Patricia suspects? A place where bigoted men rule the roost, "good brave men on their way to Paradise," as a voice very close to Patricia's sarcastically thinks (201–02)? Is it a place of peace, as Richard imagines, a cancellation of conquest and empire and violent America? When he thinks of the divided town as a "hard-won heaven" (306), he is remaking it in the image of his own hopes: "How exquisitely human was the wish for permanent happiness, and how thin human imagination became trying to achieve it" (306). Richard thinks he is analyzing the mentality of the town, but he is really converting it into a place he can like better, and can decide to stay in, as he does so decide a sentence or two later. His decision is one of very few weak spots in the novel, and also one of its most beautiful moments—beautiful because of its weakness. Having decided to stay Richard thinks of these people who so recently enraged him—and who even more recently slaughtered a group of harmless women—as "these outrageously beautiful, flawed and proud people" (306). They are beautiful and proud, of course; outrageously beautiful maybe; but to call them, in the light of what they have done, "flawed" is to refuse history for the sake of the future, and Morrison wants us to do better than that, however sympathetic we may be (and perhaps she is) to Richard's view. We have to face the future without refusing history—we have to see what he cannot bear to see.

"I have this creepy sensation ... of loss," Morrison said in a 1978 interview. "Like something is either lost, never to be retrieved, or something is about to be lost and will never be retrieved" (Mathus 13). The losses in her work have changed over the years, and many of them were not of paradise. But paradise is a wonderful image for what we might call the suspected loss, the fear that loss is what our story will disclose, that loss is what we have. Morrison's suggestion is not quite that the true paradises are lost paradises, as Proust so lucidly suggested (Proust 903); it is that we do not know the name of what we have lost and that paradise is a word which catches our disarray, a word that grieves for us. The murdering Steward Morgan may seem to be the polar opposite of the peace-dreaming Richard Misner, and a long way from paradise, but he too has his vision, none the less compelling for being so stately and hierarchical. Long ago, he and his twin brother

Deacon went on a trip with the menfolk of their family. In a prosperous town they saw

> nineteen Negro ladies arrange themselves on the steps of the town hall. They wore summer dresses of material the lightness, the delicacy of which neither of them had ever seen. Most of the dresses were white, but two were lemon yellow and one a salmon color. They wore small, pale hats of beige, dusty rose, powdery blue: hats that called attention to the wide, sparkly eyes of the wearers. Their waists were not much bigger than their necks. Laughing and teasing, they preened for a photographer.... Deek heard musical voices, low, full of delight and secret information, and in their tow a gust of verbena.... Deek's image of the nineteen summertime ladies was unlike the photographer's. His remembrance was pastel colored and eternal. (109–10)

Negro ladies, we note, not black women. Black and white photography, but colored words and memories. It is for such ladies that men of a certain generation might want to build a world. The ladies would be gracious and grateful, would acknowledge the gift and know their place. They would be Eves aloof from temptation—or at least from Eve's temptation to mastery. And it is because they represent a mockery of this memory—for Steward even more than for Deacon—that the murdered women have to die. Paradise can be lethal, an accomplice in crime, particularly for a man with "innocent eyes": "The women ... were for him a flaunting parody of nineteen Negro ladies of his and his brother's youthful memory and perfect understanding. They were a degradation of that moment they'd shared of sunlit skin and verbena. They, with their mindless giggles, outraged the dulcet tones ... of the nineteen ladies who, scheduled to live forever in pastel shaded dreams, were now doomed to extinction by this new and obscene breed of female" (279). The language ("mindless"/"dulcet," "pastel"/"obscene," and the brilliantly critical "scheduled") makes clear we are not being asked to endorse this view. But we are being asked to understand it, to see that it contains, in its way, a conflictless dream of grace and honor not unlike Richard's. Morrison's "creepy sensation ... of loss" includes the awareness that even the loss of error is still a loss. Or that there are very few enduring errors which are not haunted by truths hard to find elsewhere. So that when the narrator describes the offending women as "bodacious black Eves unredeemed by Mary" (18), she is both miming Steward's view and refuting it. When Connie tells the women that "Eve is Mary's mother" and "Mary is the daughter of

Eve" (263), she is denying the difference that means so much to Steward, but remembering that temptation and purity do not ordinarily or easily go together.

I have not yet mentioned the most obvious reference to paradise in the novel, which occurs in its last sentence, and indeed forms its last word. This is a vision not of loss but of homecoming, or of loss redeemed, but then three short words make clear that the difficult historical world has not been abandoned, only momentarily transfigured. An old black woman named Piedade is singing to another, younger black woman who is Connie dead and reborn. They are on a beach, surrounded by gleaming "sea trash." Heaving waves mark the arrival of something, "another ship, perhaps," of which we learn only that it contains "crew and passengers, lost and saved," and that they are "atremble, for they have been disconsolate for some time" (318). "Disconsolate," as Mathus points out, is a lovely pun, since Connie's full name is Consolata, and those who are arriving have lost her and needed her—needed what she is and what she knows (167). The travelers have come, perhaps, from life to the life after death; or have crossed an earthly ocean as slaves or as free people. Either way, they are here, and their subjection is over. But not their labor. And here is "down here," where we are, where we always were. "Now," the book concludes, "they will rest before shouldering the endless work they were created to do down here in Paradise" (318). This is not the paradise of Adam and Eve; it is the paradise they, and we, might have built beyond its gate.

Might have built but did not. "They shoot the white girl first," is how *Paradise* memorably opens. On a July morning of 1976 nine men have arrived at the remote house they call the Convent, determined to eradicate the evil they believe to be represented by the five straying or abandoned women who live there. But it is not until the last but one chapter of the book that the narration of this slaughter is completed, and we learn the names of the men. In the first chapter they are only shadowy roles and relations haunted by snatches of history, identified only as "the youngest," "the leading man," "his brother," "a father and his son," "the nephew"—as if their names were a secret we have to be ready for, or as if unnamed killers cannot kill. Finally we see them shoot two women indoors, and we hear one of the men say they have shot the other three as they ran across a clover field. But mysteriously, at the end of the chapter, there are no bodies inside or outside, and even the women's car, an ancient Cadillac, is gone.

What has happened? The novel itself is rife with speculation. There are "two editions of the official story": the men went out to the Convent, there was a fight, "the women took other shapes and disappeared into thin air"; the men went out to the Convent, there was a fight, and one woman, the oldest, was killed by "some" of the men (296–97). Patricia, who is passing on these versions to Richard Misner, has her own firm theory: nine coal-black men murdered five harmless women because the women were either not black or not black enough, because the women were "unholy," and "because they could"—because they felt they belonged to a black world above the law (297). But then what happened to the bodies? The town midwife, also a psychic, who knew what was going to happen and arrived at the Convent in time to witness the tail end of it, including two bodies, is distressed by the way everyone tells a different version of the story, but settles for an acceptance of God's will: "God had given Ruby a second chance. Had made Himself so visible and unarguable a presence that even the outrageously prideful ... and the uncorrectably stupid ... ought to be able to see it. He had actually swept up and received His servants in broad daylight ..." (297–98). One of the young women in the town has a more down-to-earth story: "'One of them or maybe more wasn't dead. Nobody actually looked—they just assumed. Then ... they got the hell out of there. Taking the killed ones with them. Simple, right?'" (303–04) But then this same young woman, out at the Convent, suddenly sees what she calls a door into what may be another world: "What would be on the other side? What on earth would it be? What on earth?" (305) We know that the women at the Convent have practiced magic, black or white according to your point of judgment, and that one of them has the power to raise the dead.

If the novel ended here, we could perhaps settle for the way these versions correct and refute and corroborate each other—although even then we would need to emphasize the unmistakable dead bodies and their equally unmistakable vanishing. But the novel has a short epilogue following on from these events and interpretations, in which each of the women is seen revisiting her life, in all cases but one reconciled to a loved one before she returns to wherever she is going. Are these figures ghosts, dreams? This is precisely the question we do not have to answer in fiction, where ghosts and dreams are the original inhabitants. Are the women dead? Probably, or as dead as fictional characters can get. Are they alive after death? Of course, they are there in front of us on the page, talking, swimming, looking for a favorite pair of shoes, eating grits and eggs, falling on glass. What more could a live body do?

There are all kinds of ways of thinking about this situation. Much depends on our own actual beliefs about death and what follows death. At the very least we are being asked, not to solve a difficult puzzle, but to reflect on the way fiction and memory resemble and reinforce each other, and the way both of them, inestimable consolations that they are, will also betray us if we let them. To say, for example, that fiction is fantasy or magic and nothing more, that the dead are alive if we think they are, or that active remembering abolishes death, is to reach for a comfort that will quickly fade, and that actually diminishes the horror and dignity of death, to say nothing of the crime of murder. But to say that the dead are just dead, that all possibilities end with the end of bodily life, is to miss the ongoing power of memory, and the ability of fiction to engage with the very loss it cannot deny. "They will live/and they will not die again," is what is promised to believers in the Gnostic Gospels, and cited by Morrison in the novel's epigraph. Memory promises the same: an acceptance of the first death is the condition for the avoidance of the second. But fiction's promise is slightly different. Its characters are promised that they will live, and they will die. And they will live again, and die again, and again and again, as long as there are readers who believe in them. Their voices will speak and clash, their moral persuasions will make their claims on us, and the assembly of their styles will form, as Bakhtin says, the language of the novel.

The dead and alive women of the epilogue to *Paradise*, like a number of other figures in Morrison's fiction, are pictures of possibility, of second chances. And they are reminders that possibilities themselves, outside of fiction, are often canceled by the intractable real, that for many people the first chance is also the last. The dialogue between this acknowledgment and the imagined alternative is what matters. Fiction cannot restore our losses but it can get us beyond their helpless reenactment.

RACHEL C. LEE

Missing Peace in
Toni Morrison's Sula *and* Beloved

Ｆrom her earliest fictional work *The Bluest Eye* (1970) to her latest, *Jazz* (1992), Toni Morrison cultivates an aesthetic of ambiguity. Placing Morrison in a "postmodernist" context, Robert Grant, for instance, describes both the "labor" of interpreting *Sula* and the richness evoked by its narrative "gaps." Clearly, Morrison's emphasis on absences and indeterminate meanings casts an interpretational bone in the direction of readers and critics who, as urged by Grant, transform "absence into presence." However, I would argue that the more productive endeavor may be to read the ambiguities of Morrison's texts not as aporia to be "filled ... by the reader" (Grant 94) but as signifiers of an unattainable desire for stable definitions and identities.

This essay, accordingly, explores the relationship between the slippage of words and the informing voids (desires) of Morrison's novels by examining two of her most critically recognized works, *Sula* (1973) and *Beloved* (1987). Though all of Morrison's novels play upon the variability of language, *Sula* especially throws into disequilibrium that exemplar dichotomy, good and evil, and by extension all Manichean systems which under-gird traditional linguistic and ethical orders. By bringing to light the relativity of meaning, *Sula* broaches the subject not only of semantic integrity (how we can convey what we mean) but also of epistemological integrity (how can we know anything since there is no objective perspective and no objective essence or

From *Understanding Toni Morrison's Beloved and Sula: Selected Essays and Criticisms of the works by the Nobel Prize-winning author*, edited by Solomon O. Iyasere and Marla W. Iyasere. © 2000 by Solomon O. Iyasere and Marla W. Iyasere.

truth to know). While the aforementioned questions bristle under each of Morrison's texts, in *Sula*, Morrison offers to her readers a main character who telescopes that scandal of epistemology. How can we understand or know Sula, who is not only egoless or without a self (and hence undeterminable) but who also is unable to know anything herself?

By contrast, *Beloved*, set almost a century earlier (c. 1852–1873), deals less with the metaphysical premises of good and evil to focus instead upon the institution of slavery and its overwhelming perversion of meaning. Inspired by a newspaper clipping from the 1850s (Davis 151), *Beloved* reconstructs the nuances of a black woman's killing of her infant daughter in response to the Fugitive Slave Act. Symbolic and discursive substitutions become emblematic in this latter narrative, where a ghost stands in for the lost living, where memory only approximates event, and where gestures and words struggle to fill the gaps of unvoiced longings. In *Beloved*, Morrison again highlights the variability of meaning and identity, yet in this case she links approximations of meaning to the historical condition of being enslaved.

Taking the cue from Eva's suggestion that there are no such things as innocent words or gestures—"'How you gone not mean something by it'" (*Sula* 68)—I engage in close readings of Morrison's texts with an eye toward the overdetermined nature of each sign. In addition, by looking at two of her works in conjunction, I hope to shed light on the different levels of language manipulation occurring in each book as well as conjecture the possible implications of these differences. How do the words of 1987 supplement, qualify, or reinforce their 1973 predecessors?

* * * * *

Sula begins with two gestures: a dedication and an epigraph. In the dedication, Morrison reconfigures a traditional signifier of loss and elegiac retrieval, to one of desire: "It is sheer good fortune to miss somebody long before they leave you. This book is for Ford and Slade, whom I miss although they have not left me." Instead of invoking the dead, Morrison places "Ford and Slade" into a "missed" situation, rewriting their future absence into the present and applying associations of loss and profound appreciation (usually reserved for the dead) to persons not yet defined by this absence. In effect, Morrison conveys a heightened sense of the variability of Ford and Slade, their probable mortality, their easy slippage into alter identities. How does the writer, then, who in essence "embalms" or fixes her subject, inscribe this changeableness of character? Does not every descriptive endeavor risk "missing" an essential, uncapturable quality (hence Morrison's play on the other meanings of to *miss*: 'to not quite capture,' 'to arrive too late,' 'to render inaccurately'—as in missing a piece, missing a train, or missing the point). With this dedication, Morrison unsettles the very sense of to *miss* and intimates the impossibility of any representation not informed by missing meanings.

The second sign in *Sula*, the epigraph drawn from Williams's *The Rose Tattoo*, foreshadows the replication of signs, the overdetermination of meanings, and the thematics of self in the subsequent text:

> Nobody knew my rose of the world but me.... I had too much glory. They don't want glory like *that* in nobody's heart.

The Rose Tattoo inscribes its sign upon Morrison's novel, not unlike the birthmark destined for Sula's eye. This birthmark remains an ambiguous sign variously esteemed; it appears "a rose" to the narrative voice, a stemmed rose to Eva and Nel, a "scary black thing" to Nel's children, "a copperhead" to Jude, "Hannah's ashes" to the community, and "a tadpole" to Shadrack. As a mark of and on Sula/*Sula*, the epigraph foreshadows Sula's final isolation and incomprehensibility. At her death, nobody "knows" Sula but herself. The epigraph also attributes to the eponymous protagonist an excess of self-centeredness. The words "I had too much glory" find a near correlative in Sula's later assertion ' " I can do it all, why can't I have it all?' " (142). Yet, this epigraphic suggestion of Sula's self-love enacts a further corruption of signs, for Morrison later suggests that Sula has no sense of self—"She had no center ... no ego" (119). Both Rose Tattoos (birthmark and epigraph) become for Sula/*Sula* symbols of contradictory meanings as well as marks of "missed" identification.

With those dedicatory and epigraphic signs, one enters the narrative body of *Sula*, where missed meanings between conversants proliferate. After Sula's return to Medallion, she and Nel engage in familiar yet unfamiliar banter:

> 'You been gone too long, Sula.'
> 'Not too long, but maybe too far.'
> 'What's that supposed to mean?' ...
> 'Oh, I don't know.'
> 'Want some cool tea?' (96)

While the reader may variously interpret Sula's suggestion that she has gone "too far" (i.e., she has reached a different value system, or has over-stepped consensus boundaries), Nel doesn't conjecture these meanings. Rather, the conversation turns to the distancing etiquette of proffered "tea." Nel's puzzlement over what Sula "mean[s]" is, in itself, an oddity, for the two women's history has been marked by an uncanny unison of thinking and movement that does not require words. Most memorable of that synchronicity is the prelude to Chicken Little's death, where the two girls "in concert, without ever meeting each other's eyes" dig two holes in the ground, furrowing deeper and deeper "until the two holes were one and the same," finally "replac[ing] the soil and cover[ing] the entire grave with uprooted grass [all during which] neither one had spoken a word" (58–59). This ensemble performance significantly occurs in silence, the implications being that words would disrupt the unity of action and, correlatively, that the necessity for words indicates a lesser degree of intimacy. Imbedded in the textual appeal to wordlessness, then, is the notion of language as the site and symptom of difference. Thus, when Nel recalls her former closeness with Sula, she describes them as "two throats and one eye" (147), emphasizing both perceptual "sameness" and discursive "difference." That is, even during the period in which the two girls shared "one eye," their means of articulating themselves were differentiated as "two."

In addition to the slips in language occurring *between* speakers, Morrison shows the schism between word and delayed/deferred significance that transpires within an individual's mind. When Eva describes her reasons for killing Plum, she speaks "with two voices. Like two people were talking at the same time, saying the same thing, one a fraction of a second behind the other" (71). The two voices say the "same thing"—but with a difference, one articulating, for Hannah, Plum's decline and Eva's response to it; the other translating for Eva, herself, the same scenario but with all the unsaid qualifications of motive and recollected vividness which encompass that "fraction of a second" delay. The "ambiguities of mercy" (Spillers 314), intoned but not made explicit in either Eva's act or her subsequent explanation, suggest that the "two voices" have not adequately justified her killing of Plum; perhaps the clarification required to assess Eva's act as a mercy killing or not lies in the reserve of that delayed moment—in the missing or sublimated text.

Contending with language's slippage presents a dilemma not only for Morrison's characters, but also for the author/narrator. For instance, the words "pig meat" (50) remain inadequate to describe the flavor of Ajax's utterance, the implicit "compliment" of his stylized delivery. The significance of pig meat lies less in the literal content of the term than in the way [Ajax] handled the words. When he said "hell" he hit the *h* with his lungs and the impact was greater than the achievement of the most imaginative foul mouth in the town. He could say "shit" with a nastiness impossible to imitate. So, when he said "pig meat" as Nel and Sula passed, they guarded their eyes lest someone see their delight. (50)

This qualification acknowledges the distance between the words at the writer's disposal and the nuances conveyed in the hissing of a particular *h*. While Morrison elaborates on the *h*'s transformative effects on the word *hell*, she leaves absent how Ajax utters *pig meat* to give it a complimentary texture; like *shit* it remains "impossible to imitate." Thus, despite the supplement that Morrison provides, *pig meat* as Ajax delivers it, remains missing from the text, only associatively colored by the description of Ajax's hissing *hell*.

Through such proximal associations, Morrison manages to absent the utterance and, through such absence, deliver the sense. That is, Ajax says aloud what was "in all their minds" yet difficult or prohibitive to express (e.g., "the taste of young sweat on tight skin," or the "mystery curled" beneath "cream-colored trousers" [50]). The emphasis on the way in which Ajax mouths the words subordinates their referential function to highlight instead the process of meaning's construction. More important than the referent of "pig meat" is the utterance's capacity to inspire for the men in front of the pool hall and for the two walking girls a breeze of sexual (re)awakening. Moreover, the very slips and deviances in both Ajax's intonation and Morrison's description of it provide a stylistic correlative to Sula's and Nel's burgeoning sense of sexuality: They were "like tightrope walkers, as thrilled by the possibility of a slip as by the maintenance of tension and balance" (51). The playfulness in both Ajax's and Morrison's words simultaneously create and avoid the desire for sexual and semantic gratification.

The absence of Ajax's "pig meat" utterance, yet its evocation through supplemental conceit, reveals its simultaneous properties as both missed yet not missing from the narrative. This liminal straddling between absence and presence becomes characteristic of the metonymic device which Morrison shows operating for herself as well as her characters. For instance, Jude's tie and Ajax's license evolve into metonyms for persons with whom they are associated. For Nel, Jude's tie becomes both the sign of his absence and the single remnant of all that he took: "... you walked past me saying, 'I'll be back for my things.' And you did but you left your tie" (106). Jude's tie remains liminally situated, as a signifier of absence, only through being present and metaphorically bringing into presence the remembered Jude.

It would seem that Ajax's license would likewise provide Sula with a "tie" to her former lover; however, in this instance, Morrison reflects on the relevance of linguistic error to one's sense of knowing. As Sula searches for signs of Ajax's former presence, she eventually stumbles across physical evidence, which ironically negates Ajax's identity as Sula knows it:

> Then one day ... she found ... proof that he had been there, his driver's license.... But what was this? Albert Jacks? His name was Albert Jacks? A. Jacks. She had thought it was Ajax ... when for the first time in her life she had lain in bed with a man and said his name involuntarily or said it truly meaning *him*, the name she was screaming and saying was not his at all.
>
> (135–136)

Although she truly "means *him*," Sula misses saying Albert Jacks's name with its inscribed difference. This mistake leads Sula to question her knowledge in general: ' "... there is nothing I did know and I have known nothing since the one thing I wanted was to know his name ..." ' (136). Her conclusion on knowing nothing applies beyond herself—how can anyone know anything when the purveyors of meaning slip, deviate, and deceive?

A correlative question—How can anyone convey anything when words limit and elude?—bristles under Morrison's text. Instead of released verbal expression, Morrison often presents only the gestures toward possible expressions:

> The body *must* move and throw itself about, the eyes *must* roll, the hands *should* have no peace, and the throat *should* release all the yearning, despair and outrage that accompany the stupidity of loss.
>
> (107; italics added)

The imperative thrust of *must* declines into its subjunctive *should*, a pattern which defers mandatory urgency. Desire and purpose replace definitive action, as Morrison thwarts her character's attempt to "release all yearning": "Nel waited ... for the oldest cry ... her very own howl. But it did not come" (108).

The inadequacy of words and the desire for meaningful expression infuse Morrison's novel. Yet Sula's statement on "know[ing] nothing" presents an even graver problem. In the silence of one's interior consciousness, meaning becomes variable or meaningless—knowledge a mere ruse. Variability of meaning, whether articulated or silent, derives from a relativity of perspective. If one could stabilize for a moment the relational connotations of the word *bottom*, one could not fix the variable viewpoint from which it refers. That is, the Bottom remains "'high up for us,' said the master, 'but when God looks down, it's the bottom. That's why we call it so. It's the bottom of heaven—best land there is'" (5). The white farmer argues from God's "viewpoint" not because he deems it right, but because it allows him to swindle his black slave out of valley or "bottom" land. However, genuine investment in God's point of view informs Eva's judgments of right and wrong as well as communal assessments of good and evil. It remains for Sula to question that fundamental reliance upon God's authority, bringing into focus the implied perspective from which consensus meaning derives:

> 'Bible say honor thy father and thy mother that thy days may be long upon the land thy God giveth thee,' [says Eva].
> 'Mamma must have skipped that part. Her days wasn't too long,' [responds Sula].
> 'Pus mouth! God's going to strike you!'
> 'Which God? The one watched you burn Plum?' (93)

By asking "Which God?" Sula poses the relativity of even this monolith and questions both Eva's version of good and evil and good and evil in general. Additionally, Sula flaunts "falling," saying "'What the hell do I care about falling?'" since falling/Falling no longer *means* the descent into evil implied in Eva's Biblical aphorism ("'Pride goeth before a fall'") (93). Sula accepts this slippage, this fall (in language), and opposes the community's investment in a monolithic God as determiner of meaning.

Interestingly, while Sula here undermines God as monolith, she later seeks an unfallen language to describe the loneliness she seeks in coition —

> a loneliness so profound the word itself had no meaning. For loneliness assumed the absence of other people, and the solitude she found in that desperate terrain had never admitted the possibility of other people. (123)

Sula and Morrison seek to describe an absence that antedates presence—a loneliness existing without relation to another. Yet language falls short. Morrison can only approximate Sula's loneliness through a catalog of "lost" items:

> She wept then. Tears for the deaths of the littlest things: the castaway shoes of children; broken stems of marsh grass battered

and drowned by the sea; prom photographs of dead women she
never knew; wedding rings in pawn-shop windows; the tidy
bodies of Cornish hens in a nest of rice.   (123)

This list supplements the idea of loneliness-as-void, yet does not achieve it
and, paradoxically, erases it by filling it in.

Morrison later makes more explicit this loneliness defined by another
against a loneliness which is "mine." In response to Nel's implicit
condemnation of Sula's self-reliant lifestyle ("'Lonely, ain't it?'"), Sula
replies, "'Yes. But my lonely is *mine*. Now your lonely is somebody else's....
Ain't that something? A secondhand lonely'" (143). Although Sula has
slipped into a "secondhand lonely" for Ajax, the loneliness she describes to
Nel consists of a yearning or missing without object. In effect, Sula wishes to
describe and achieve an Adamic loneliness, an unfallen, originary loneliness.

Sula/*Sula* thus exhibits a desire for absolute meaning, though only
briefly. Shortly after Nel's departure, Sula contemplates her own lack of
permanence and her correlative lack of meaning:

'If I live a hundred years my urine will flow the same way, my
armpits and breath will smell the same.... *I didn't mean anything. I
never meant anything.* I stood there watching her burn and was
thrilled. I wanted her to keep on jerking like that, to keep on
dancing.'

                                              (147; italics added)

Sula describes her unvariability (what one would think implies a stable
identity), but also her meaninglessness (perhaps confirming de Sausserian
notions of meaning's contingency upon differences [Derrida 140]). Despite
this self-evaluation, Sula, rather than meaning nothing, produces an excess of
meanings. Her words "I didn't mean anything" can be variously interpreted:
Sula cannot intend meaning since meaning and the purveyors of meaning
remain corrupt, or Sula hasn't made an impact on the world other than being
"a body, a name and an address" (173). The latter interpretation confirms
Sula as egoless or only a striving toward identity rather than a completion or,
as Deborah McDowell phrases it, "character as *process*" rather than
"character as *essence*" (81). The context in which Sula "speaks" these thoughts
compound their overdetermination. As the last quoted words before her
death, these thoughts take on a confessional tone, especially in juxtaposition
to her recollection of Hannah's burning. Sula's "I never meant anything" may
refer to her gesture of ambivalence, of looking at Hannah's fiery dance,

feeling neither remorse nor delight. Thus, Sula reaffirms her non-relation to another, while also denying any substantive presence unto herself. Rather than "never mean[ing] anything," Sula's meanings are endless, incomplete— always missed.

The seeming contradiction of Sula as neither in relation to another nor defined as present unto herself resolves itself in the notion of Sula as open-ended or "never achiev[ing] completeness of being" (McDowell 81). That is, to pose Sula's relation to another (effectively writing in what she desires) would be to project a closure to her identity. In *Sula*, however, closure consistently eludes both author and title character. For instance, the narrative closing of Chicken Little's life, initially described as "the closed place in the water," quickly transforms into "something newly missing" (61), as if closure were always informed by some missing piece (and thus not closed or complete at all). Chicken Little's "ending" oddly remains unseen by most of the community; and because his remains are withheld from viewing by the "closed coffin" (64), closure paradoxically creates a void in perception—a new lack in the text.

Sula's death creates similar gaps in the text. Her narrative continues beyond her last breath, and her post-mortem thoughts "'Well, I'll be damned ... it didn't even hurt. Wait'll I tell Nel'" (149) not only write her beyond her own ending but also reinforce Sula's striving after supplementation. Sula/*Sula* asks the reader to "wait" until a doubtful future moment (since she is dead, she cannot tell Nel), deferring infinitely the closure of both book and "self."

Not surprisingly, then, *Sula* concludes with an open-ended description which re-emphasizes the ambiguous borders of personal and discursive definitions. Nel's contemplation of the Peace gravestones conflates people, words, and desires:

> Together they read like a chant: PEACE 1895–1921, PEACE 1890–1923, PEACE 1910–1940, PEACE 1892–1959.
> They were not dead people. They were words. Not even words. Wishes, longings. (171)

The associative ambiguity of "Peace" clues the reader into the thematic suggestion that Peace, both the people and the word, remains missing and that this missing Peace (piece) inspires desire. Morrison takes the conventional sentiment of "rest-in-peace" out of equilibrium and overlays grave, book, language, and identity with inconclusiveness. Nel's final cry "'O Lord, Sula ... girl, girl, girlgirlgirl'" (174) echoes this triple intersection of words, people, and desires. The variable referent of "girl" (Nel's invocation to Sula or to herself) points to language's plurisignifying potential to evoke missed people (others), the missed self, missed meanings, and all the desire encompassed in those yearnings for the "missed." The novel's inconclusiveness, then, reiterates Sula's identity as desire without object, as the narrative itself embodies that same sense of desire for the reader.

* * * * *

Whereas, in *Sula*, words fail to explain conversational objects (a restroom) or concepts (God), in *Beloved*, language and expression in general fall short because the experiences they strive to capture are peculiar—always circumscribed by the legacy of having been owned. In her later work, Morrison highlights the lack of vocabulary to speak the experience of the enslaved self as well as the often perilous relation of the former enslaved to a historically specific language which commodifies African-Americans. *Beloved*, then, redefines the duplicity of language with an eye toward its historical warping.

One might begin to define the "something missing" in *Beloved* through language and its often incomprehensible meanings. Morrison shows that the mutations of time often place language out of reach, so that former words cannot be recollected:

> What Nan told her [Sethe] had forgotten, along with the language she told it in ... she was picking meaning out of a code she no longer understood. (62)

Facing near hieroglyphs in memory, Sethe must bypass the language and the words for the meaning behind them. Thus, Morrison presents a gap in what Nan says, and instead proposes what Nan "means:"

> [Nan] told Sethe that her mother and Nan were together from the sea. Both were taken up many times by the crew. 'She threw them all away but you. The one from the crew she threw away on the island.... Without names, she threw them. You she gave the name of the black man. She put her arms around him. The others she did not put her arms around.' (62)

Morrison switches from third-person paraphrase of Nan's "meaning" to direct quotations—fabricated quotations, however, since the original words and language have been lost. In Sethe's distillation of meaning from a forgotten "code," Morrison implies the dual construction of meaning. The words here are as much fabricated by Sethe as they are delivered by Nan, who, in turn, wishes to convey some elusive meaning from Sethe's mother. This last meaning finally surfaces through a series of deferrals, leaving the reader uncertain as to how to interpret Nan's "words." Are they indicators of Sethe's relative importance to her mother (since she has not met the fate of her half-siblings)? Do they create a threatening picture of mother-love, as Sethe's killing of Beloved has done for Howard and Buglar?

The difficulties of interpreting meaning pose dilemmas not only for those recollecting the past, but also among characters sharing the same narrative present. When Stamp Paid goes to visit the women of 124, he encounters an incomprehensible language:

> Out on Bluestone Road he thought he heard a conflagration of hasty voices—loud, urgent, all speaking at once.... All he could make out was the word *mine*. The rest of it stayed outside his mind's reach. (172)

Though Stamp Paid "couldn't describe [this speech] to save his life," the narrator (through Stamp Paid's perspective) supplements this initial description with yet another approximation of these "sounds":

> [It was] like the interior sounds a woman makes when she believes she is alone and unobserved at her work; a *sth* when she misses the needle's eye; a soft moan when she sees another chip in her one good platter; the low, friendly argument with which she greets the hens. Nothing fierce or startling. Just that eternal, private conversation that takes place between women and their tasks. (172)

One wonders whether Morrison, here, portrays more about the perceiver than the perceived. That is, the male figure, representative of the public workplace, glances in the window of the female privatized home, and sees an alien space defined by domestic tasks and an exclusive female presence (down to the hens). To him, the sounds remain unintelligible, the significance of the "argument with which she greets the hens" unfathomable.

As these two examples attest, slippage of language in *Beloved* occurs between persons who have lost contact. Unlike Sula and Nel, the main characters of this later novel, with the exception of Beloved, remain discrete entities, none having achieved the closeness implied in "two throats and one eye." Even family members do not realize an affinity like Sula's and Nel's. Sethe only knows her mother through two gestures: her mother's revealing to Sethe her circle and cross brand, and the slap Sethe receives upon requesting a similar mark (61); Joshua/Stamp Paid displaces his emotional attachment to his wife Vashti by changing his name rather than snapping her neck (233). In both cases, the distance between mother-daughter and husband-wife must be maintained, for in the pressurized atmosphere of slavery, close ties risk implosion. Thus, Morrison implies how historical realities perpetuate a system that precludes intimate contact: As Denver later articulates, "Slaves not supposed to have pleasurable feelings on their own; their bodies not supposed to be like that ..." (209). Language's slippage and missed meanings take place across migratory (and chronological) stretches, allowing Morrison to contextualize the corruption of signifiers within the historical exigencies of slavery and its aftermath.

In particular, Morrison shows how certain symbols become overdetermined in meaning. Sethe's breasts, for instance, begin as signifiers of nurturing. Sethe, who is pregnant with Denver but still has "'milk for [her] baby girl,'" must get to Ohio where her daughter awaits her. Yet, before Sethe leaves Sweet Home, Schoolteacher's nephews forcibly "rape" her milk (16–17), reinscribing her breasts as sites of violation and instruments through which to deprive her children of sustenance; they also epitomize how "private" body parts become commodified, public, and un-"own"-ed by the self. The overdetermined meaning of Sethe's breasts results, in part, from the lack of an appropriate language to speak the outrage of slavery. How can one describe the multiple injustices and rage which slavery yields—the "unspeakable thoughts, unspoken" (199)? Thus, tropes such as Sethe's breasts come to approximate the confluence of emotions (guilt, shame, rage, grief, insecurity, terror, numbness...) begotten from the "Peculiar Institution."

Likewise, Paul D's rooster becomes the only way for him to express a degradation so severe that it remains unnamed by the narrative's conclusion. In a conversation which begins reluctantly, with intentions both not to tell and not to hear, Paul D finally tells Sethe of the roosters:

> 'Mister [the rooster], he looked so ... free. Better than me. Stronger, tougher. Son a bitch couldn't even get out the shell by hisself but he was still king and I was....' Paul D stopped and squeezed his left hand with his right.... 'Mister was allowed to be and stay what he was. But I wasn't allowed to be and stay what I

was. Even if you cooked him you'd be cooking a rooster named Mister. But wasn't no way I'd ever be Paul D again, living or dead.... I was something else and that something was less than a chicken sitting in the sun on a tub.' (72)

The ellipses and hesitations throughout Paul D's speech tell of gaps and deferrals in meaning. Paul D doesn't know whether he can "say it right," or say it fully, and, in fact, as the narrative reveals, "... what he was telling her was only the beginning" (72).

Morrison further compounds the meaning of roosters by associating Mister's comb with Paul D's missing or buried "red heart": "... there was no red heart bright as Mister's comb beating in him" (73). Red heart and rooster approximate each other, even as they trope toward some more ambiguous meaning. That meaning becomes further complicated by Paul D's chanting "'Red heart'" as he touches Beloved "'on the inside part'" (117)—an act which further shames him.

Morrison finally articulates a clearer image of Paul D's unnamed hurt through a catalog of items:

> A shudder ran through Paul D.... He didn't know if it was bad whiskey, nights in the cellar, pig fever, iron bits, *smiling roosters*, fired feet, laughing dead men, hissing grass, rain, apple blossoms, neck jewelry, Judy in the slaughterhouse, Halle in the butter, ghost-white stairs, chokecherry trees, cameo pins, aspens, Paul A's face, sausage or the loss of a *red, red heart*.
> 'Tell me something, Stamp,' Paul D's eyes were rheumy. 'Tell me this one thing. *How much is a nigger supposed to take?*'
> (235; italics added)

A shudder and exasperation flavor Morrison's "meaning," which one might conjecture as the degradation of having no agency, of being transformed or moved at will by another. The breasts and roosters, as overdetermined metaphors for the "weight" of being black in America during the late nineteenth-century, hint at how this "burden" cannot be expressed simply or singularly. Techniques such as cataloging and metaphorical substitution, displacement, and approximation aid Morrison in conveying the lack of vocabulary to describe fully the degradation of slavery.

Not only words but also gestures become subject to slippage; and often gestures (in themselves a comment on the need for supplements to words) remain the expression of choice for those who have no access to the "master language." Beloved, who returns from the dead, relies heavily upon gesture to supplement her words. In response to Denver's question "'What's it like over there, where you were before?'" Beloved replies, "'Dark ... I'm small in that place. I'm like this here.' She raised her head off the bed, lay down on her side and curled up" (75). Beloved's gesture seems to indicate a womb of darkness, but her later assertions of her "crouching" with a "dead man on my face" (211) carry suggestions of slave ship passage. More simply, the place "over there" could be death, pre-birth, or void. To say that Beloved's words exhibit missing pieces would be not only to state the obvious but also to overlook Morrison's more masterful troping by gesture. Instead of supplementing Beloved's meaning through additional words, Morrison leaves Beloved's gesture literally *at rest*—not closed in meaning but accepting of the gaps that already exist in memory and that widen during the conveyance of meaning.

Beloved's "massage-stranglehold" of Sethe's neck becomes another gesture of ambivalent meaning. Denver insists that Beloved has "choked [Sethe's] neck,'" whereas Beloved claims that she has "'kissed her neck'" (101). Beloved's counter-statement does not necessarily negate Denver's words. A too-strong kiss may strangle, just as a "too-thick love" can result in "unmotherly" acts. Interestingly, Paul D characterizes Sethe's love as "'too thick,'" to which Sethe responds, "'Love is or it ain't. Thin love ain't love at all'" (164). Sethe denies any texture or variable quality to love, while Paul D shows that "love" inadequately describes the emotional relation one has to another. He, thus, exposes "love" as a synecdoche of sorts that only partially names Sethe's relationship to her children. Likewise, the different interpretations of the "massage" as either choke-hold or kiss emerge from a similarly reductive (is or ain't) determination of benevolent or malevolent intent. Yet Morrison consistently undermines this benevolent/malevolent dichotomy, showing how love for the captive female can manifest itself in both.

Morrison also shows how characters besides Beloved choose approximating gestures over words. For instance, after Sethe discovers Beloved's identity (as her returned "ghost" daughter), Sethe falls into a flurry of mothering activity: playing with Beloved, braiding her hair, feeding her "fancy food," and clothing her in "ribbon and dress goods" (240). Presumably trying to make up for lost time, Sethe condenses her gestures of care into two months, yet succeeds only in making Beloved, Denver, and herself look "like carnival women with nothing to do" (240). The narrative voice reveals the disjunction between Sethe's pattern-making and the shallowness of result. Instead of the "real thing," one has carnivalesque trappings without substance—the displaced substitute of some unrealizable desire.

The scapegoating of Sethe by various members in the community enacts a similar substitutive gesture. Instead of accusing themselves, Ella and Paul D, for instance, transfer selfcensure onto the already publicly identified "criminal," Sethe. Ella, who shuns Sethe after the Misery (as Stamp Paid calls the Fugitive Slave Act and Sethe's desperate response to it [171]), has herself orchestrated a child's death, "a hairy white thing, fathered by 'the lowest yet,'" whom she "delivered, but would not nurse" (258–259). Likewise, Paul D displaces his own shame onto Sethe's recorded public act. As he listens to her explanation of the newspaper article, Paul D judges Sethe's action as "'wrong.' ... 'You got two feet, Sethe, not four.' ... Later he would wonder what made him say it.... How fast he had moved from his shame to hers" (165). The two displacements allow Ella and Paul D, and by extension the community, to voice the violence engendered by slavery in an already constructed language. That is, they use the language of the white judiciary, white newspapers, and white opinion to assess and fix judgment upon Sethe's act. Instead of arriving at a new discourse to express, encompass, and comprehend (but not necessarily mitigate) Sethe's act, Ella and Paul D misappropriate Sethe's "crime" in order to overlook and keep silent what they have no alternative words for.

"Missing" from the community, then, is a discourse for and about public/private shame. Sethe has ruptured secreted guilt by displaying "on the lawn"[1] the communally shared guilt over child abandonment, malevolent love, and infanticide. Sethe's killing of Beloved remains an inconceivable gesture whose meaning *Beloved* spends its entire length trying to approximate. In Schoolteacher's nephew's reaction to Sethe's killing in the woodshed, Morrison highlights the mistaken meanings derived from decontextualized judgments:

> What she go and do that for? On account of a beating?
> Hell, he'd been beat a million times and he was white. ... 'What
> she go and do that for?' (150)

The nephew reduces Sethe's act to a response to a whipping. He compares it to his own projected reaction, that "no way ... could [he] have" done what she did (150). Not being a slave, he cannot grasp the meaning of Sethe's action, as perhaps that meaning may never be grasped through forgotten agony and "official" versions of history.

Perhaps what is desired, then, is a language to explain and absolve, to encompass all the nuance and ambiguity of motive and emotion—a language which allows the women of 124 "to be what they liked, see whatever they saw and say whatever was on their minds" (199). Morrison approximates this desired language in the lyric section running from pages 200 to 217, a rendition of interior consciousness, for, as Sethe asserts, she doesn't need to vocally explain herself because Beloved "understands everything already" (200). Only an unfallen language would exhibit a unity of thought and word that would render verbalization obsolete—a language in the beginning: "In the beginning there were no words. In the beginning was the sound, and they all knew what that sounded like" (259). Morrison allows that unfallen sounding to become realized for an instant, which recalls the healing work of the Clearing:

> For Sethe it was as though the Clearing had come to her with all its heat and simmering leaves, where the voices of women searched for ... the sound that broke the back of words. ... It broke over Sethe and she trembled like the baptized in its wash. (261)

Morrison presents the "roaring" of the unspoken, which spiritually blesses and absolves. Yet, this triumphant moment of wordless song lasts only briefly, perhaps a glimpse of Paradise after the Fall. Morrison makes clear that this type of language, though desired, cannot often be realized—that the women of 124, for instance, can "say whatever was on their minds. *Almost*" (199; italics added). Amongst Sethe, Beloved, and Denver, much remains "unspeakable thoughts, unspoken" (200). Sethe's monologue, for instance, projects into an indeterminate future her "telling" of a specific knowledge: "I know what it is to be without the milk that belongs to you. ... I'll tell Beloved about that; she'll understand" (200). Like Paul D's rooster, Sethe's stolen milk signals such inexpressible emotions that Sethe defers voicing them, even as she desires to make the incident "under stand[able]."

Morrison soberly returns the narrative to language's limitations. Words, akin to the "spores of bluefern growing in the hollows along the riverbank," have the potential to "live out [their] days as planned" (84); i.e., to express authentically. Instead of realizing that intent, however, the spore collapses and the certainty of its expression—its full bloom—"lasts no longer than [a moment]; longer, perhaps than the spore itself" (84).

Morrison does not simply refer to language here. The spore also represents the promise of human life and the fragility of that promise for the enslaved. As former slave Harriet Jacobs observed while watching "two beautiful children playing together" (one a "fair white child," the other her slave), "I foresaw the inevitable blight that would fall on the little slave's heart. I knew how soon her laughter would be changed to sighs" (Jacobs 29). The slave, denied possession of her body, will never realize the promise implied by and borne out in the fruition of her white counterpart. Possessed by another, the enslaved suffers from a fragmentation of self (literal as well as figurative),[2] or as Paul D phrases it, not being able "'to be and stay what I was" (72). Morrison's characters can only obliquely refer to the situation of being denied a self. For instance, Sethe mentions that "there was no nursing milk to call my own" (200), referring to the shared milk she took as a child from Nan's breasts and her own milk forcibly taken from her by Schoolteacher's nephews. After escaping to Ohio, she claims her post-slavery sense of self by reappropriating her milk for no one but "my own children" (200); through reclaimed agency over her milk, Sethe points to herself as no longer the possession of another.

However, Sethe still evokes her self through others: For Sethe, "the best thing she was, was her children" (251). Even when she earlier conjectures her possible death, Sethe couches it in terms of her baby, "'I believe this baby's ma'am is gonna die in wild onions on the bloody side of the Ohio River.' ... And it didn't seem such a bad idea ..." (31). Yet, because she is the "baby's ma'am," Sethe attempts to survive, a decision born of concern not for herself but for her baby. Thus, akin to Morrison's Sula, whose identity remains incomplete, Sethe, too, only proceeds toward an investment in herself as her own, "'best thing'" (273). Nel's voiced realization of herself as separate from her mother's influence "'I'm me.... Me'" (*Sula* 28)—becomes echoed in Sethe's concluding remarks which indicate a recognition of the self—but with a difference: "'Me? Me?'" (273). This faux-conclusion to Sethe's narrative revises the stable self implied in Nel's "'I'm me.... Me,'" emphasizing the striving toward rather than any realized definition of self.

Beloved's other conclusion (an epilogue?) also thematizes an open-endedness to words, narrative, and desires. In one phrase, "This is not a story to pass on" (275), Morrison seemingly closes her story as well as gestures toward unwriting her narrative. Like the "footprints" by the stream which "come and go, come and go," her narrative seems to imprint and efface itself—much as Beloved has done within collective memory. The community deliberately forgets her "like a bad dream" (274), actively absenting her from their recollections; however, the narrative announces her as the final word of the text—"Beloved"—that which is desired, missing, yet elusively present.

* * * * *

While *Sula* appears overtly to thematize the notion of signification's duplicity, *Beloved* grounds language's slippage to the not so distant history of slavery in America. Perhaps Morrison signifies[3] on the earlier text, attempting a redefinition or respecifying of postmodernism's general emphasis on the instability of meaning; that is, whereas *Sula* capitalizes on the notion of language as aprioristically corrupt, *Beloved* does not take for granted that there is only one language (i.e., that defined by semioticians or that practiced by Schoolteacher and his nephews). Morrison contextualizes "corrupt" language as historically specific, even against deconstructionist theories which atemporalize and universalize language. Her historicization in *Beloved* thus speaks on some level about the limits of poststructuralist findings for African-American writers who remain doubly circumscribed by a language which can no longer convey authentically, but which has hitherto effectively constructed black subjects as less than human. Her grounding of discursive slippage to historical circumstances thus offers a praxis of resistance to these theories which would subsume all narratives as corruptions, just when alternate narratives taking the formerly enslaved as their subjects are beginning to emerge. Thus, whereas in *Sula*, language's slippage exists a priori, in *Beloved*, gaps and missed meanings evolve from specific sites of corruption due to historical circumstances. In neither text, however, are lapses elided or desires achieved. In effect, Morrison wishes to indulge two seemingly contradictory gestures: to make "Peace" a longing, and to make people "at rest" with thislonging piece.

NOTES

1. In *Thinking Through the Body*, Jane Gallop describes Joanne Michulski's 1974 killing and dismemberment of her two children as bringing "violence by and to the mother—out of the home and onto the lawn, into the public eye ... [effectively] reinscrib[ing] it in the world of work and meaning, power and knowledge" (2). Likewise, Sethe, rather than having fallen away from a community's mores, has actually enacted a public spectacle of the community's already shared, secreted history. She effectively reinscribes private crime onto public space.

2. Morrison symbolizes this literal fragmentation in Schoolteacher's dissection of his slaves' body parts: their division into animal characteristics on the right side of the page and human characteristics on the left (*Beloved* 193).

3. The practice of "Signifyin(g)," according to Henry Louis Gates, Jr., is "repetition and revision, or repetition with a signal difference" (*Monkey* xxiv). Gates expands the purview of "signifyin(g)" to include African-American intertextuality or the activity of "black writers read[ing] and critiqu[ing] other black texts as an act of rhetorical self-definition" (*Figures* 242). I suggest that Morrison, in *Beloved*, signifies on the very work of signification in *Sula*. That is, she repeats with a signal difference the thematics of language

slippage so apparent in *Sula*, the difference being the grounding of that language slippage to historical event.

WORKS CITED

Davis, Christina. "Beloved: A Question of Identity." *Presence Africaine* 145 (1988): 151–156.

Derrida, Jacques. "Difference." *Speech and Phenomena and Other Essays on Husserl's Theory of Signs.* Evanston: Northwestern University Press, 1973. 129–60.

Gallop, Jane. *Thinking Through the Body.* New York: Columbia University Press, 1988.

Gates, Henry Louis, Jr. *Figures in Black: Words, Signs, and the "Racial" Self.* New York: Oxford University Press, 1987.

———. *The Signifying Monkey: A Theory of African-American Literary Criticism.* New York: Oxford University Press, 1988.

Grant, Robert. "Absence into Presence: The Themetics of Memory and 'Missing' Subjects in Toni Morrison's *Sula.*" McKay 90–103.

Jacobs, Harriet. *Incidents in the Life of a Slave Girl.* Ed. Jean Fagan Yellin. Cambridge: Harvard University Press, 1987.

McDowell, Deborah. "'The Self and the Other: Reading Toni Morrison's *Sula* and the Black Female Text." McKay 77–89.

McKay, Nellie Y., ed. *Critical Essays on Toni Morrison.* Boston: Hall, 1988.

Morrison, Toni. *Beloved.* New York: Knopf, 1987.

———. *Sula.* 1973. New York: Plume, 1982.

Spillers. Hortense J. "A Hateful Passion, A Lost Love." *Feminist Studies* 9.2 (1983): 293–323.

Chronology

1931	Born Chloe Anthony Wofford on February 18 in Lorain, Ohio, the second child of Ramah (Willis) and George Wofford.
1953	Graduates with B.A. in English from Howard University. Changes her name to Toni during the years at Howard.
1955	Receives M.A. in English from Cornell University for thesis on the theme of suicide in William Faulkner and Virginia Woolf.
1955–57	Instructor in English at Texas Southern University.
1957–64	Instructor in English at Howard University.
1958	Marries Harold Morrison, a Jamaican architect.
1961	Morrison's first son, Harold Ford is born.
1964	Divorces Harold Morrison and returns with her two sons to Lorain.
1965	Becomes editor for a textbook subsidiary of Random House in Syracuse, New York.
1970	Publishes her first novel, *The Bluest Eye*. Takes editorial position at Random House in New York, eventually becoming a senior editor.
1971–72	Associate Professor of English at the State University of New York at Purchase.
1974	Publishes *Sula* and an edition of Middleton Harris's *The Black Book*.

1975	*Sula* nominated for the National Book Award.
1976–77	Visiting Lecturer at Yale University.
1977	Publishes *Song of Solomon*, which receives the National Book Critics Circle Award and the American Academy and Institute of Arts and Letters Award. Is appointed to the National Council on the Arts.
1981	Publishes *Tar Baby*.
1983	Morrison leaves her editorial job at Random House.
1984–89	Schweitzer Professor of the Humanities at the State University of New York at Albany.
1986	Receives the New York State Governor's Art Award. *Dreaming Emmett*, Morrison's play about the murder of Emmett Till, premiers in Albany.
1986–88	Visiting Lecturer at Bard College.
1987	Publishes *Beloved*, which is nominated for the National Book Award and the National Book Critics Award.
1988	Receives Pulitzer Prize in Fiction and the Robert F. Kennedy Award for *Beloved*.
1989	Becomes Robert F. Goheen Professor of the Humanities at Princeton University.
1992	Publishes *Jazz* and *Playing in the Dark: Whiteness and the Literary Imagination*.
1993	Receives Nobel Prize in literature.
1994	Morrison's mother, Ella Ramah Wofford, dies.
1996	Receives the National Book Foundation Medal for Distinguished Contribution to American Letters.
1997	Publishes *Paradise*.
2002	Toni and her son, Slade, start work on a book series called *Who's Got Game?*. They also write the picture book *The Book of Mean People*.
2003	Publishes *Love*. Publishes with Slade, *The Ant or the Grasshopper?* and *The Lion or the Mouse?*
2004	Publishes with Slade *Poppy or the Snake?*

Contributors

HAROLD BLOOM is Sterling Professor of the Humanities at Yale University. He is the author of over 20 books, including *Shelley's Mythmaking* (1959), *The Visionary Company* (1961), *Blake's Apocalypse* (1963), *Yeats* (1970), *A Map of Misreading* (1975), *Kabbalah and Criticism* (1975), *Agon: Toward a Theory of Revisionism* (1982), *The American Religion* (1992), *The Western Canon* (1994), and *Omens of Millennium: The Gnosis of Angels, Dreams, and Resurrection* (1996). *The Anxiety of Influence* (1973) sets forth Professor Bloom's provocative theory of the literary relationships between the great writers and their predecessors. His most recent books include *Shakespeare: The Invention of the Human* (1998), a 1998 National Book Award finalist, *How to Read and Why* (2000), *Genius: A Mosaic of One Hundred Exemplary Creative Minds* (2002), and *Hamlet: Poem Unlimited* (2003). In 1999, Professor Bloom received the prestigious American Academy of Arts and Letters Gold Medal for Criticism, and in 2002 he received the Catalonia International Prize.

MADONNE M. MINER is Assistant Professor of English at the University of Wyoming. She is author of *Insatiable Appetites* (1984) and essays on American fiction.

MELVIN DIXON was Assistant Professor of English at Williams College (1976–80) and Professor of English at Queens College, CUNY (1980–92). He is author of *Ride Out the Wilderness: Geography and Identity in Afro-American Literature* (1987), two novels and a book of poetry.

DEBORAH E. MCDOWELL is Professor of English at the University of Virginia. She is author of 'The Changing Same': Studies in Fiction by Black Women (1994), coeditor of Slavery and the Literary Imagination (1989) and editor the forthcoming Norton Anthology of African-American Literature. She is on the editorial board of Black American Literature Forum.

MARILYN SANDERS MOBLEY is Associate Professor of English at George Mason University where she serves as Director of African American Studies. Her book, Folk Roots and Mythic Wings in Sarah Orne Jewett and Toni Morrison: The Cultural Function of Narrative (1991), was published by Louisiana State University Press. She has served as president and vice president for the Toni Morrison Society.

TRUDIER HARRIS is J. Carlyle Sitterson Professor of English and Chair of the Curriculum in African and Afro-American Studies at the University of North Carolina at Chapel Hill.

PHILIP PAGE is a Professor of English at California State University, San Bernardino. He is the author of Dangerous Freedom: Fusion and Fragmentation in Toni Morrison's Novels (1995) and Reclaiming Community in Contemporary African-American Fiction (1999).

J. BROOKS BOUSON is Associate Professor of English at Loyola University in Chicago. She is the author of The Empathetic Reader: A Study of the Narcissistic Character and the Drama of the Self and Brutal Choreographies: Oppositional Strategies and Narrative Design in the Novels of Margaret Atwood.

MARIA DIBATTISTA is a Professor of English and comparative literature at Princeton University, where she teaches modern literature and film. She is the author of First Love: The Affections of Modern Fiction (1991), Virginia Woolf's Major Novels: The Fables of Anon (1979), and coeditor of High and Low Moderns (1997).

MICHAEL WOOD is Charles Barnwell Stuart Professor of English at Princeton University, and the author of books on Stendhal, García Márquez, and Nabokov. His most recent work is Children of Silence: On Contemporary Fiction (1998). He writes frequently on literature and film for the New York Review of Books and the London Review of Books.

RACHEL C. LEE is an Assistant Professor in the departments of English and Women's Studies at UCLA. She is author of *The Americas of Asian American Literature: Gendered Fictions of Nation and Transnation*. Her work spans the fields of twentieth-century American literature, feminist theory, ethnic studies, and cultural studies.

Bibliography

Baker, Houston, A., Jr. *Afro-American Poetics: Revisions of Harlem and the Black Aesthetic*. Madison: University of Wisconsin Press, 1988.

———. *Blues, Ideology, and Afro-American Literature: A Vernacular Theory*. Chicago: University of Chicago Press, 1984.

———. *The Journey Back: Issues in Black Literature and Criticism*. Chicago: University of Chicago Press, 1980.

———. *Long Black Song: Essays in Black American Literature and Culture*. Charlottesville: University Press of Virginia, 1972.

———. *Singers of Daybreak: Essays in Black American Literature*. Washington, D.C.: Howard University Press, 1974.

Bakerman, Jane S. "Failures of Love: Female Initiation in the Novels of Toni Morrison." *American Literature* 52 (1980): 541–63.

———. "The Seams Can't Show: An Interview with Toni Morrison." *Black American Literature Forum* 12 (1978): 56–60.

Barthold, Bonnie J. *Black Time: Fiction of Africa, the Caribbean, and the United States*. New Haven: Yale University Press, 1981.

Beaulieu, Elizabeth Ann. *The Toni Morrison Encyclopedia*. Westport, CT: Greenwood Press, 2003.

Blake, Susan L. "Folklore and Community in *Song of Solomon*." MELUS 7 (1980): 77–82.

Brenner, Gerry. "*Song of Solomon*: Morrison's Rejection of Rank's Monomyth and Feminism." *Studies in American Fiction* 15 (1987): 13–24.

Bruck, Peter, and Wolfgang Karrer, eds. *The Afro-American Novel since 1960*. Amsterdam: Grüner, 1982.

Callahan, John F. *In the African-American Grain: The Pursuit of Voice in Twentieth-Century Black Fiction*. Urbana: University of Illinois Press, 1988.

Campbell, Jane. *Mythic Black Fiction: The Transformation of History*. Knoxville: University of Tennessee Press, 1986.

Carmean, Karen. *Toni Morrison's World of Fiction*. Troy, New York: Whitston Pub. Co., 1993.

Christian, Barbara. *Black Feminist Criticism: Perspectives on Black Women Writers*. New York: Pergamon Press, 1985.

———. *Black Women Novelists: The Development of a Tradition 1892–1976*. Westport, CT: Greenwood Press, 1980.

Cooke, Michael G. *Afro-American Literature in the Twentieth Century: The Achievement of Intimacy*. New Haven: Yale University Press, 1984.

David, Ron. *Toni Morrison Explained: A Reader's Road Map to the Novels*. New York: Random House, 2000.

Davis, Arthur P. *From the Dark Tower: Afro-American Writers (1900 to 1960)*. Washington, D.C.: Howard University Press, 1974.

Davis, Charles T. *Black Is the Color of the Cosmos: Essays on Afro-American Literature and Culture 1942–1981*. Edited by Henry Louis Gates, Jr. New York: Garland, 1982.

De Arman, Charles. "Milkman as the Archetypal Hero: 'Thursday's Child Has Far to Go.'" *Obsidian* 6 (1980): 56–59.

Dundes, Alan, ed. *Mother Wit from the Laughing Barrel: Readings in the Interpretation of Afro-American Folklore*. Englewood Cliffs, NJ: Prentice-Hall, 1973.

Edelberg, Cynthia Dubin. "Morrison's Voices: Formal Education, the Work Ethic and the Bible." *American Literature* 58 (1986): 217–37.

Fikes, Robert J. "Echoes from Small Town Ohio: A Toni Morrison Bibliography." *Obsidian* 7 (1979): 142–48.

Fultz, Lucille P. *Toni Morrison: Playing With Difference*. Urbana: University of Illinois Press, 2003.

Furman, Jan. *Toni Morrison's Fiction*. Columbia, South Carolina: University of South Carolina Press, 1996.

Gates, Henry Louis, Jr. *Figures in Black: Words, Signs, and the "Racial" Self*. New York: Oxford University Press, 1987.

————. *The Signifying Monkey: A Theory of Afro-American Literary Criticism.* New York: Oxford University Press, 1988.

————, ed. *Black Literature and Literary Theory.* New York: Methuen, 1984.

————, ed. *"Race," Writing, and Difference.* Chicago: University of Chicago Press, 1986.

———— and K.A. Appiah, eds. *Toni Morrison: Critical Perspectives Past and Present.* New York: Amistad, 1993.

Harris, A. Leslie. "Myth as Structure in Toni Morrison's *Song of Solomon.*" MELUS 7 (1980): 69–76.

Hedin, Raymond. "The Structuring of Emotion in Black American Fiction." *Novel* 16 (1982–83): 50–64.

Hogue, W. Lawrence. *Discourse and the Other: The Production of the Afro-American Text.* Durham, NC: Duke University Press, 1986.

Holloway, Karla F.C., and Stephane Demetrakopoulous. *New Dimensions of Spirituality: A Biracial and Bicultural Reading of the Novels of Toni Morrison.* New York: Greenwood Press, 1987.

House, Elizabeth B. "Artists and the Art of Living: Order and Disorder in Toni Morrison's Fiction." *Modern Fiction Studies* 34 (1988): 27–44.

————. "The 'Sweet Life' in Toni Morrison's Fiction." *American Literature* 56 (1984): 181–202.

Hovet, Grace Ann, and Barbara Lounsberry. "Flying as Symbol and Legend in Toni Morrison's *The Bluest Eye, Sula,* and *Song of Solomon.*" *CLA Journal* 27 (1983–84): 119–40.

————. "Principles of Perception in Toni Morrison's *Sula.*" *Black American Literature Forum* 18 (1979): 126–29.

Hull, Gloria T.; Scott, Patricia Bell; and Smith, Barbara, ed. *All the Women Are White, All the Blacks Are Men, but Some of Us Are Brave: Black Women's Studies.* Old Westbury, NY: Feminist Press, 1982.

Iannone, Carol. "Toni Morrison's Career." *Commentary* 84 (December 1987): 50–63.

Jones, Bessie W. *The World of Toni Morrison.* Dubuque, IA: Kendall/Hunt, 1985.

Kent, George E. *Blackness and the Adventure of Western Culture.* Chicago: Third World Press, 1972.

Klotman, Phyllis Rauch. "Dick and Jane and the Shirley Temple Sensibility in *The Bluest Eye.*" *Black American Literature Forum* 13 (1979): 123–125.

Lange, Bonnie Shipman. "Toni Morrison's Rainbow Code." *Critique* 24 (1983): 173–181.

Lee, A. Robert, ed. *Black Fiction: New Studies in the Afro-American Novel since 1945.* New York: Barnes & Noble, 1980.

Lee, Dorothy H. "To Ride the Air." *Black American Literature Forum* 16 (1982): 64–70.

Lepow, Lauren. "Paradise Lost and Found: Dualism and Edenic Myth in Toni Morrison's *Tar Baby.*" *Contemporary Literature* 28 (1987): 363–77.

Levine, Lawrence W. *Black Culture and Black Consciousness: Afro-American Folk Thought from Slavery to Freedom.* New York: Oxford University Press, 1977.

Lupton, Mary Jane. "Clothes and Closure in Three Novels by Black Women." *Black American Literature Forum* 20 (1986): 409–22.

Marks, Kathleen. *Toni Morrison's* Beloved *and the Apotropaic Imagination.* Columbia: University of Missouri Press, 2002.

Mbalia, Doreatha Drummond. *Toni Morrison's Developing Class Consciousness.* Selinsgrove, PA: Susquehanna University Press, 1991.

McKay, Nellie Y., ed. *Critical Essays on Toni Morrison.* Boston: G.K. Hall, 1988.

Middleton, David L. *Toni Morrison: An Annotated Bibliography.* New York: Garland, 1987.

———. *Toni Morrison's Fiction: Contemporary Criticism.* New York: Garland, 1997.

Mobley, Marilyn E. "Narrative Dilemma: Jadine as Cultural Orphan in Toni Morrison's *Tar Baby.*" *Southern Review* 23 (1987): 761–70.

Montgomery, Maxine Lavon. "A Pilgrimage to the Origins: The Apocalypse as Structure and Theme in Toni Morrison's *Sula.*" *Black American Literature Forum* 23 (1989): 127–38.

Mori, Aoi. *Toni Morrison and Womanist Discourse.* New York: Peter Lang, 1999.

Morrison, Toni. *The Bluest Eye*, 1970.

———. *Sula.* 1974.

———. *Song of Solomon.* 1977.

———. *Tar Baby.* New York: Alfred A. Knopf, 1981.

———. *Dreaming Emmett* (play). 1985.

———. *Beloved.* 1987.

———. *Jazz.* New York: Alfred A. Knopf, 1992.

———. *Playing in the Dark: Whiteness and the Literary Imagination.* Cambridge, MA: Harvard University Press, 1992.

————. *Race-ing Justice, En-Gendering Power: Essays on Anita Hill, Clarence Thomas, and the Construction of Social Reality*. Pantheon Books, 1992.

————. *The Nobel Lecture in Literature*. New York: Alfred A. Knopf, 1993.

————. *Conversations with Toni Morrison*. Edited by Danille Taylor-Guthrie. Jackson: University of Mississippi Press, 1994.

————. *Paradise*. New York: Alfred A. Knopf, 1997.

————. *Love*. New York: Alfred A. Knopf, 2003.

Page, Philip. *Dangerous Freedom: Fusion and Fragmentation in Toni Morrison's Novels*. Jackson: University Press of Mississippi, 1995.

Peterson, Nancy J. *Toni Morrison: Critical and Theoretical Approaches*. Baltimore: John Hopkins University Press, 1997.

Reyes, Angelita Dianne. "Ancient Properties in the New World: The Paradox of the 'Other' in Toni Morrison's *Tar Baby*." *Black Scholar* 17 (March–April 1986): 19–25.

Rosenblatt, Roger. *Black Fiction*. Cambridge, MA: Harvard University Press, 1974.

Scruggs, Charles. "The Nature of Desire in Toni Morrison's *Song of Solomon*." *Arizona Quarterly* 38 (1982): 311–35.

Smith, Valerie. *Self-Discovery and Authority in Afro-American Narrative*. Cambridge, MA: Harvard University Press, 1987.

Stepto, Robert B. *From Behind the Veil: A Study of Afro-American Narrative*. Urbana: University of Illinois Press, 1979.

————. "'Intimate Things in Place': A Conversation with Toni Morrison." In *Chant of Saints: A Gathering of Afro-American Literature, Art, and Scholarship*, edited by Michael S. Harper and Robert B. Stepto. Urbana: University of Illinois Press, 1979.

Story, Ralph. "An Excursion into the Black World: The 'Seven Days' in Toni Morrison's *Song of Solomon*." *Black American Literature Forum* 23 (1989): 14–58.

Tally, Justine. *Toni Morrison's Histories and Truths*. Hamburg: Lit; Piscataway, NJ: Distributed in North America by Transaction Publishers, 1999.

Thomas, H. Nigel. *From Folklore to Fiction: A Study of Heroes and Rituals in the Black American Novel*. Westport, CT: Greenwood Press, 1988.

Weixlmann, Joe, and Houston A. Baker, JR., ed. *Black Feminist Criticism and Critical Theory*. Greenwood, FL: Fenkevill, 1988.

Werner, Craig Hansen. *Paradoxical Resolutions: American Fiction since James Joyce*. Urbana: University of Illinois Press, 1982.

————. "Tell Old Pharaoah: The Afro-American Response to Faulkner." *Southern Review* 19 (1983): 711–35.

Willis, Susan. *Specifying: Black Women Writing the American Experience.* Madison: University of Wisconsin Press, 1987.

Acknowledgments

"Lady No Longer Sings the Blues: Rape, Madness, and Silence in The Bluest Eye" by Madonne M. Miner. From *Conjuring: Black Women, Fiction, and Literary Tradition*, edited by Marjorie Pryse and Hortense J. Spillers. 176–189. © 1985 by Indiana University Press. Reprinted by permission.

"Like an Eagle in the air: Toni Morrison" from *Ride Out the Wilderness: Geography and Identity in Afro-American Literature* by Melvin Dixon. 141–169. © 1987 by the Board of Trustees of the University of Illinois. Reprinted by permission.

"'The Self and the Other': Reading Toni Morrison's *Sula* and the Black Female Text" by Deborah E. McDowell. From *Critical Essays on Toni Morrison* by Nellie Y. McKay. 77–90. © 1988 by Nellie Y. McKay. Reprinted with permisison of the Gale Group.

"A Different Remembering: Memory, History, and Meaning in Toni Morrison's Beloved" by Marilyn Sanders Mobley. From *Toni Morrison* (Modern Critical Views), Harold Bloom, editor. 189–199. © 1990 by Chelsea House Publishers.

"Sula" from *Fiction and Folklore: The Novels of Toni Morrison* by Trudier Harris. 52–71. © 1991 by Trudier Harris. Reprinted by permission.

"Putting It All Together: Attempted Unification in Song of Solomon" from *Dangerous Freedom: Fusion and Fragmentation in Toni Morrison's Novels* by Philip Page. 84–107. © 1995 by the University Press of Mississippi. Reprinted by permission.

"Speaking the Unspeakable" from *Quiet As It's Kept: Shame, Trauma, and Race in the Novels of Toni Morrison* by J. Brooks Bouson. 1–21. © 2000 by State University of New York. Reprinted by permission.

"Contentions in The House of Chloe: Morrison's Tar Baby" by Maria DiBattista. From *The Aesthetics of Toni Morrison: Speaking the Unspeakable*, edited by Marc C. Conner. 92–112. © 2000 by University Press of Mississippi. Reprinted by permission.

"Sensations of Loss" by Michael Wood from *The Aesthetics of Toni Morrison: Speaking the Unspeakable*, edited by Marc C. Conner. 113–124. © 2000 by University Press of Mississippi. Reprinted by permission.

"Missing Peace in Toni Morrison's Sula and Beloved" by Rachel C. Lee. From *Understanding Toni Morrison's Beloved and Sula: Selected Essays and Criticisms of the works by the Nobel Prize-winning author*, edited by Solomon O. Iyasere and Marla W. Iyasere. 277–296. © 2000 by Solomon O. Iyasere and Marla W. Iyasere. Reprinted by permission of the author.

Index